D0760159

# THE ANTIQUITIES
# OF
# CONSTANTINOPLE

Other Historical Travel Guides

Published by

Italica Press

*The Marvels of Rome*
*Mirabilia Urbis Romae*

Theoderich
*Guide to the Holy Land*

DR
720
.G513
1988

# PIERRE GILLES

# THE ANTIQUITIES
# OF
# CONSTANTINOPLE

BASED ON THE TRANSLATION
BY
JOHN BALL

\*

SECOND EDITION
WITH NEW INTRODUCTION
AND BIBLIOGRAPHY
BY
RONALD G. MUSTO

ITALICA PRESS
NEW YORK
1988

HIEBERT LIBRARY 62732
Fresno Pacific College - M.B. Seminary
Fresno, CA 93702

First Published 1729
Private Edition
London

\*

Second Edition
Copyright © 1988 by Italica Press

ITALICA PRESS, INC.
595 Main Street
New York, New York 10044

All rights reserved. No part of this publication may be reproduced, stored in a retrieval system, or transmitted, in any form or by any means, electronic, mechanical, photocopying, recording, or otherwise, without prior permission of Italica Press.

**Library of Congress Cataloging-in-Publication Data**

Gilles, Pierre, 1490-1555.
    The antiquities of Constantinople.

    Translation of: De Topographia Constantinopoleos.
    Bibliography: p.
    Includes index.
    1. Istanbul (Turkey) -- Description. 2. Istanbul
(Turkey) -- Antiquities. 3. Turkey -- Antiquities.
I. Title.
DR720-G513      1987        939'.8        86-82697
ISBN      0-934977-09-7
ISBN      0-934977-01-1 (pbk.)

Printed in the United States of America
5 4 3 2

Cover design by James Stokoe.
The Church of Hagia Sophia in a computer image digitized and edited from a photograph of the west facade.

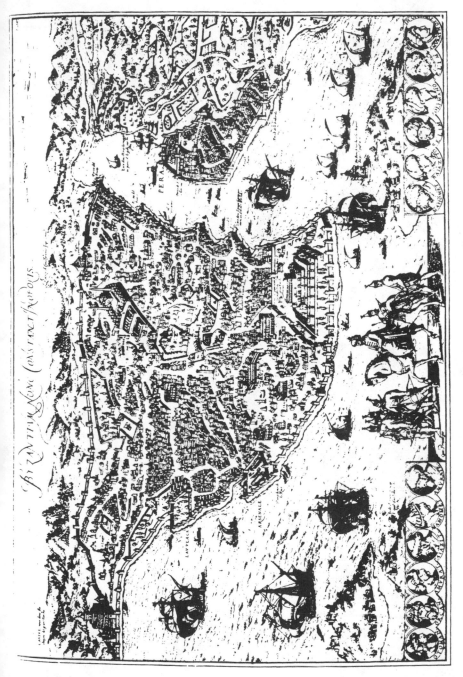

CONSTANTINOPLE IN 1576

# CONTENTS

# ILLUSTRATIONS

# PREFACE

THIS VOLUME PRESENTS A SECOND EDITION OF JOHN Ball's 1729 English translation of *The Four Books of the Antiquities of Constantinople,* which was written by Pierre Gilles and published posthumously in 1561. No other edition of an English translation of this work has been available since that time, despite the fact that this is a fundamental text on one of the principal cities of both East and West.

In an attempt to make this work accessible to the modern reader — as with Italica Press's entire series of Historical Travel Guides — the editors have followed certain stylistic principles. The language, punctuation, capitalization and spelling of Ball's translation of both the text and Gilles' preface have been modernized. The Latin has been consulted occasionally, but this is neither an attempt at a new translation nor simply a reprint of the Ball translation. Ball's own English preface has been reprinted verbatim with only the capitalization modernized. Ball's translation has its own historical interest and obviously, a life of its own beyond the work of Gilles. Although it is not a perfect translation, apparently not always thorough and complete, we have chosen to work with this text rather than allow the work of Gilles to remain unknown to an English-speaking audience while waiting for another translation.

Several features have been added to this edition. An introduction brings the entire work into perspective for a modern audience, giving the historical background of the city, the period, the book and its author. A series of four new maps are keyed to the four books of the text and a fifth provides a perspective on Turkish Constantinople under Süleiyman the Magnificent, when Gilles visited the city. These are not exact topographical maps; they attempt, however, to give the relative locations of the sites mentioned in the text. The illustrations of Constantinople that appear throughout the text are either by contemporaries of Gilles or are reproduced from Ball's 1729 edition.

A glossary of architectural terms will help the reader with the types of buildings, architectural details and units of measurement used in the text. There is also a select bibliography for further reading and research on Constantinople and Pierre Gilles. The index alone will be a great resource to help the reader find sites in the city and references in the text to earlier writers on Constantinople. The task of annotating the text and pursuing the references to earlier authors has, however, been left to the scholar prepared to undertake a new critical edition of the text.

Finally, this edition has not included the letter from John Roe to John Ball nor *The Ancient Description of the Wards,* which were included in the original Ball edition. The intention of this edition throughout is to introduce Gilles' work to the modern reader in the hope that this will spur further interest both in the author and in the fascinations of Constantinople.

*Eileen Gardiner*

\* \*
\*

# INTRODUCTION

*And therefore I have sailed the seas and come
to the holy city of Byzantium*

W.B. Yeats, "Sailing to Byzantium"

## THE SETTING

On May 30, 1453 the Ottoman Sultan Mohamet II rode into the conquered city of Constantinople, the capital and last stronghold of the Byzantine Empire, entered the Church of Hagia Sophia, and there prayed to Allah. The ancient capital of the Roman Empire of the East now lay under the Turkish sword, and a millennium of history had come to an end. Byzantium, Constantinople, Istanbul: the different names all describe the same and ever-changing city, but touch only facets of its fabled life — Greek, Roman, Byzantine and Moslem — that have symbolized magic and power for the peoples of the West and East.

Already a thriving commercial center in 431 B.C.E. at the start of the Peloponnesian War when it was allied with Athens against Sparta, Byzantium occupied the golden triangle of land at the confluence of the Bosporus, the Sea of Marmara, and the Golden Horn and dominated the passages between the Black Sea and the Mediterranean, Europe and Asia. The city was originally founded in 667 B.C.E. by Greeks from Megara. While the Romans held most of the Bosporus region from 74 B.C.E., Byzantium itself fell to Emperor Septimus Severus only in 196 C.E. during a fierce and bitter siege that resulted in the destruction of most of the city. Realizing the commercial and strategic importance of the site, however, Severus set about rebuilding the ancient Greek polis perched atop its acropolis on the Promontory and encircled it with a belt of walls that are vaguely mirrored today by the walls of the Topkapi Palace precinct.

Soon after his accession in 324 Constantine the Great realized that the Roman state's true strengths lay in the population, culture, and wealth of the East. Contemplating the future strategic needs of the empire, he decided to move the capital from Rome to northwestern Asia Minor. After investigating several cites on the coast, including Troy, where he began building his city, he decided that Byzantium, with its seven hills and glorious, commanding position was the ideal site. In 330, therefore, he began work on his New Rome, stripping old Rome and many of the richest cities of the East of much of their wealth, best art, and costliest ornaments.

Constantinople, as his new city came to be known, soon became the greatest city of Rome, especially after the division of the Empire into East and West by Theodosius in 395. While its culture and language gradually and definitely became Greek, its inhabitants continued to call themselves *Romanoi*, Romans, and this is how they were known to subjects of the Empire and to its enemies for a millennium. The Roman Empire of the East, what today we call the Byzantine Empire, outlived its western partner, which fell finally in 476, and continued to grow and to change for the next thousand years.

The Byzantine Empire of Constantinople not only preserved the culture and imperial rule of ancient Rome, it transformed it into an eastern, despotic empire and civilization, one hierarchical yet at the same time one infused with a profound Christian ethic and mysticism, one based on imperial power and great commercial wealth, but one of subtle diplomacy and intelligence, of clever alliance and brilliant military force. For centuries, now contracted, now expanding, the Empire was able to balance off the aggressive forces of Islam on the south and east, the Slavs to the north and west, and the Latins — Italians, Franks, Germans and Normans — from the West. The empire reached its zenith under Emperor Justinian I (527-68), then lost vast areas, including Egypt, Syria, and North Africa, to Islam but recovered and expanded from 827 to 1025. In 1071, however, Emperor Romanus IV suffered a disastrous defeat at the hands of the Seljuk Turks at Manzikert in Eastern Anatolia; and from that point on the history of the empire and of its capital, Constantinople, was one of holding on: both against the Turks to the east and the newly aggressive Latins to the west, often in uneasy alliance with the Byzantines in their attempts to win back the Holy Land from the Moslems. In 1204 the Fourth Crusade, instigated and aided by the Venetians, turned back upon the heart of Eastern Christendom itself, and conquered and looted Constantinople. The sack was the worst disaster suffered by the city since Severus' conquest and saw the installation of a Latin empire. Venice was glutted with booty from the sack for years. The four bronze horses until recently atop San Marco's, for example, were stripped from Constantinople. They had been brought there by Constantine the Great from a shrine at Delphi.

In 1261 the Byzantines under the Paleologi emperors regained the city, but by the early 1300s the Turks had already crossed the Bosporus and were occupying Thrace. By 1450 the empire of Constantinople controlled nothing more than its suburbs, and in April 1453 the Ottoman Sultan Mohamet II attacked the city, which held out for fifty days in one of the most desperate, and myth-inspiring sieges in history. Its mighty double walls built by Theodosius the symbol of the age, crumbled under the constant bombardment of Mohamet's new artillery. After a desperate pitched battle at the Saint Romanus Gate, in which Emperor Constantine XI died in the fray,

Mohamet took the city, made it the Ottoman capital, and raised the crescent in the place of the cross.[1]

The Ottoman sultans, the new emperors of Constantinople, soon turned their holy war of Islam against the heart of Europe. Every year, the Golden Horn bristled with the new armaments of Turkish war fleets sent against the Christian princes of the Mediterranean. Ottoman armies rolled against the fortresses of Eastern Europe in an unstoppable tide of conquest. By 1520, when Sultan Selim I died, the Ottoman Empire stretched from Alexandria in Egypt to Mosul in Syria, from Bodrum in southwestern Anatolia to the Danube. In 1566, by the end of of the reign of his son Süleiyman I, it had come to rest at the gates of Vienna, at Kars in Georgia, at Baghdad and Basra in Iraq, and it stretched from Tripoli in Libya to Oran in Algeria.

The mid-sixteenth century was an age of great fear and struggle throughout Europe and the Mediterranean world. The age saw the fall of Belgrade (1521) and Rhodes (1522), the siege of Vienna (1529) and of Malta (1565), the Battle of Mohacs (1526) and of Lepanto (1572). The Ottoman Empire became the obsession of Europe's rulers. Unravelling the policy of the Sublime Porte of Constantinople was the waking obsession and haunting dream of Europe's most famous rulers, from the Hapsburg Emperor Charles V to Philip II of Spain, from Pope Leo X to François I of France. It clouded the thought and fueled the fears of Martin Luther and Erasmus, of Thomas More and Juan Luis Vives. The problem of "the Turk" and what to do about this new and menacing "evil empire" obsessed the Christian West and produced treatise, political alliance and a literature on aggression and the Western response to it that equal anything in the twentieth century. The Turk was cruel and tyrannical, murderous to both the Christian and his own, treacherous and sadistic, keeper of slave harems and of Christian boys turned into murderous Janissaries, a creature in love with war and conquest, delighting in blood and torture.

Yet, anyone who has visited Istanbul or has studied the civilization of the age of Süleiyman must come away confused and surprised, asking how such an evil empire could create such bold and enduring architecture, such dazzling ceramics and textiles, such literature and history, such religious zeal and philosophical thought.

It also comes as a surprise that to his fellow Turks Süleiyman was known as the "Lawgiver," a just ruler who provided hospitals, schools, orphanages and facilities for the poor, who protected and beautified the holy places of the Empire — Jerusalem, Mecca and Medina — unsparingly. This is the sultan who, with his beloved Roxelana, composed poetry and strolled in gardens scented with blossoming fruit trees and roses. Not since the golden age of the Byzantine Empire under Justinian had the city of Constantinople seen such wealth and activity, so much building and innovation, so many schools and artists making anew and crystallizing the beauty and genius of a culture. This brilliant age of arts and material culture focused the power, wealth and intellect of an entire empire and civilization on Constantinople; this was truly the age of Süleiyman the Magnificent.

By the time of Gilles' visit in 1544 Constantinople was the largest and wealthiest city of the Mediterranean, in fact of the Western, world. Its population of 700,000 was larger than the combined populations of Venice, Palermo, Messina, Catania and Naples. Its Turks, Greeks, Jews, Armenians, Gypsies, Arabs and Africans, Slavs, Italians, French and others worshipped at over 400 mosques and dozens of Christian churches; they bought and sold in tens of thousands of small shops, they plied its waters in thousands of barks, ferries and small ships. Each year the city consumed over 100,000 tons of wheat and other cereals and hundreds of thousands of head of cattle and sheep.[2]

Just as Süleiyman owed so much of his empire's success to his own brilliance as a military and cultural leader and to the abilities of his generals, including Barbarossa and Ali Pasha, he also owed much to the disunity and varying purposes of the West; for the age of Süleiyman was also the age of the Reformation, of the Italian wars that ended its Renaissance, of the apogee of the Holy Roman Empire and of the rise of the great Atlantic states: France, England and Spain. Amid this whirlwind of change neither politics nor religion created any clear-cut divisions or alliances.

The French king, the Most Catholic Monarch, as often as not fought against the Holy Roman Emperor in alliance with both Protestants and Turks. François I saw French interests more closely tied to the Ottomans than with the Hapsburgs, who threatened to surround and humiliate him. He called for Ottoman aid as early as 1525. In 1536 Süleiyman granted the French commercial privileges in his empire. The capture of Nice by a combined French-Turkish fleet in 1543, and the Turks' wintering in Toulon disgusted the rest of Christian Europe but provided a needed balance to Charles V's power. Playing the Turkish card was one of François I's trumps, and his close ties with the Sublime Porte allowed his ambassadors and other servants free access to the city, as free, that is, as any infidels were granted.

PIERRE GILLES

It is, therefore, in this context that we should understand the life and works of Pierre Gilles, that faithful servant of the French crown, and the description of Constantinople in the age of Süleiyman the Magnificent that he has left for us.

Pierre Gilles, or Petrus Gyllius as he is known from his Latin texts, was born in Albi in 1490. We do not know very much about his youth and early education. Judging from his later work and interests, however, it is clear that he shared the education and enthusiasms of the new generation of French Humanists. This included his contemporaries François Rabelais, Jacques Lefevre D'Etaples, and Guillaume Budé, all Humanist friends or disciples of Erasmus and the Italian Humanists. These scholars and writers excelled equally in the worlds of science and letters that owed so much to the newly discovered or edited texts of antiquity, whether Classical or Christian. Gilles' command of classical languages, especially Greek and Latin, was excellent, and he was well versed in the works of Aristotle, Aelian and Pliny, among the most important of the ancient naturalists.

Gilles took an early interest in natural science, especially ichthyology, and studied the marine life along the southern coast of France and the Adriatic, in 1533 publishing his *One Book on the French and Latin Names of the Fish*,[3] dedicated to King François I, a patron of the new Humanists. Like his contemporary, the physician Rabelais who notes him in his *Gargantua*,[4] Gilles saw no modern distinction between the worlds of "science" and other, more literary learning. He followed the example of the best Humanists by editing the works of his contemporaries and preparing new philological tools for the scientific study of antiquity through the careful discovery, assemblage and presentation of its classic texts — both sacred and secular — and writing commentaries on them. Among these are his edition of Elio Antonio de Nebrija's *A Dictionary of Place Names*[5] and of the great Italian Humanist philosopher and philologist Lorenzo Valla's *History of King Ferdinand of Aragon*.[6] He also published a *Greek-Latin Lexicon*,[7] a translation of the Greek Father Theoderit's *Commentary* on the twelve minor prophets, and a selection of texts from Aelian, Porphyry, Heliodorus and Oppian, among others.

Sometime in the early 1520s, like Erasmus and many other Humanists, Gilles took up the duties of tutor to princes, in this case the young Georges d'Armagnac, one of the great nobles of the realm, who eventually went on to become bishop of Rodez and a cardinal of the Catholic church and who remained Gilles' faithful patron and friend until his death. D'Armagnac persuaded Gilles to dedicate his *On the Life and Nature of Animals*[8] to François I, and through this opened for him a whole new world of royal support and commission.

Among the favorite interests of François was his useful alliance with the Ottoman Empire and its powerful Sultan Süleiyman the Magnificent. Royal embassies to the East had long served a variety of purposes: diplomatic, scientific, intelligence gathering and goodwill, what we might today call "cultural exchange." In addition, royally supported missions to the seats of classical antiquity — the Holy Land, Greece and Asia Minor — could only enhance the reputation of the French king among the makers of public opinion in the Christian West. Therefore, in 1544 Gilles left France on a fact-finding mission with a French embassy that included the king's royal cosmographer, André Thevet d'Angoulême.[9]

Gilles seems to have spent the years 1544 to 1547 in Constantinople, gathering literary sources and investigating the physical remains of the ancient city. We know for certain that he was in the city in 1546, when the Grand Bezestan was burned down, allowing Gilles to examine the ancient basilicas left standing in its ruins.[10] Out of money, in 1548 he enlisted in Süleiyman's army and joined the expedition mounted by the sultan against Persia. In winter quarters outside Aleppo in 1548 he met the French ambassador to the Sublime Porte, Gabriel d'Aramon, who took Gilles with him to the Holy Land and Egypt. While in Jerusalem in 1549 Gilles met a friend of André Thevet, the expelled Jesuit millenniarist, Guillaume Postel, whose speculations on the divine plan of history and on the Holy City's place in the New Age would end in his death as a heretic. Before he left for Rome to join the Jesuits, Postel had had an interview with François I, in which he told the king that he was prophesied to be the millennial king of the Last Days, and that the Jesuit Order would be instrumental in ushering in these times.[11] The meeting of Gilles and Postel in Jerusalem is emblematic of the age: the naturalist geographer and the explorer of sacred geography had both ventured to the East to rediscover the ancient sources of Christian life and to draw on them to reconstruct holy cities more fitting a new age of enlightenment.

In January 1550, still in d'Aramon's company, Gilles returned to Constantinople. That same year he travelled with the ambassador back to France. Almost immediately upon his return, however, Gilles headed south to Rome, where his patron, Cardinal d'Armagnac, now resided. D'Aramagnac took him into his protection and secured for him the absentee priorage of Durenque in Aveyron to guarantee him some income. While in Rome Gilles began the work of sifting through the large number of source materials and notes that he had accumulated on the history of Constantinople. Gilles had made great progress in completing his book on Constantinople by 1555; but then — as the epitaph on his tomb tells us — he was stricken by a severe fever that he fought for eleven days before finally dying at the fourth hour on January 5, 1555.[12] His patron Georges d'Armagnac provided for his funeral and his tomb, in the church of San Marcello in Rome.

From his epitaph we learn that Gilles was hard at work organizing his notes for his two works on Constantinople when he died. He apparently left these incomplete, however; and his nephew, Antoine Gilles, then took up the task of finishing his work. This he did faithfully; and in the 1560s a string of books emerged from his stewardship. The most important for our purposes appeared in Lyon in 1561 and were his *Three Books on the Thracian*

*Bosporus*[13] and the *Four Books On the Topography of Constantinople and On Its Antiquities.*[14]

## THE *ANTIQUITIES OF CONSTANTINOPLE*

*Four Books on the Topography of Constantinople and On Its Antiquities,* or *The Antiquities of Constantinople,* is Gilles best known work today. The text describes the city of Constantinople in four books, discussed through the various wards of the city with their monuments as one proceeds east to west from the Promontory to the double land walls and then back across the Golden Horn to Galata, where the account concludes. The overall methodology is very modern: like the historians of the *Annales* school or other structuralists, Gilles begins with an introductory account of the physical surroundings of the city, its waters, geographical location, its natural resources, wealth and physical conditions.

Book I then deals with the mythological and historical background: the city's founding, its early growth, and its present extent. Gilles then proceeds from the first hill and a brief overview of its present monuments through all seven hills and the land walls, gates and towers. Book II returns to the same ground, once again beginning on the first hill and first ward, and starts Gilles' uncovering of the ancient monuments of the city, moving west but concentrating on the area of the ancient forum, around the Augustaeum with its surrounding buildings, the heart of ancient Constantinople, taking up the first to the fourth wards and nearly half of the entire text.

Book III then moves eastward on the third hill and from the fifth ward to the tenth ward, surveying most of the north and central sections of the city. Book IV proceeds from the eleventh ward and the fourth hill west to the seventh hill and then north to the fourteenth ward before crossing the Golden Horn to the thirteenth ward of

Galata or Sycae. Gilles briefly concludes with a survey of contemporary Ottoman monuments, mentioning the major ones but simply enumerating the mosques, palaces and other sites in medieval itinerary style. The author then briefly reviews his use of sources and ends with some very personal remarks on his investigations and his journey.

## GILLES' METHOD

Not only is *The Antiquities of Constantinople* the "first truly scholarly account of the city,"[15] but it is also one of the most entertaining travel books and one of the most fascinating journals of discovery yet produced. Not that Gilles' discoveries ranged the broad distances or the wild terrains and peoples of a Marco Polo or Columbus; instead, his discoveries were of invisible cities — the topography of a long lost imperial capital —the monuments, churches, public buildings, theaters and circuses, the palaces, harbors and docks of Constantinople as it existed not during the age of Süleiyman, or in the more recent Byzantine past, or even in ancient Greek Byzantium, but in the great Christian age of Justinian and the late Roman Empire.

His geography is mapped first from the surviving literary texts of Greek historians, and only then from actual physical retracing of the steps that they laid out. In this Gilles was both the faithful devotee of the Humanist method of carefully reading the prize texts of late Christian antiquity and a forerunner of the modern science of topography and archeology. He applied the same careful analysis to texts that he then put into practice in the field: verifying one source against another, carefully measuring the mental geography of the ancient sources against the physical geography of Constantinople's streets, pillars and columns. By the time

he has completed his four books Gilles has resurrected for
the reader the monuments of a long vanished city, ward
by ward, hill by hill, neighborhood after neighborhood.
While not always accurate in his attributions or locations
for buildings, he is surprisingly accurate for the majority
of ancient sites that he reconstructs: for him the city is a
lost and only partially recovered text, pieced together
carefully by the best-known exegetical methods of his
day. One must admit that the result of his editing is not
really the original city that modern archeology and
topography have constructed, but a Renaissance text, a
contemporary image of ancient glory made — like all texts
— in the image of its times.

When the modern reader and traveler is able to
compare still-existing sites to Gilles' descriptions, his
accuracy and keen powers of observation become ap-
parent immediately. His detailed descriptions of Hagia
Sophia, of the Hippodrome and its sculpted columns, of
the Basilica Cistern, of the Süleimaniye Mosque complex,
of the layout of the city on its seven hills, its harbors and
inlets, are all astonishingly accurate.

While Gilles also gives due notice to the most
important building projects under way during the reign
of Süleiyman the Magnificent, which he witnessed first-
hand, his vision of the present is always obscured by the
shadow — and the brilliance — of the past: he seeks not the
present mosque or ruined chapel, but the original ancient
monument behind or beneath them. In the walls and
courtyards of Ottoman buildings he finds the acanthus
leaf and the ovolo, the cherub, goddess, and ancient
mosaic; in the medieval church he uncovers the columns,
capitals and architraves of a Classical city and people long
gone.

Like so many of his Humanist contemporaries, Gilles
has little patience or attention for what must have been the
vast remains of medieval Constantinople: the palaces,
wharves, fortifications and churches of the Latin Empire,

of the Paleologi emperors and of the trading emporiums and neighborhoods of the Venetians, Pisans, Genoese and other Westerners. The Blachernae, the Galata Tower, St. Savior in Chora are barely mentioned. In this single-hearted devotion to Christian antiquity Gilles shares much of the Humanist outlook, but in his reliance on first-hand examination of the monuments he joins the company of only a few Renaissance scholars, among them Petrarch and Poggio Bracciolini, and looks forward to the Romantic, and then scientific, archeological study of antiquity. His knowledge of ancient sculpture, inscriptions, and architecture, of their vocabulary and syntax, is excellent: his sources have taught him how to see, describe and to appreciate their remains in the city.

Gilles method, repeated over and over again through the course of these four books, is a simple one. Using the *Ancient Description of the Wards of the City,* a catalog itinerary produced in early fifth century,[16] as his broad outline, Gilles first introduces a general area of the city: the hills, or the wards, or a forum area, and briefly introduces the reader to a particular ancient site in it. He then briefly reviews the existing state of knowledge on this site: whether his evidence is an existing monument in full use or in abandoned ruin, inscriptions or poems, the stories of Constantinople's older residents who remember physical remains or stories, or the literary sources of ancient and more recent Byzantine historians. He then attempts to compare his sources, both to one another to derive a consensus, and then against other forms of evidence: physical or oral. When all these are in agreement, all is well, and Gilles is able to paint a fairly accurate picture; when they are not, he then strikes out on his own, discrediting a source through various scholarly or empirical judgments, comparing literary with physical remains. Often he actually goes out to the supposed site of a monument and attempts to retrace the building or area under discussion, sometimes with the help of a Turkish assistant, who did the climbing, entering and counting. Often such a physical examination is so far different from the literary sources that Gilles is forced to reject his written text's accuracy; often he will choose one sight with the same name over another precisely because his own physical examination leads to no other possible conclusion. Having thus fixed one more piece into the larger puzzle, he then goes on methodically to the next area discussed in the *Ancient Description*.

## THE *ANTIQUITIES* AS TRAVEL JOURNAL

*The Antiquities of Constantinople* also stands on its own as a brilliant piece of travel literature, quite aside from its use as a historical source or its appeal as a Renaissance text. Gilles' study of the ancient city under the rule of the Ottomans was no mere academic task: he faced great difficulties every step of the way, not only in his uncovering of sites and sources but from the hostility of both Turkish and Greek residents of the city. Yet the book also breathes the air of great travels: his interest in marine life emerges very clearly in the introductory passages, in which he enumerates the great variety of fish that thrive in the swift currents of the Bosporus and are enjoyed by the inhabitants, a fact to which the modern traveler to Istanbul can well attest. It conveys his delight in the city's parks and gardens, its country paths and busy thoroughfares, in its vistas from the heights of Pera or the Promontory over the seven hills of Constantinople, the Sea of Marmara, the shores of Asia, the distant hills of Bithynia, and Mount Olympus, always covered with snow, and the blue waters and the darting sails of all types of boats and ships that cross the sea passages commanded by the city.

Like all good travelers, Gilles also retains his wry sense of the ironic and the humorous: his descriptions of attempts to measure columns and buildings, the interruptions by Turkish onlookers and his implied attempts to distract them while his guide works feverishly away counting courses of stone, turnings of steps, moldings, cornices and windows, all faithfully recorded in a certain quite triumph, brick by brick, later in his account.[17] His narrative style of events he has witnessed is sparse and emblematic. He captures the atmosphere of the place and time in vivid scenes of everyday life: two acrobats vie for popular approval in the Hippodrome by jumping, unaided, from the Colossus set up there. One lands on his feet unhurt; the other loses his balance, slips, and is dashed to pieces amid the crowd.[18] His humorous self-revelations are just as sparse and dry. He tells us how he has discovered the true dimensions of the Chalca of Constantine: as he was scrambling around the site, he accidentally fell into a hole left by the ruins; climbing back out he counted the courses of its foundations, bases, tores and shafts.[19]

As we have already noted, Gilles seems to have worked extensively from journal books and to have compiled his final account from them during his years in Rome. We know that his nephew eventually finished his book, and we can infer that he followed his uncle's journal's rather closely toward the end, completing the works directly from the journals, with only light editing. In Antoine's almost verbatim copying of these notebooks he preserved for us a treasure house of the traveler's diary.

In these final sections, in his reflections on his trip, Gilles steps uncharacteristically to the fore, abandoning his measured, reasoned description of sites and sources, and interjects his own very personal feelings about his trip. We know he has come to the end of a long, obviously rewarding, but sometimes difficult and frustrating journey. He tells us that he was a stranger in the land: the people were not only unhelpful, they were downright hostile, both Greeks and Turks. The only way to keep on their good side was to put up with their coarse manners and dull conversation and to promise them lots of wine. They are also Philistines, with no regard for the glories of antiquity all around them. Not only that: they are ignorant and contemptuous of classical learning. His trip drained him of health, money and, obviously toward the end, spirit. While he concludes in proper Humanist fashion with a quote from the Platonists, Gilles tells us that he would never undertake such a journey ever again, and never knew why he ever undertook it to begin with. One can only speculate how many journals of wondrous trips through the ages have ended with similar private thoughts not intended to see the light of day.

## THE *ANTIQUITIES* AS TRAVEL LITERATURE

While we have discussed the nature of the *Antiquities of Constantinople* and touched on the life, method and personality of its author, we should now place the book itself in its place in the history of travel literature. Pilgrimage to the East, for religious, social, military or economic reasons had been an essential part of life in Western Europe since antiquity. Descriptions of ancient Greek sites are as old as Herodotus' *Histories* or Pausanias' *Guide to Greece*. From late antiquity on accounts of voyages to the East, especially to the Holy Land, were common reading in the West and reached an apogee in the era of the Crusades.[20] Among the most important sites for pilgrimages were Jerusalem itself and then Rome and Constantinople. All these cities held a special place for the Christians of the Middle Ages and Renaissance as seats both of Christian glory and suffering, and as focuses of imperial power, dreams, and memories.

Of these Constantinople held a special magical place, both for its religious associations and for the fact that it remained the vibrant center of a mighty Christian empire, the successor of Rome itself in power and glory. It was a magic city to the West: ringed with strong double walls and mighty towers, the city of the new Golden Gate, with palaces rising high above the glittering waters of the Golden Horn and the Bosporus: a city that at one breath called to mind spiritual and temporal wealth and power, a city unlike anything else in the Western world.

Among the earliest descriptions of the city or accounts of journeys to Constantinople[21] are Arculf's c. 670 and that of Ibn bin Iahya in the ninth century. In 968 Bishop Liutprand of Cremona recounts his frustrations and embarrassments as the envoy of German emperor Otto I to the splendid court of Nicephoras Phocas. During the age of the crusades we have accounts as disparate as those of Benjamin of Tudela from Spain and Anthony of Novgorod from Russia; while with the Crusades the narratives of Odo of Deuil, Geoffrey of Villhardouin and Robert of Clari trace vivid, if tragic, encounters of Latins and Byzantines. The last two give startling histories of the capture and sack of the city in 1204 by participants in the events.

During the late Middle Ages accounts abound; among them are the journals of Ludolf von Sudheim and Stephen of Novgorod (c. 1350), Ruy Gonzalez de Clavijo (1403), and Gilbert de Lannot (c.1420). Also around 1420 Cristoforo Buondelmonti visited and brought back to the West vivid images of the great city. This tradition was followed in the fifteenth century by Matteo de Pasti and Gentile Bellini, who left us striking portraits of Ottoman rulers and nobility. We can also mention here the views of the city later printed by Hartmann Schedel and Melchior Lorch. Among late fifteenth-century travelers we should also mention Pero Tafur and Angiolello. From 1453 we have an eye-witness account of the city's siege and capture from Nicolo Barbaro.

By the time Pierre Gilles visited the city, then, there had been a long and continuous tradition of Western travel literature there. While he draws on much of the medieval literature of the itinerary and city description, Gilles' keen observation and methods produce something new that seems to have captured the imagination of his contemporaries and his successors. His was definitely the most influential and well-known guide in the sixteenth century;[22] and his influence can be traced straight through the work of later travelers like Charles du Fresne du Cange (c.1650), Heinrich von Reimers (1793) and even in that of Julia Pardoe (1839). Gilles is still the basis for much of the speculation of modern guides and topographical surveys. One need only page through the *Blue Guide: Istanbul* to see the debt we owe to Gilles' speculations, daring and discoveries.

Each age has created its own spiritual vision of Constantinople: a city of Greek thieves, of Turkish princesses, of plotting princes, of otherworldly saints or Philistine traders. Each age has built its own physical city: ancient and Classical, medieval, Islamic and modern; yet each vision, each construct is only an approximation, a text discovered, reconstructed, edited and glossed. Pierre Gilles left his own text for his own age; yet it is a text that can still inform and delight the modern mind and eye.

*Ronald G. Musto*

# NOTES

1. Constantinople retained its Greek name until 1923, when modern Turkey was born and the city became Istanbul.

2. See, for example, Fernand Braudel, *The Mediterranean and the Mediterranean World in the Age of Philip II,* 2 vols., New York: Harper & Row, 1972-73, 1: 410-11, 418-19.

3. *Liber unus de Galicis et Latinis nominibus piscium,* Lyon: S. Gryphius, 1533.

4. See Louis Pascal, "Pierre Gilles," in *Nouvelle Biographie Générale,* Paris: Didot Frères, 1857, 20: 543, n.1.

5. *Dictionarium oppidorum,* Paris. No date.

6. *Historiae Ferdinandi regis Aragoniae,* Paris: Simon de Colines, 1521.

7. *Lexicon graecolatinum,* Basil: V. Curio, 1532.

8. *De vi et natura animalium,* Lyon: S. Gryphius, 1533.

9. Author of *Le grand insulaire et pilotage cosmographie de Levant* (Lyon, 1554); and the *Cosmographie universelle* (Paris 1575).

10. See below, p. 30.

11. See Marjorie Reeves, *The Influence of Prophesy in the Later Middle Ages,* Oxford: Clarendon Press, 1969, pp. 287-89, 381-84, 479-81; *Joachim of Fiore and the Prophetic Future,* London: SPCK, 1976, pp. 121-24, 149.

12. "Non. Ian. MDLV. Po. Cn. vixit annos LXV menses, dies V, hor. iiii."

13. *De Bosporo Thracio libri tres,* Lyon: Guillaume Rovillium, 1561.

14. *De topographia Constantinopoleos et de illius antiquitatibus libri quatuor,* Lyon: Guillaume Rovillium, 1561.

15. Cyril Mango, in "Introduction," Jean Ebersolt, *Constantinople byzantine et les voyageurs du Levant,* London: Pindar Press, 1986, p. 1.

16. The *Notitia urbis Constantinopolitanae,* ed. O. Seeck as *Notitia dignitatum,* Berlin, 1876, pp. 229-43; and translated as an appendix in Ball, *Antiquities.*

17. See, for example, his description of the Column of Constantine, p. 135; or of the Pillar of Arcadius, pp. 197-99.

18. See p. 81 below.

19. See p. 104 below.

20. See introduction to Theoderich, *Guide to the Holy Land,* New York: Italica Press, 1987.

21. See J.P.A. van der Vin, *Travellers to Greece and Constantinople. Ancient Monuments and Old Traditions in Medieval Travellers' Tales,* 2 vols., Leiden: Nederlands Historisch-Archaeologisch Instituut te Istanbul, 1980; James Phillips, *Early Christian and Byzantine Constantinople,* 2 vols., Monticello, IL: Vance Bibliographies, 1982, vol. 1; and Ebersolt, *Constantinople byzantine.*

22. See R. Janin, *Constantinople byzantine,* 2nd ed., Paris: Institut français d'études byzantines, 1964, p. xx.

\* \*
\*

CONSTANTINOPLE IN 1493

The made Prospect of the church of Sancta Sophia from Dr Greges Lib. 3 Plate

I. Tinney Sculp.

HAGIA SOPHIA, INTERIOR ELEVATION

# TRANSLATOR'S PREFACE

IT IS CUSTOMARY UPON A TRANSLATION TO GIVE SOME account both of the author and his writings. The author, Petrus Gyllius, as he stands enrolled among the men of eminency, and figure in polite learning , I find to be a native of Abi in France. He was in great reputation in the Sixteenth Century and was looked upon as a writer of so good a taste, and so comprehensive a genius, that there was scarce anything in the polite languages, which had escaped him. As he had a particular regard of men of distinguished learning, so was he equally honoured and esteemed by them. Francis, the First, king of France, the great patron of literature, and who was also a good judge of his abilities, sent him into Italy, and Greece, to make a collection of all the choice manuscripts which had never been printed, but in his passage it was his misfortune to be taken by the Corsairs. Some time after, by the application and generosity of Cardinal d'Armanac, he was redeemed from slavery. The just sense this munificent patron had of his merit, incited him, when my author had finished more than forty years travels over all Greece, Asia, and the greatest part of Africa, in the search of antiquities to receive him into his friendship, and family; where, while he was digesting, and methodizing his labours for the service of the public, he died in the year 1555, and in the sixty-fifth year of his age.

Although it was his intention to have published all the learned observations he had made in his travels, yet he lived to give us only a description of the Bosporus,

Thrace, and Constantinople, with an account of the antiquities of each of those places. In his search of what was curious he was indefatigable, and had a perfect knowledge of it in all its parts. He had also translated into Latin Theodore's *Commentaries on the Minor Prophets*, and sixteen books of Aelian's *History of Animals*. Petrus Belonius is highly reflected upon, in that being his domestic, and a companion with him in his travels, he took the freedom to publish several of his works under his own name: and indeed such a flagrant dishonesty in acting the plagiary in so gross a manner, was justly punished with the most severe censures; since it had been merit enough to have deserved the praises of the learned world for publishing such valuable pieces, with an honorable acknowledgement of the author of them.

I have no occasion to vindicate the worth and credit of my author, whose fame will live, and flourish, while the characters, given him by Gronovious, Thuanus, Morreri, Tournefort, and Montfaucon are of any weight. These great men have recorded him to future times, for his deep insight into natural knowledge, his unwearied application to the study of antiquity, and his great accuracy and exactness in writing.

In the following treatise, the reader had before him a full and lively view of one of the most magnificent cities in the universe; stately and beautiful in its natural situation, improved with all the art and advantages of fine architecture, and furnished with the most costly remains of antiquity; so that New Rome, in many instances of that kind, may seem to excel the Old.

I hope my author will not be thought too particular and exact in describing the several hills and vales, upon which Constantinople stands when it is considered, that he is delineating the finest situation in the world.

The manner in which he treats on this subject is very entertaining; and his descriptions, though with the greatest regard to truth, are embellished with a grace and beauty, almost poetical. This, I look upon it, was occasioned by the agreeable variety of delightful prospects and situations, which the subject naturally led him to describe.

The present state of Constantinople, I mean as to the meanness and poverty of its buildings, is attested by all those, who have either seen of wrote concerning it; so that it is not now to be compared with itself, as it stood in its ancient glory. The Turks have such an aversion to all that is curious in learning, or magnificent in architecture, or valuable in antiquity, that they have made it a piece of merit, for above two hundred years, to demolish, and efface everything of that kind; so that this account of the antiquities of that city given us by Gyllius, is not only the best, but indeed the only collective history of them.

In tracing out the buildings of Old Byzantium, the ancient Greek historians, which he perfectly understood, were of great service to him; this, with his own personal observations, as residing for some years at Constantinople, furnished him with materials sufficient for the present history.

The curious, who have always admired the accuracy of this work of Gyllius, have yet been highly concerned, that it wanted the advantage of cuts, by which the reader might have the agreeable pleasure of surveying with the eye what my author has so exactly described with the pen.

I have therefore endeavored to supply this defect, by presenting to the view of the reader a collection of figures, which do not only refer to such curiosities as he will find mentioned in the several parts of my author, but such as have been described by other later travelers, and by this means I hope I have given a complete view of whatsoever is most remarkable in the Antiquities of Constantinople.

*John Ball*
*1729*

\* \*
\*

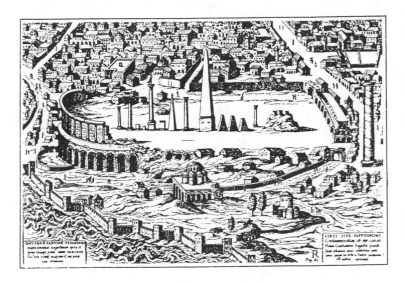

# AUTHOR'S PREFACE

CONSTANTINOPLE IS SO SITUATED ON A PENINSULA
that it is scarcely bounded by the Continent; for on three
sides it is enclosed by the sea. It is not only well fortified
by its natural situation, but it is also well guarded by forts
erected in large fields, extending from the city at least two
days' journey and more than twenty miles in length. The
seas that bound the peninsula are Pontus, or the Black Sea,
the Bosporus, and the Propontis. The city is enclosed by a
wall formerly built by Anastasius. It is for this reason
that being secured by a double peninsula, as it were, it
calls itself the fortress of all Europe and claims the
preeminence over all the cities of the world, extending
over the straits of both Europe and Asia.

For besides other immense advantages peculiar to it,
this is considerd a principle convenience of its situation,
that it is encompassed by a sea abounding with the finest
harbors for ships: on the south by the Propontis, on the
east by the Bosporus, and on the north by a bay full of
ports, which cannot only be secured by a boom, but even
without such a security can greatly annoy the enemy.
With the walls of Constantinople and Galata straitening its
latitude into less than half a mile over, it has often
destroyed the enemy's ships by liquid fire and other
instruments of war. I would remark further, that were it
secured according to the improvements of modern
fortification, it would be the strongest fortress in the
world. That is, if the four ancient ports, formerly
enclosed within its walls by booms, were rebuilt. Two of
these, which were not only the ornament, but the defense
of old Byzantium, held out a siege against Severus for the

space of three years; nor could it ever be obliged to surrender, except by famine.

Besides the profits and advantages it receives from the Propontis and the Aegean Sea, it holds an absolute dominion over the Black Sea. By one door only, namely by the Bosporus, it shuts up its communication with any other part of the world; for no ship can pass this sea, if the port thinks it fit to dispute its passage. By which means it appears that all riches of the Black Sea, whether exported or imported, are at its command. And indeed such considerable exports are made from here of hides of all kinds, of honey, wax, slaves, and other commodities as supply a great part of Europe, Asia, and Africa.

On the other hand, there are imported from those places such extraordinary quantities of wine, oil, corn, and other goods without number, that Mysia, Dacia, Pannonia, Sarmatia, Maeotis, Colchis, Spain, Albania, Cappadocia, Armenia, Media, Parthia, and both parts of Scythia share in the great abundance.

For this reason all foreign nations, if they want to entitle themselves to any property in the immense wealth of the Black Sea, and all seaport and island towns are obliged to court the friendship of this city. Besides, it is impossible for any ships to pass or repass, either from Asia or Europe, but at its pleasure, since it is, so to speak, the bridge and port of both those worlds. In fact, I might call it the continent that joins them, if the Hellespont did not divide them. But this sea is thought in many respects to be inferior to that of Constantinople. First, since it is much larger, and then, since it does not have a bay as that has, by which its city might be made a peninsula, nor a commodious port for ships. Indeed, if it had such a bay, it could still not reap any advantage of commerce from the Black Sea, except by the permission of the people of Constantinople.

Constantine at first began to build a city upon Sigeum, a promontory hanging over the straits of the Hellespont;

but quitting that situation he afterwards pitched upon a promontory of Byzantium. Troy, I acknowledge, is a magnificent city, but they were blind who could not discover the situation of Byzantium; all stark blind, who founded cities within view of it, either on the coast of the Hellespont or the Propontis. Though they maintained their grandeur for some time, yet at present they are quite in ruins, or they have only a few streets remaining. And if they were all rebuilt they must be subject to Constantinople, which is superior in power to all of them. Wherefore we may justly call it the key; not only of the Black Sea, but also of the Propontis and the Mediterranean Sea.

Cyzicus, now called Chazico, is highly esteemed since it joins the island to the Continent by two bridges, and unites two opposite bays and is, as Aristides informs us, the bond of the Black and the Mediterranean Sea. But any man who has his eyes in his head may see that it is only a very weak one. The Propontis flows in a broad sea between Cyzicus and Europe, by which means a passage is open into both seas, even though the people of Cyzicus might pretend to dispute it. So on the other hand, the people of Hellespont or Constantinople should contest it with them, they could have no advantage of the commerce of either of those seas.

I shall say nothing at present of Heraclea, Selymbria, and Chalcedon seated on the coast of the Propontis, anciently cities of renown both for the industry of their inhabitants and the agreeableness of their situation. But they could never share the principal commodities of other commercial towns in the neighborhood of the port of Constantinople, which was always looked upon as impregnable. The harbors of those cities have lain all under water for a considerable time, so that they were not of sufficient force to sail the Bosporus and the Hellespont without the permission of the inhabitants of those places.

But the Byzantines rode masters of the Black Sea in defiance of them all.

Byzantium therefore seems alone exempted from those inconveniences and incapacities that have happened to its neighbors and to many other potent and flourishing cities. Having lain in their own ruins for several years these are either not rebuilt with their ancient grandeur or they have changed their former situation. All its neighboring towns are still lost. Only the name of Memphis remains. Whereas Babylon, seated in its neighborhood, from a small fort, has become a large and populous city. Yet neither of them is as commodious as Constantinople. I shall take no notice of Babylon in Assyria, who, when it was in its most flourishing state, had the mortification to see a city built near it as large as itself. Why is not Alexandria rebuilt, except because it must support itself more by the industry of its people than its agreeable situation? It was the sanctity of St. Peter and the grandeur of the Roman name that contributed more to the rebuilding old Rome than the natural situation of the place itself, since it had no convenience for ships and harbors.

I pass in silence Athens and Lacedaemon, which were more remarkable for the learning and resolute bravery of their people than the situation of their city. I omit the two eyes of the sea coast, Corinth and Carthage, both of which, falling into ruins at the same time, were first repaired by Julius Caesar. Afterwards, when they fell entirely into decay, nobody rebuilt them. And although Carthage is situated on a peninsula with several havens about it, in no part of it are there two seas that fall into each other. For although Corinth may be said to lie between two seas and is called the fort of Peloponneseus, the key and door of Greece, yet is it so far from uniting two seas in one channel or two bays adjoining to the peninsula, that it was never able to make head against the Macedonians or Romans, as Cyzico and Negropont did;

one by its well-built forts and other war-like means, and the other by the strength of its natural situation.

But Constantinople is the key both of the Mediterranean and Black Sea. If you were to make a voyage around the world by the best skill in navigation you will meet it only in one point, that is, the mouth of the port. I shall say nothing of Venice, which does not so much enclose the sea for proper harbors as it is enclosed by it and labors under greater difficulties to keep off the swellings and inundations of the seas than to unite them together. I pass by the situations of the whole universe, wherever there are, have, or shall be cities; in none of them shall you find a port abounding with so many and so great conveniences, both for the maintenance of its dominion over the seas and the support of life as in this city.

It is furnished with plenty of all manner of provisions, being supplied with corn by the very large plain of Thrace, which extends in some parts a length of seven days and in others of more than twenty days journey. I shall say nothing of Asia, adjoining to it, abounding with the greatest fruitfulness both of corn and pasture, and the best conveniences for their import from both seas. As to the immense quantity of its wines, besides what is the product of its own soil, it is furnished with that commodity from all the coasts of the Bosporus, the Propontis, and the Hellespont, which are all well stocked with vineyards. Without the danger of a long voyage, Constantinople can, at its pleasure, import the choicest wines of all kinds, and whatever else may contribute to its own gratification and delight.

It is for this reason that Theopompus gives it the characteristic that ever since it became a market town its people were wholly taken up either in the market, in the port, or at taverns, giving themselves up entirely to wine. Menander, in his comedy *Auletris*, tells us that Constantinople makes all its merchants sots. "I booze it," says one of his actors, "all night; and upon my waking after the dose, I fancy I have no less than four hundred heads upon my shoulders." The comedians play handsomely upon them in giving us an account that when their city was besieged, their general had no other way to keep his soldiers from deserting but by building taverns within the walls. This is though a fault proceeding from their popular form of government, yet at the same time this denotes to us the great fruitfulness of their soil and the great plenty they have of wine. They who have been eyewitnesses can best attest how well they are provided with flesh, with venison and fowls. They might share these more abundantly, except that they are only indifferent sportsmen. Their markets are always stored with the richest fruits of all kinds. If any objection is made to this I would have it considered what quantities the Turks use, after hard drinking, to allay their thirst.

As to timber, Constantinople is so plentifully supplied with that, both from Europe and Asia, and will in all probability continue to be so, that it can be under no apprehensions of a scarcity that way as long as it remains a city. Woods of immeasurable length, extending themselves from the Propontis beyond Colchis, a more-than-forty-days journey, contribute to its store; so that it does not only supply the neighboring parts with timber for building ships and houses; but even Egypt, Arabia and Africa partake in the inexhaustible abundance. Meanwhile of all the cities of the world it cannot possibly need wood of any kind, in need of which even in our time, we have observed the most flourishing cities, both of Europe and Asia, sometimes to have fallen.

Marseilles, Venice, Taranto are all famous for fish; yet Constantinople exceeds them all in its abundance of this. The port is supplied with vast quantities from both seas; nor do they swim only in thick shoals through the Bosporus, but also from Chalcedon to this port so much so that twenty fish boats have been laden with one net.

Indeed they are so numberless that often from the continent you may take them out of the sea with your hands. In fact, when they swim up into the Black Sea in the spring you may kill them with stones. The women with osier baskets tied to a rope, angle for them out of the windows; and the fishermen with bare hooks take a sort of tunny fish in quantities sufficient to supply all Greece and a great part of Asia and Europe.

But not to recount the different kinds of fish they are stocked with, they catch such multitudes of oysters and other shellfish that in the fish market every day you may see so many boats full of them that there are enough for the Greeks all their fast days when they abstain from all sorts of fish that have blood in them. If there was not so considerable an abundance of flesh in Constantinople and if the people took any pleasure in eating fish and their fishermen were as industrious as those of Venice and Marseilles and were also allowed a freedom in their fishery, they would have it in their power not only to pay as a tribute a third part of their fish at least to the Grand Seignior, but also to supply all the lesser towns in its neighborhood.

If we consider the climate of New Rome, it must be allowed by proper judges, that it far excels that of Pontus. For my own part I have often experienced it to be a more healthy air than that of Old Rome; and for many years past I have hardly observed more than a winter or two to have been very cold and the summer heats have been allayed by the northern breezes, which generally clear the air for the whole season. In the winter it is a little warmed by the southern winds, which have the same effect. When the wind is from the north it generally brings rain, though it is quite otherwise in Italy and France. As to the plague, it is less raging, less mortal and no more rife among them than it is, commonly speaking, in great cities. Indeed, it would be less rife were it not for the multitudes of the common people and the foul way of eating among their slaves.

But that I may not seem to wax to much in praise of this city, never to be defamed by the most sour cynic, I must confess that there is one great inconvenience it labors under, which is that it is more frequently inhabited by a savage than a genteel, civilized people. Not that it is not capable of refining the manners of the most rude and unpolished, but because its inhabitants, by their luxurious way of living, emasculate themselves and for that reason are wholly incapable of making any resistance against those barbarous people by whom, for a vast distance, they are encompassed on all sides.

For this reason, although Constantinople seems, as it were by nature, formed for government, its people have neither the decencies of education nor any strictness of discipline. Their affluence make them slothful and their pride renders them averse to open familiarity and generous conversation. For that reason they avoid all opportunities of being thrust out of company for their insolence or of falling into dissensions among themselves, by which means the Christian inhabitants of the place formerly lost both their city and government. But even if quarrels and divisions never run so high as to throw the whole city aflame, as they have many times done, even though they should raze it even with the ground, nevertheless it would soon rise again again out of its own ruins because of the pleasantness of its situation.

Without this the Black Sea could not so much properly be called Euxine, as the Axine Sea — the inhabitants of the whole coast used to kill all strangers that fell into their hands — because of the great numbers of barbarous people who dwell round the Black Sea. It would be dangerous venturing on the coasts of the Black Sea, either by land or water, which are full of pirates and robbers, unless they were kept in a tolerable order by the government of the port. There would be no passing the straits of the

Bosporus, which is inhabited on both shores by a barbarous people except for the same reason. And though a man was never so secure of a safe passage he might mistake his road at the mouth of the Bosporus, being misguided by the false lights that the Thracians, who inhabit the coast of the Black Sea, formerly used to hang out, instead of a pharos.

It is therefore not only in the power of Constantinople to prevent any foreigners sailing in the Black Sea, but in reality no powers can sail it without some assistance from her. Since, therefore, Constantinople is the fortress of all Europe, both against the pirates of Pontus and the savages of Asia, even if it were effectually demolished to all appearance, nevertheless it would rise again out of its ruins to its former grandeur and magnificence. With what fury did Severus pursue this city to final destruction? Yet when he cooled his resentments against these people he realized that he had destroyed a city that had been the common benefactor of the universe and the grand bulwark of the Eastern Empire. Soon after he began to rebuild it, and he ordered that, in honor of his son, it would be called Antonina. I shall end with this reflection: that though all other cities have their periods of government and are subject to the decays of time, Constantinople alone seems to claim a kind of immortality and will continue to be a city as long as humanity shall live either to inhabit or rebuild it.

*Pierre Gilles*

\* \*
\*

The SERRAGLIO POINT of CONSTANTINOPLE.

A  The Entrance into ỹ Serraglio from ỹ City.
B  Lodgings for the Guards.
C  The great Hall for publick Audience.
D  The Grand Signor's Lodgings.
E  The Womens Lodgings.
F  Pleasure Houses.
G  The Grand Signor's Barge-houses.
H  Part of Constantinople called Balat.
I  The Entrance into the Serraglio from Sea.
K  Sancta Sophia now ỹ Grand Signors Mosque.
L  Part of the Asia Shear.
M  The Bosporus w.ch divides Europe from Asia.

From H. Randolph

# BOOK ONE

## I

## Of the Founders of Byzantium
## And the Different Successes
## And Revolutions of that City

IT IS RECORDED BY STEPHANUS AND PAUSANIAS THAT Byzantium, now called Constantinople, was first founded by Byzas the son of Neptune and Corossa, or by a person named Byzes, admiral of the fleet of the Megarians, who transplanted a colony there. I am of the opinion that this was the same person as Byzas. For had it taken its name from Byzes, this city would more properly have been called Byzeum rather than Byzantium. In the *Life of Marcus* Philostratus, a Sophist of Byzantium, calls the admiral of the fleet by the name of Byzas when he informs us that Marcus, who, he claims, was descended from the ancient family of Byzas, made a voyage to Megara and was favored greatly by the people there who had formerly sent a colony over to Byzantium. When they had consulted Apollo about where they should found a city, these people received an answer from the oracle that they should seek out a position opposite the Land of the Blind. The people of Chalcedon were given to understand by this mystical answer that though they had made a landing there before and had an opportunity of viewing the commodious situation of that and other

1

adjacent places, at last they had encamped at the most improper place of all.

As to what is mentioned by Justin, that Byzantium was first founded by Pausanias a Spartan, I take it to mean no more than this: that they who affirm that Sycae, presently called Galata, was first founded by the Genoese, as was Constantinople by Constantine, their meaning was that they either rebuilt or enlarged those places, and not that they were the first founders of them. For I find in Herodotus that upon the invasion of Thrace by Darius, the people of Byzantium and Chalcedon did not in the least expect the arrival of the Phoenician fleet. Having left their cities, they retired to the inland shores of the Black Sea and there founded Mesembria, and that the Phoenicians burnt Byzantium and Chalcedon. I am therefore of the opinion that the Lacedaemonians, under the command of Pausanias, sent a colony there and rebuilt Byzantium, which was previously either a colony of the Megarians or the center of the subjects of Byzas, the son of Neptune, its first founder.

Eustathius assures us that in antiquity it was called Antonina from Antoninus Bassianus, the son of Severus Caesar but that it lasted with that name no longer than his father lived, and that many years after it was called New Rome, Constantinople, Anthusa or Florentia by Constantine the Great; because of which Priscian called it New Constantinopolitan Rome.

It was foretold by the oracle that its inhabitants would be a successful and flourishing people, but a constant course of prosperity did not always attend them. It was with great difficulty that this city first began to make a figure in the world in the struggles it underwent with the Thracians, Bithynians, and Gallo-grecians, and in paying a yearly tribute of eighty talents to the Gauls who controlled part of Asia. It was through greater struggles that it rose to higher degrees of eminence, while being frequently harassed not only with foreign but domestic enemies. It underwent mighty changes sometimes under the popular, sometimes under the aristocratic, form of government, widely extending its conquests in Europe and Asia, but especially in Bithynia. Philarcus observes in the sixth book of his *History* that the Byzantines have the same power over the Bithynians as the Lacedaemonians had over their Helotae. This commonwealth had so great a veneration for the Ptolemaei kings of Egypt, that they paid divine honors to one of them named Philadelphus and erected a temple to him within sight of their city. So great a regard had they for the Roman name that they assisted them against the king of Macedon, to whom they gave the nickname Pseudo-Philippus as if he were a degenerate descendent of his predecessors. I need not mention the powerful aid they sent against Antiochus, Perseus, Aristonicus and the assistance they gave Antonius when engaged in a war against pirates. This city alone withstood the brunt of Mithridates' whole army that had landed in their territory and at last, though with great difficulty, bravely repelled the invader. It immediately assisted Sulla, Lucullus and Pompey when they laid siege to any town or fortification that might prove to be a haven for their auxiliary forces on their march, either by sea or land, or might prove a convenient port either for export or import of provisions.

Finally, joining its forces with Niger against Severus, it became subject to the Perinthians and was despoiled of all the honors of its government. All its stately baths and theaters, its strong and lofty walls with which it was fortified, were entirely ruined. These had been built of square stone, much of the same hardness as that of a grindstone, not brought from Miletus, as Politianus fancies. I say that this stone was cut out of no quarry, either from ancient Miletus or Miletopolis, because Miletus lies at too great a distance from it, and Miletopolis, which is situated near the River Rhyndacus, is in no way famous for quarries. I saw this last city, by

3

the way, adjoining the lake of Apolloniatus, entirely demolished, retaining only its present name.

The walls of Byzantium, as Herodian relates, were cemented with so thin a mortar that you would think them not a constructed building but one huge stone. They who saw them in ruins in Herodian's time were equally surprised at those who built and those who defaced them. Dion, whom Zonaras quotes, reports that their copings were built with stones three feet thick pressed together with links of brass. It was so firmly compacted inwardly that the whole building seemed to be one solid wall.

It is adorned with numerous and large towers with gates placed in them one above another. The walls on land side are very lofty; towards the sea they are not quite so high. There were two ports within the walls, secured with booms, as was their entrance by two high forts. At the time I had no opportunity to consult Xenophon in the original. However, I was of the opinion from the Latin translation that a passage in that author, which is as follows, relates to one of those ports:

> When the soldiers had passed over from Chrysopolis to Byzantium and were denied entrance to the city, they threatened to force the gates unless the inhabitants opened them of their own accord. Immediately hastening to the sea, they scaled the walls and leaped into the town, close by the sides of the port, which the Greeks call χηλαι, that is by the piles; because they jut out into the sea, winding into the figure of a crab's claw.

But afterwards, meeting that author in Greek, I found no mention there of the port, but only τὴν χηλὴν τοῦ τείχους, that is, near "the copings of the wall" or rather the buttresses that support it. Had the original read χηλὴ τοῦ λιμένος it ought rather to have been translated the "leg," or the "arm."

Dionysius of Byzantium mentions that the first winding of the Bosporus contains three ports. In their time the Byzantines had five hundred ships, some of which were two-decked galleys; some had rudders both at stem and stern and also had pilots at each end, and two sets of hands aboard, so that there was no need for them to tack about either in an engagement or on a retreat.

Both in the lifetime and after the death of Niger, the Byzantines worked wonders when besieged for three years; for they not only took the enemies' ships as they sailed by them but dragged their three-decked galleys from their moorings. Diving under water, they cut their anchors, and by fastening small ropes from the stern around their ankles, they hauled off their ships, which seemed to float merely on the natural tide of the sea. Nor were the Byzantines the first to practice this stratagem. Under the pretence of gathering shell-fish, the Tyrians frequently would play the same trick; which Alexander had no sooner discovered that he gave orders that the anchors of his whole fleet should be fastened to iron chains instead of cables.

In this siege the Byzantines were reduced to great straits but they still refused to surrender, making the best defense they could with timber taken from their houses. They also braided cables for their ships out of their women's hair; in fact, sometimes they threw down statues and horses on the heads of their enemies. At last their provisions were entirely spent, so they took to hides softened in water. These gone, they were brought to the extreme necessity of eating one another. At last, wholly reduced by famine, that were forced to surrender. The Romans gave no quarter to the soldiers nor to the principal men of the city. The whole town, with all its stately walls in which it gloried, was levelled to the ground; and all its theaters and baths were demolished to the narrow width of a single street. Severus was highly pleased with so noble a conquest. He took away the freedom of the city, and having deprived it of the dignity of a commonwealth, he confiscated the goods of the inhabitants. Afterwards making it a tributary, he gave it to the Perinthians with all the neighboring country. He later entered the city. Seeing the inhabitants coming to meet him with olive branches in their hands, begging quarter and excusing themselves for making so long a defense, he ended the slaughter; yet he left the Perinthians in possession of the town. Nevertheless, allowing them a theater, he gave orders for building them a portico for hunting and a hippodrome, to which he joined some baths, which he built near the Temple of Jupiter, who was called Zeuxippus. He also rebuilt the Strategium. All the works that were begun by Severus in his lifetime were finished by his son Antoninus.

# II

# The Extent of Old Byzantium

THE PRESENT INHABITANTS OF CONSTANTINOPLE TELL you that old Byzantium stood inside the compass of the first hill in the imperial precinct, where the Grand Seignor's Seraglio now stands. From what follows, however, it will appear that I am of the opinion that it was of larger extent. Our modern writers describe its situation thus: it began at the wall of the citadel, stretched to the tower of Eugenius, and rose gradually up to the Strategium, the Baths of Achilles and the Urbicion. From there it passed on to Chalcopratia and the Miliarium

Aureum, where there was another Urbicion of the Byzantines. From there it stretched to the Pillars of Zonarius, from which, after a gentle descent, it wound around by the Mangana and the Baths of Arcadius up to the Acropolis. I am inclined to believe all these writers, except Eustathius, who tells us that the Athenians made use of Byzantium, a small city, to keep their treasure in. But Zosimus, a more ancient historian, describes Byzantium in this manner:

It was seated on a hill that took up part of the isthmus and was bounded by a bay called Ceras and the Propontis. At then end of the porticos built by Emperor Severus there was a gate set up upon his reconciliation with the inhabitants for giving protection to Niger, his enemy. The wall of Byzantium extended from the eastern part of the city to the Temple of Venus and to the sea opposite Chrysopolis. From the north it descended to the dock and so onward to the sea that faces the Black Sea and through which you sail into it.

This, he says, was the ancient city.

Dionysius, a more ancient writer than Zosimus, as appears from his account written before the city's destruction by Severus, tells us that Byzantium was at least forty furlongs in circumference, which is a much greater extent than the previous writers reported it. Herodian informs us that in the time of Severus Byzantium was the greatest city in all Thrace.

# III

## The Rebuilding of Byzantium
## By
## Constantine the Great
## And its Extent in his Time

ZONARAS RECORDS THAT CONSTANTINE DECIDED to build a city and to give it his own name. At first, therefore, he settled on Sardicus, a plain in Asia, afterwards on the Sigeum promontory, and last of all on Chalcedon and Byzantium. Georgius Cedrinus is of the opinion that he first settled on Thessalonica, and after he had lived there two years wonderfully taken with the delights of the place, he built the most magnificent temples, baths, and aqueducts. Interrupted in his great designs by the plague that raged there, he was obliged to leave it. Crossing toward Chalcedon, formerly overthrown by the Persians but then being rebuilt, he was directed by eagles frequently carrying the small stones for the workmen from there to Byzantium, where Constantinople was to be built.

Zonaras is of the same opinion and only differs as to the story of the stones and says that they were small ropes that they used in building. But this seems to be a fable taken from the writer, Dionysius of Byzantium, who tells us that Byzas would have founded Byzantium in a place called Semystra at the mouth of the rivers Cydarus and Barbysa had not a crow snatched a piece of the sacrifice out of the flames and carried it to a promontory of the Bosporus. This directed Byzas to found Byzantium in that place.

But Constantine does not seem to me to have been so nearsighted as were the ancient Chalcedonians, for which they stand recorded in the histories of all ages. No, it is discernable by anyone of tolerable judgment that Byzantium was a much more appropriate site for the Roman Empire than Chalcedon. The far more ancient historians, among whom are Sozomen of Salamis and Zosimus, who wrote in the reign of Theodosius II, judged the event more rationally. They tell us, without taking any notice of Sardica, Thessalonica or Chalcedon, that Constantine debated where he might build a city equal in glory and magnificence to Rome and call it by his own name. He had found a convenient site for that purpose between old Troy and the Hellespont; he laid the foundations and raised part of the wall to a considerable height, which is still to be seen today on the promontory of Sigeum. Pliny called this Ajantium because the sepulcher of Ajax, which was in that place, hung over the cliffs of the Hellespont. They also relate that some ships were stationed there and that the Greeks, when at war with the Trojans, pitched their tents in that place.

Constantine afterwards came to the opinion that Byzantium was a more suitable site. Three hundred and sixty-two years after the reign of Augustus he rebuilt, enlarged and fortified it with great and strong walls. With an edict engraved on a stone pillar and publicly set up in the Strategium, near his own equestrian statue, he ordered it to be called Nova Roma Constantinopolitana. After computing that the natives were not a sufficient number to populate the city, he built several fine houses in and around the forums, of which he made a present to the senators and other men of quality whom he brought with him from Rome and other nations. He also built several forums, some as an ornament and others for the service of the city. He beautified the Hippodrome with temples, fountains, porticos, and a Senate House; and he allowed its members equal honors and privileges with those of Rome. He also built himself a palace, little inferior to the royal one at Rome. In short, he was so ambitious to make it rival Rome itself in all it grandeurs and magnificence that at length, as Sozomen assures us, it far surpassed it both in the number of its inhabitants and in its affluence of all kinds.

Eunapius, a Sardian and no mean writer even though an enemy of Constantine, describes the vast extent of Constantinople in these words:

> Constantinople, formerly called Byzantium, allowed the ancient Athenians the liberty of importing corn in great quantities. But at present not all the cargo ships from Egypt, Asia, Syria, Phoenicia, and many other nations can import a quantity sufficient for the support of those people, whom Constantine — by unpeopling the other cities — has transported there.

Zosimus also, though otherwise no very good friend of Constantine on the score of his religion, frankly admits that he wonderfully enlarged it and that the isthmus was enclosed by a wall from sea to sea a distance of fifteen furlongs beyond the walls of old Byzantium.

But to whatever extent Constantine might have enlarged its boundaries, the emperors who succeeded him have extended them further and have enclosed the city with much wider walls than those built by Constantine and have permitted them to build one house so closely to another even in their market places that they could not walk in the streets without danger since they were so crowded with people and cattle. For this reason a great part of the sea that runs around the city was drained in some places. Here by fixing posts in a circle and building houses on them they made their city large enough for the reception of an infinite multitude of people. Thus Zosimus expresses himself on the vast extent of this city as it stood in the time either of Arcadius or Theodosius.

Agathius says that in the time of Justinian the buildings were so close and crowded together that it was very difficult to see the sky when looking up through their rooftops. We may reconstruct the large size of this city before Justinian's time to some extent from an *Ancient Description of the City* by an anonymous but seemingly very faithful writer. He assures us that the length of the city from the Porta Aurea to the seashore in a direct line was fourteen thousand and seventy-five feet and that it was six thousand, one hundred and fifty feet in width. Yet we cannot reconstruct from Procopius that in the reign of Justinian the Blachernae were enclosed within the walls, although before his time the city was enlarged by Theodosius II, who — as Zonaras and others write — gave orders to Cyrus the governor of the city for that purpose. With great diligence and wonderful dispatch this man built a wall over the land side from sea to sea in sixty days. Astonished that so immense a work should be finished in so short a time, the inhabitants cried out publicly in the theater, in the presence of Theodosius the emperor, "Constantine built this city, but Cyrus rebuilt it." This drew the envy of his prince on him and rendered him suspect. Therefore he was tonsured by command of Theodosius against his inclinations and was made bishop of Smyrna.

The following inscriptions made to Constantius and carved over the gate of Xylocerum (Xylocercon or Xylocricum) and Rhegium, note of him in these verses:

These walls by Theodosius' royal will,
And Constantinus Prefect of the East,
In sixty days, surprizing speed! were built.

Over the Gate of Rhegium is this inscription:

> Great Constantinus, Prefect of the East,
> In sixty days this stately building finished.

The reason why Constantine ordered Byzantium to be called New Rome, or Queen of the Roman Empire, is mentioned by Sozomen and others: God appeared by night to Constantine and advised him to build a city at Byzantium worthy of his own name. Some say that just as Julius Caesar, discovering a plot against him, judged it necessary to move to Alexandria or Troy, stripped Italy at the same time of everything that was valuable and carried off all the riches of the Roman Empire, leaving the administration in the hands of his friends; so it is said that Constantine, perceiving himself to be obnoxious to the people of Rome — having drained the city of its wealth — went over at first to Troy and afterwards to Byzantium.

Zosimus, an implacable enemy to the Christian name, alleges an execrable piece of villainy as the cause of his removal. He says:

> Constantine, when he had murdered Crispus and had been guilty of other flagrant crimes, desired an expiation for them from the priests. Their answer was that his offences were so many and enormous that they did not know how to atone for them. They told him at the same time that there was a certain Egyptian who came from Spain to Rome, who, if he had an opportunity of speaking to him, could procure him an expiation if he would establish in his dominions this belief of the Christians, namely that men of the most profligate lives, immediately upon their repentance, obtained the remission of sins. Constantine readily closed this deal, and his sins were pardoned. At the approach of the festival on which it was usual for

him and his army to go to the Capitol to perform the customary rites of their religion, Constantine feared to be present at the solemnity, being warned against it by a dream that was sent him from the Egyptian. By not attending the holy sacrifice, he highly disgusted the Senate and the whole body of the people of Rome. But unable to bear the curses and scandal they threw upon him on that account, he went in search of some place or other equally famous to Rome where he might build a palace and that he might make the seat of the Roman Empire. At last he discovered a place between Troas and Old Ilium fit for that purpose. There he built a palace, laid the foundations of a city, and raised part of a wall for its defense. Afterwards, disapproving the site, he left his works unfinished and settled at Byzantium. Wonderfully taken with the agreeableness of the place, he judged it to be very appropriate for an imperial seat in all respects.

This according to Zosimus, a great favorite of Julian the Apostate and an inveterate enemy to Constantine on account of his religion. I have so perfect an aversion to his sentiments that I cannot give the least credit to the enormities he charges Constantine with, and of which Constantine had the greatest abhorrence, being a prince of remarkable clemency and goodness. I am capable of proving this fully, but it would prove too great a digression in the present history. The truth of it is that Sozomen and Evagrius both have sufficiently refuted these malicious reflections.

In these calumnies, I say, I entirely differ from Zosimus, yet with his description of the extent and compass of the city I am wholly in agreement. Though an enemy of Constantine, he is forced to acknowledge him to have built so large, so noble, so magnificent a city. I am even more induced to give credit to his history in this respect because he lived many ages closer to the time of Constantine that our modern monks. In the books they have written on Constantinople they give the following account: Constantine built a wall from the tower of Eugenius, which was the boundary of old Byzantium, to St. Anthony's Church and the Church of the Blessed Virgin, called Rabdon, right up to the Exacionion. At a mile's distance it passed into the old gates of the Church of St. John the Baptist, stretching farther to the cistern of Bonus, from which it extended to the Armation and so wound round to St. Anthony's Church again. I would give myself the trouble of verifying this account, except that I know the authors are so fantastic that they cannot be depended on in any way. But I take it to be an intolerable blunder that they place the Church of St. John the Baptist within the walls built by Constantine, whereas for many years after his death it continued to be outside this city. I shall note this and many other errors in the following history.

# IV

# The Present Shape, Circuit, Length and Width Of Constantinople

THE SHAPE OF CONSTANTINOPLE IS TRIANGULAR, THE base of which is the part that lies westward. The top angle points to the east where the peninsula begins. But the sides of this triangle are not equal; for the side that lies westward winds around the angle of the bay in the figure of a half-moon. At a great distance from there it winds around again from north to south. But the south side of this triangle veers around to such an extent that, should you draw a straight line from one angle of it to the other, it would cut off a creek, the middle of which is at least a quarter mile over. Next is the side that faces the north and is called Ceras, the "bay" or "horn." Should you draw a straight line over it from one angle to another, it would cut off not only the whole bay but also a part of Galata, for this side turns inward in such a manner that from each point it curves in the form of a bow, with two smaller windings of the same figure in its middle. It lies so far into the Continent, that the two horns or ends of the bow that includes them in no way interrupt the view of the angles of the larger arc.

Because of this Constantinople may seem to be rather a triarcular than a triangular form. For right angles never project beyond their sides, nor do they inflect inward. But all semicircular forms are in a way both convex and concave. So that if these three angles, so far as they project beyond the main body of the city, were divided from it, Constantinople would form a rectangular figure little more than a mile broad and almost three times as long. But be that as it may, all are of the opinion that this city ought to be considered a triangle because it has three sides. The one that faces the Propontis and the other on the side of the Thracian continent are of equal length; the third adjoining the bay is about a mile shorter that the other two.

This city is computed to be nearly thirteen miles in circumference, although Laonicus Chalcondylus, in his *History of the Ottomans*, assures us that Constantinople was a hundred and eleven furlongs in circumference. Its length, extending over the Promontory with six hills, is more than thirty furlongs, but if its shape were an equilateral triangle, it would not be much more than nine miles in circumference. If we supposed its hilly site to be widened into one large plain, then it would not be as large in circumference as the inhabitants generally reckon it, namely eighteen miles. One could observe that Constantinople does not contain more building sites since it is situated on hills than it would if it were built on a plain; because you cannot build on a decline, as conveniently as you can on level ground. But such reasoning does not hold equally good as to the number of its houses and the number of its inhabitants. For Constantinople can contain more people, since it is situated on hills, than it could if it were sited on a plain.

The width of this city varies in several places. From the east to the middle it is at least a mile in width but in no place broader than a mile and a half. It then divides into two branches, where it is almost as broad as it is long. I can compare its shape to nothing more properly than an eagle stretching out its wings and looking obliquely to the left. On its beak stands the first hill, where the Grand Seignor's Palace is. In his eye stands the Church of St. Sophia; on the lower part of the head is the Hippodrome; upon his neck are the second and third hills; and the remaining part of the city fill up his wings and his whole body.

# V

# A General Description
# Of
# Constantinople

IN CIRCUMFERENCE CONSTANTINOPLE TAKES UP THE whole peninsula, which contains seven hills. Of those the eastern angle of the city includes one rising at the

Promontory that Pliny calls Chrysoceras and Dionysius of Byzantium, Bosporium. The first hill is divided from the second by a broad valley. The Promontory of Bosporium contains the other six, extending from the entrance of the peninsula on the east, its ridge continuing westward somewhat curved, and ending over the bay. Six hills and five valleys shoot from its right side, and it is divided only by the third and fifth valleys on its left side, all on the descent. It has only some small hills and vales, which are more steep than the hills themselves. It also has two windings that rise from the top of the first hill, from which it ascends by degrees almost to another winding, which begins from the top of the third hill. Sinking to a gentle descent here, it opens to the valley that lies between the third and fourth hill. From there is rises again with a moderate ascent and continues level westward almost to the Urbicion, where it rises again.

The plains adjoining the Promontory have different levels. Those that divide the Promontory at the top and those at its foot are very uneven in many places. The plain at the top of the first hill is seven hundred paces long and two hundred wide. Shooting out from here it rises almost imperceptibly to the top of the second hill, where it is five hundred paces wide, and constantly descends to the top of that hill. Here the second valley, which is also overhanging and very narrow, makes its rise. On the third hill the plain is more than six hundred paces in width but is somewhat wider at the level of the entrance of the third valley, which is six hundred paces wide. From here you rise by a gentle ascent to the plain on top of the fourth hill, which is not more than two hundred paces wide. On the fifth hill it widens to seven hundred paces. On the hill from which the fifth valley rises it is more narrow; and on the sixth hill it ascends a little again.

The plain that extends between the sea and the bottom of the Promontory is also not as level in some places as it is in others; for it is narrower under the hills. In the valleys it is half as wide again. Winding from the Promontory —where it begins —over the three valleys, it widens at that distance to a thousand paces. At the foot of the hills, however, it is not more than an acre, or a hundred and twenty feet, in breadth, except at the bottom of the third and fifth hills, where it is very narrow. It extends over the fourth valley both in length and width to a great degree. At the foot of the sixth hill it contracts again, except at the foot of the two smaller hills, situated behind the first and second hills; one of which projects almost to the sea, the other is no great distance from it.

But to describe Constantinople in a more easy and comprehensive manner, I will give the reader a particular account of its hills and vales, which make a very lovely and agreeable prospect indeed. For the six hills that shoot from the Promontory —which you might call brothers for their resemblance —stand in so regular an order that none of them blocks the view of another. As you sail up the bay you see them all hanging over it in such a manner that all around the city you see both sides of every one of them.

The first of these hills juts out to the east and bounds the bay; the second and third lie more inward to the south; the others lie more open to the north so that at one view you have a full prospect of them. The first lies lower than the second; the second than the third; the fourth, fifth and sixth are higher in some places, in others somewhat lower than the third. This you may discover by the level of the Aqueduct. That the first hill is lower that the third and the fourth may be discovered by the tower that supports the Aqueduct by which the water is raised more than fifty feet into the air.

To make this more intelligible, I will divide the city's length from the land's point on the shore of the Bosporus to the walls on the neck of the isthmus and consider its width as it broadens from the Propontis to the bay called Ceras. The reason why I divide the city's width into six parts is due to the natural location of the Promontory, which itself is divided into six hills, with valleys running between them. It was not very difficult to distinguish the Roman hills, because they were entirely separated by valleys, but it is not as easy to distinguish those of Constantinople because they are joined at the top. Besides, their backs do not project in so mountainous a way as they do in front; so that I cannot better describe them than by calling them a continued ridge of hills, each divided by valleys. Therefore, to proceed regularly, I shall first give the reader a description of the right side of the Promontory, with its hills and vales, and then note its left side, which stands behind them.

# VI

## A Description
## Of the Position
## Of All the Parts
## Of the City

THE FIRST PART OF THE PROMONTORY'S WIDTH IS ITS shorefront. This opens a distance of a thousand paces eastwards and joins the opening of the Bosporus. This sea winds around the back of the Promontory in such a manner that from the point where the Bosporus is divided into the bay called Ceras and the land's point of that sea, it extends from north to south a distance of fourteen furlongs. From there it winds around from the southeast to the south-southwest another four furlongs all the way to the mouth of the Propontis. Joining the Bosporus, this winds around the city to the southwest a distance of two miles or more. This side of the hill is bounded at the

bottom by a plain of the same width as itself, which is two
hundred paces. On the plain there rise some smaller hills,
which are not more than four hundred paces in height.
On the top of the left side of these hills stands the
Hippodrome. On the right side, which faces southwest, is
the Palace of the Grand Seignor. I might not improperly
call it the front of the Promontory, since it is almost an
equal ascent on all sides with a plain running along its
entire length. Besides, it adjoins the first hill. For these
reasons I might call it a part of the first hill, but to
understand it more distinctly I shall treat it by itself.

# VII

# The First Hill,
## The Palace of the Grand Seignor,
## The Church of St. Sophia,
## And
## The Hippodrome

THE FIRST HILL, EXTENDING FROM THE SOUTHEAST TO
the southwest, has an entrance thirty paces wide. From
there it widens gradually until it is almost as broad as it is
long. It rises at the corner of the isthmus that joins the
peninsula to the Continent. It projects out in the form of a
scimitar or a hawk's beak, and almost divides the straits of
the Bosporus and the bay called Ceras. The whole hill
projects beyond the others almost to the mouth of the bay.
It has a descending angle except at the top, where there is
a plain that joins the plain of the Promontory.

The lesser eminences that stand on it, and which face
the east and north, have a moderate descent. Others are
more steep, so that in some places you are obliged to

climb them by steps; but the tallest of them is not more than four hundred paces high.

The plain at the foot of this hill is very different. Its eastern part it is greatly extended by the seashore, which juts out in a semicircle. The width of its southeast and northern part is increased by the valley that divides the first from the second hill. The plain on the top of the hill is about seven hundred paces in length. This hill is not only fortified by nature, being encompassed on the east by the Bosporus, on the north by the Bay of Ceras, and on the west by a cool valley; but it is also enclosed within the walls of the Seraglio, which are guarded with numberless ramparts and towers that are equal in strength to the walls of the city. Towards the foot of the hill and the plain near the sea lie the gardens of the Grand Seignor. The Imperial Palace, which is partly situated on the top of the hill and partly on the eminences below it, affords an almost immeasurable prospect both by sea and land.

On this plain there are two imperial areas or courts; the first of these courts is seven hundred paces long and two hundred broad. You pass through this into another inner court, which is a quadrangle two hundred paces long and has a magnificent portico around it supported by a multitude of fine marble pillars curiously variegated. In the middle of the court there is a fine shady walk of plane and cypress trees for the lawyers; and in the north angle of the city is the *Forum Judiciale*, which the Ottomans call their Divan.

On the southeast side of a large court stands the magnificent and stately palace of the Grand Seignor, on the north of which are built many imperial baths and kitchens with eight arched roofs rising like hemispherical cupolas. Each of these cupolas, resembling a little house, is nothing else but a chimney with windows, light at top, made like a lantern.

There is a two-doored iron gate that lets you into the first court, the doors of which, when opened, stand twenty paces apart. The porters or Capoochees always stand on duty at these gates. Just above them the hill rises up to a smooth level with the ridge of the Promontory. The porch or gate house is lined on each side with glittering armour and shines, as do the jambs of the gate, with rich marble. Over the porch there rises a square building covered with lead, as are all the other edifices of the palace.

There is a passage out of the first court through another two-doored gate into the second inner court. This is the station of the Drudging Porters. The gate house here also blazes with brightly shining arms. This gate has nothing like a porch outside, though it does inside. It is supported by ten pillars of different kinds of marble; its roof proudly glitters with gold and is beautified with the most rich and lively colors of Persian work.

At the third gate, where the entrance opens onto the Seraglio, there are other porters or Capoochees attending. These are under the command of the Capoochee-Pasha, or Captain of the Porters, who is also Chamberlain to the Grand Seignor. Nobody is allowed to enter the palace without his permission, except the servants and other officers of the household. However, his noblemen may freely enter to pay homage to him while he is sitting near the door of the Seraglio.

All ambassadors, when introduced into his presence, are allowed to kiss his hand. He receives them sitting on a low couch, curiously embroidered, in a little apartment built with marble, adorned with gold and silver, and sparkling with diamonds and precious stones. This Room of State is encircled with a portico that is supported by pillars of the finest marble, the capitals and pedestals of which are all gilded.

Besides these that I have mentioned there are many other gates around the Seraglio, through which none are admitted except those who are in the highest favor with the emperor. If I am not mistaken, I counted twelve that were all ironwork; seven of them near the city; two of them, through which they carried their hay to the Seraglio, were near the sea; on the seaside there were five more. The first of these stands to the north of the Seraglio, towards the bay; the second stands on the ridge of a hill. It is very large, has a porch with an arched roof in front of it, is gilded and adorned in a surprising manner with Persian paintings, supported with pillars of ophitic marble, and looks into the Bosporus.

At some distance eastward there is another gate facing Chalcedon. Just before it are moored the vessels in which the Grand Seignor sails to some different shore when he goes hunting or is inclined to divert himself in his gardens. The fourth gate stands southeast near the ruins of a Christian church, some tokens of which still remain in a wall to which the Greeks in their frequent visits, continue to pay a kind of devotional reverence to this day.

Beyond this there is a fifth port or gate where a room is built, though it is only raftered, from which you may have the diversion of seeing the fish that were caught, since it is also a kind of repository where the Grand Seignor's fishermen lay up their tackle. I would observe, by the way, that though all the hills of Constantinople afford a very pleasing prospect, there is none that entertains you with such peculiar delight as the first hill, where the Sultan lives in a licentious and luxurious manner.

He has before him, whether he is walking in his gardens or in his chambers of the Seraglio, a full view of the Bosporus and both its shores, which are green and flourishing with woods belonging to the neighboring farms. On the right hand he beholds a spacious field of Chalcedon covered with his own gardens; he sees the Propontis, islands without number, and the woody mountains of Asia. If he looks an immense distance behind him he beholds Mount Olympus always clothed in snow. If he takes a shorter prospect he views before him the wonders of his own city, the Church of St. Sophia and the Hippodrome. If he casts his eyes to the left, he beholds the seven hills on which the city is seated, and more remotely he looks around the immeasurable, spacious fields of Thrace. If he extends his prospect over the seas, he views a moving scene of ships passing and repassing before him; some sailing from the Hellespont or the Black Sea, others again coming into his port from all the coasts of the Propontis; while at the same time other vessels are sailing up and down the Bay of Ceras, where there is also an abundance of ferries and small boats always rowing from side to side. And if he looks below him, he has the agreeable pleasure of beholding the three sides of the first hill, dressed with trees, flowers, and plants of all kinds.

He not only has a fine prospect from the palace but is entertained with several delightful vistas from the top of the gardens rising on the hills. If he has an inclination to take a view of his Seraglio from the point of land that projects so far into the sea and that, as I observed, divided the Bosporus, here he beholds it in all its glory, strengthened with large pillars of marble and fanned with gentle, refreshing breezes. Here he often sits with small osier lattices before him, so that, like another Gyges, he discerns all that sail near him, though he himself is visible to none. And if at any time he is weary of the company of his domestics, he can divert himself with the ridiculous drollery of the watermen fixing their oars and boat-poles to the shore as they tug against the violent stream of the Bosporus, which is much more rapid than the Rhone.

Outside the Seraglio stands the Church of St. Sophia, which is about seventy paces from the gate of the first court. It is situated on the brow of the first hill, upon an eminence that hangs over the garden of the first valley. From there you ascend by stone steps to the gate of the Seraglio and the Church of St. Sophia, which from the southeast falls with so easy a descent that it almost imperceptibly terminates on a plain both above and below it. In short, all the descents from the Imperial Palace to the Hippodrome are moderate and gentle.

Southwest of the Church of St. Sophia a plain extends to the end of the Hippodrome, which is more than seven hundred paces long. The Hippodrome is more than two furlongs in length and one furlong in width. It stands on perfectly level ground; but this is more to be ascribed to industry than its natural situation. The middle part of the hill, stretching as far as the Propontis, which is on three sides of it, is an overhanging ground. On the east it falls with a small declivity, on the west it is more on the descent; on the side of the Propontis it drops directly perpendicular to a depth of fifty feet, more or less.

The whole facade of the Hippodrome is built on arches, which makes it stand on a level table and entertains the spectator with a very delectable view of the Propontis, so that you may not only see men sailing to and fro before you, but you may also see the dolphins frequently tumbling about in the waters. The steps on the north side of the Hippodrome, which survived until only a few years ago, were demolished by Ibraham Pasha and were used in building his own house. Between the Hippodrome and the Propontis there stretches a plain that widens out to the width of four hundred paces, where the churches of Bacchus and Sergius anciently stood; both of which I shall note in the following history. Below the Hippodrome, to the south, is the gate called Porta Leonis, which is situated outside the city on the ruins of the Palace of Leo Macellus; the windows of which, of antique workmanship, still remain in the walls. The Palace was built on a hill adjoining the sea that was about a hundred paces high.

# VIII

# The First Valley

FROM THE UPPERMOST PLAIN OF THE PROMONTORY, on which, as I observed, stood the Church of St. Sophia and the Hippodrome, by an easy ascent of a thousand paces you climb the ridge of the second hill up to the Porphyry Pillar erected on the top of the second hill. This is bounded on the east by the first valley, which divides the first from the second hill. It rises at the plain of St. Sophia and extends from south to north. This valley represents exactly the figure of the letter V; one of whose sides extends directly east, the other north. Through the middle of it runs the wall that divides the Grand Seignor's palace from the rest of the city. The lowermost plain of the Promontory extends in length and breadth so far into this valley that from the bay to the Church of St. Sophia you may walk a thousand paces almost level. From its entrance on the sea side it is a plain five hundred paces long; then winding into this vale it rises on a small ascent that is more easily perceivable by the gentle fall of the water than by the eye or the foot. It is somewhat wide at the beginning, afterwards it is narrower, and at the end it straightens into two smaller valleys; one of which, near the Church of St. Sophia, is four hundred paces long. It rises gradually and is so narrow that the public way takes up its whole width.

# IX

# The Second Hill

THE RIDGE OF THE PROMONTORY RISES A LITTLE higher, and the two valleys adjoin to make the second hill. The first valley divides the first hill from the second hill; on the west the other valley divides ths second from the third. On the north it is bounded by a plain on the seashore. The ridge of the Promontory extends from south to north a distance of one thousand paces in length and four hundred in width. The different width of the vales varies along the width of the whole hill. For the point where the valleys that bound its sides at the top are more contracted the hill widens; and at the foot of the hill, where they are much wider, the hill is less so. The smaller hills that stand on it extend its length. Two of these hang over the bay. Its height varies according to the different height of the three cliffs, or small hills, that rise upon it. The cliff lying to the southeast rises moderately from the lowest part of the valley to the top of the hill a height of about a thousand paces. Afterwards, as the valley widens, it grows smaller and is rendered more steep by two small valleys — branching out of the great valley — that indeed descend gradually not more than a hundred paces.

The different height of the cliffs that hang over the bay may be best discovered by considering the different heights of the five public ways that stretch from the ridge to the foot of the hill. The first of these streets rises to a height of five hundred paces, two hundred of which from the foot of the hill are very easy to ascend, the other three hundred are very steep. The second road is six hundred paces high, a hundred of which rise through the lowest of the small valleys on a gentle ascent, the next hundred are almost perpendicular, so that you must climb them by steps; the other four hundred rise gradually to the top of the hill, which is sixty paces wide. The ridge of this hill shoots south a distance of a hundred and fifty paces, almost from the Church of St. Sophia to the Porphyry Pillar. The other three public ways from the bottom of the hill rise gently for the first three hundred paces, the next two hundred are so steep that you are obliged to ascend them by windings and turnings; the remaining five hundred up to the plain on the hill rise moderately.

I would observe further that on the side of the cliffs that project over the bay, two small hills jut out, one to the north, and the other to the east. Uniting they form a little valley, which is bounded on the east by a hill that rises eighty paces high and has very agreeable descents in some places. This is the reason that most of the smaller cliffs that bear upon this hill stand to the east and that the side of the hill that looks west is more sloping in some parts than others. Its heights fall into the lowest plain in the valley a length of three hundred paces from the foot of the hill to its middle and are almost perpendicular; and from the middle to the top they slope only a little.

The hills that project over the head of the valley are no more than two hundred paces high, and often on a different ascent. For as the valley rises, the cliffs seem lower. Indeed, all the lower cliffs of this hill have a double ascent: one lengthways and the other sideways. For those that stand east and west are situated in such a manner that they also lie to the north. In short, all the sides of this hill, in their steepest ascents are no more than a furlong high; in other places they fall into a moderate declivity; and at the bottom they gradually enlarge into a plain. The tops of the upper cliffs are half sloping and half on the plain. The plain adjoins the sea; dividing the hill from the bay, it spreads out three hundred paces but immediately widens again to a width of five hundred paces and so visibly enlarges the farther it extends into the valleys.

Thus, having given the reader some account of the front and fore part of the Promontory, I shall now give a short description of its back side, which faces the sea. Behind the second and third hills are two smaller hills that hang over the Propontis. Between these hills descends a hollow valley. These hills stand in the middle of the valley. The one that lies eastward, as well as the one that lies to the west, rises to a height of more than two hundred paces. At the end of the valley, between these hills, is a well-built harbor enclosed with a wall. It sits on the plain on the shore near the part of the sea that runs up to the front of the Hippodrome. The mouth of this harbor is three hundred paces in breadth. From the bay called Cornu the side crossing the hill to the Propontis widens a distance of two miles.

# X

## The Second Valley,
## Which Divides
## The Second Hill
## From the Third

THE VALLEY THAT DIVIDES THE SECOND HILL FROM THE third hill begins at the Promontory and ends in the plain adjoining the sea. It contains the fish market and the ferry, from which you cross the water to Sycae. From here to the entrance of the second valley a plain expands to the breadth of four hundred paces so levelly that the water falls from there into the bay with an almost imperceptible descent. When it has contracted into the narrow compass of two hundred paces in breadth it gradually straightens into a less to the middle of the valley, where it is only fifty paces wide and afterwards is no broader than the main road.

It is more than six hundred paces in length, three hundred of which are almost level, the other three hundred on a descent. It rises easily to that part of the Promontory where the second and third hills join. In the lowermost part of the valley runs the main road that faces Galata. This way is full of merchant's houses on both sides. These are covered with a kind of transparent slat, which have a small casement here and there. The merchants of Galata frequent the Grand Bezestan or Place of Exchange. It is situated partly at the head of the valley and partly on an eminence of the third hill. In the year of Our Lord 1546 it was wholly burnt to the ground, except two basilicas roofed with brickwork, which were locked up every night and their windows secured by iron bars when the fire was over.

After the fire I was allowed to view their grand forum. I found it to lie so level that it had only a small ascent either from west to east or from south to north. I observed that it stood on more than five furlongs of ground. On the highest part of it, which lies to the east, I was permitted to see a nymphaeum adorned with forty-five marble pillars, which supported a brick roof.

The fire laid open to my view the old basilica, which I could not view before because of the shops and public houses. I observed farther that it had two additional buildings like wings joining the main building, each of which was divided into sixty apartments, which were all arched overhead. The roof was covered with lead, as their shops and places of public entertainment are. The inner chambers of these apartments are always locked for privacy and are secured by an iron door. The basilica itself consists of fifteen large apartments. In the shape of a dome, it has four doors and is supported by eight pillars; the roof is brickwork and it is leaded at the top.

The new basilica is supported by twelve pillars built of a square stone; four arches bear upon these pillars, which support twenty small roofs, built in the form of domes. These stand around about sixty merchants warehouses or shops with arched roofs. Within the basilica there are two hundred and twenty more of these warehouses, which are made in the following manner. Around the walls of the basilica are built an abundance of very broad pews, where the merchants expose their goods for sale. The masters are always sitting before them. They take these out of presses —when they show them to their chapmen —that have boxes or drawers in them. These presses are fastened to the wall, have two folding doors, and are removable at pleasure.

# XI

## The Third Hill

THE THIRD HILL IS BOUNDED ON EACH SIDE BY TWO valleys. The one that lies to the east divides it from the second hill; the western valley divides it from the fourth. The ridge of this hill is more than a thousand paces in length. It shoots from the top of the Promontory southward, northward to the Bay of Ceras, almost at the same height. The second hill, on the contrary, falls with a surprising descent from the utmost height of the Promontory to the lowest plain on the bay shore. At the top of the third hill is a level plain of great length. At its foot it extends north by three hundred paces north, more than the foot of the second hill. It is not of equal breadth in all places; at the top of the Promontory itself it is about eight hundred paces in every direction. It is here that the Seraglio stands.

On the part of the plain that lies to the east stands the Merchants Forum, a caravansaray, and the Sepulcher of Emperor Beyazit. On its south side is an open area, around which stand the booksellers' shops. On the part that lies northward stands the works that the Emperor Süleiyman is now building, namely his tomb, a caravansaray, and a magnificent and expensive mosque. They are built not only on the natural site of the ground there but also on artificial foundations.

This hill descends upon three smaller hills on three sides. On the side that lies eastward, where the Tower of Hirena stands, a small hill juts out into the second valley. The long projection of this hill on the ridge towards the bay makes another small hill that lies northward. From the side that points westward, where the Church of St. Theodore stands, another little hill shoots out of the middle to the plain that lies on the seashore. Two sides of this hill descend in a double declivity, one in a straight and the other in an oblique way. After it has extended a distance of thirteen hundred paces, the eastern side of the hill abates somewhat in its winding descent, but the nearer you descend to the plain the more it falls with a direct and confined declivity.

The descents from the ridge of the hill to the valley differ very much. The uppermost of them, hanging over a very deep valley, rise to the height of five hundred paces, the lowest three hundred of which are very steep. The three hundred paces above them are scarcely half that steepness. The other descents of this hill are not as sloping where the valley rises higher.

The slope of the western sides of the hill is like the eastern. The northern side has several descents. A smaller hill, shooting from the ridge of this hill, is five hundred paces high, the lowermost three hundred of which fall so precipitously that the buildings that stand on them are all underpropped. The two hundred paces above them fall with an easy descent. The farther the descents on this side of the hill lie from the plain on the seashore, the more they are lengthened by a sidelong fall, which rises on the eastern side of the hill. The plain on the shore, interrupted by the inlet of the bay, is not more than two hundred paces in breadth; but at the other parts of the foot of the hill it visibly widens up to the entrance of the valleys.

When I first arrived in Constantinople the Grand Seraglio, seated on the side of this hill, was less than six hundred paces in compass; but at present it is more confined, since the caravansarays have been built there by Sultan Süleiyman, and the burying place for the women — which is at least half the ground — has been taken out of it and enclosed. The left side of the Promontory, which lies behind the third hill to the south, juts out with two smaller hills; from the one that shoots eastward, the side of the Promontory that winds around westward to the other hill, which is situated a little above the foot of the Promontory. At the bottom of this hill, the Promontory gives access to the third valley, which lies behind it, and from there it stretches fully north. The left side of the third therefore has a double descent; one towards the south, which is six hundred paces high, another extending south south-west seven hundred paces high; but at due west it falls very short of that height.

The plain that lies between the back southern parts of the third hill and the shore of the Propontis is in no part less than three hundred paces broad nor more than seven hundred paces long. The plain of the valley that encloses the foot of the hill westward and that divides the seventh hill from the Promontory, reaching from the shore of the Propontis where the walls are not encompassed by the sea, is almost level and is five hundred paces wide in every part.

The three hills I have mentioned may very properly be called the Promontory of the Bosporus; for they hang over the sea in such a manner that whether you sail to Constantinople out of the Black Sea or the Propontis you may see them at a great distance, prominent over the cliff sides of the Bosporus. The third valley seems to separate the other three hills, which lie farther onto the mainland, from these. The reason why I place six hills on the Promontory of the Bosporus is because these latter hills all stand in a row near the bay and are joined together both at their top and the sides. The plain that unfolds on the ridge of this hill descends gently into a plain that hangs over the third valley and is six hundred and twenty paces long and as many wide.

# XII

## The Third Valley

THE THIRD VALLEY, WHICH LIES BETWEEN THE THIRD and fourth hill, seems to be a double valley; for in the middle it rises high, which makes it doubtful whether it is a part of the valley or of the Promontory. That its height is a part of the valley seems plain from the height of the arches that reach from one side of the valley to the other. It may be considered the ridge of the Promontory because of the descent of its outermost parts, which fall to the right and left on each side of the Promontory.

On the right side it descends onto a very low plain, which is three hundred paces broad at its entrance and continues level a length of five hundred paces more. Though it sinks at the bottom to an equal depth, its pitches or sides are higher in some places than in others. For where the plain is most hollow one of its sides is three times higher than the other. From this plain you ascend by easy steps to the top of the middle of the valley, which is six hundred paces wide, except the small part in the middle where it is not more than four hundred paces in breadth.

Through the top of this valley, or Promontory, from the fourth to the third hill, run the arches of an aqueduct, the tops of which are the same height as the hills themselves. The height of these arches reveals how great the descent is from them. For though they are all equal in height at the top, this height is very different according to the difference of their sites. For they are very high at the top of the valley, which is a plain level ground; but on the descent of these hills not nearly so high; and they continue a length of eight hundred paces at the same height, though the higher they stand on these hills, the less tall they are.

The top of this valley or Promontory descends with a gentle fall of seven hundred paces into a plain, which divides the Promontory from the seventh hill and from there extends to the Propontis. From the bay to the Propontis, passing through the third valley, the city is more than ten furlongs wide.

# XIII

## The Fourth Hill

THE FOURTH HILL IS ENCLOSED BY TWO VALLEYS, THE ridge of the Promontory, and the shore of the bay. Alongside of it stands the Tomb of Mohamet, who took Constantinople, several caravansarays, and baths. It is more than 3600 paces in circumference. The length from its ridge to the bay is a thousand paces; its breadth from east to west is at least eight hundred. As you take a view of it from the top, stretching in a square toward the bay, you perceive that it ends in two windings, very different from each other. The one that points northward stretches in a continuous ridge and descends on both sides; the one that shoots eastward lies so low that it seems to be only an ascent to the other. Its end winds westward where it forms a little valley. This hill is bounded by a valley eastward and is parted from the third hill on the north by the plain, on the shore on the east partly by a valley that divides it from the fifth hill and partly by the winding of the Promontory. This rises from top of the fourth to the top of the fifth hill in so gradual and delectable a manner that you discover that its ridge is uneven more by a fine discernment of the eye than by any difficulty in walking it. For these hills are joined together is such a way that they seem to lie on one level. They both have one plain. This, covering the top of the fourth, is not more than four hundred paces long nor more than two hundred wide, though afterwards — when continued to the fifth hill — it widens to a width of five hundred paces.

The fourth hill is equal in height to any of the other six; yet its ascents, whether they lie in a straight line or more obliquely, are more moderate because it is a long tract of ground with three declivities. The first of these descends through its whole length from southwest straight north more than a thousand paces. Two hundred of those, rising from the seashore, are a more easy ascent, the rest rise so gently that you can scarcely perceive them, although the uppermost hundred paces, which reach the top of the hill, are very steep. The cross descent, which runs athwart the width of the hill, is double. One of these falls westward; the other, which slopes eastward, rises from the valley that divides the third from fourth hill. From the highest part of this valley you ascend two hundred paces. Below its top is another ascent, which is five hundred paces high, one hundred of which rise from the bottom and are very steep.

You discover the height of the rest, which are an easy ascent, by the level of the aqueduct. From the bottom of the valley you ascend four hundred paces, the first hundred and eighty of which are very steep, after which you may walk two hundred more almost level. From here you rise to the middle, which is higher and is a hundred paces in breadth. It is also eight hundred paces high from the top to the bottom. From here you descend two hundred paces westward to the lowest part of the valley that divides the fourth and fifth hill, which is all a narrow piece of ground about four hundred paces in length. The first two hundred paces on the shore of the bay are all level; but it is uncertain whether they are a part of the valley or the seashore. For this valley is enclosed by these two hills the way the fourth is bounded by the plain on the shore, which is two hundred paces broad, whereas the fifth scarcely descends so far. The following eight hundred paces are on much the same level, the last four hundred of which stretch from the top of the Promontory and are very steep. Passing between the bay and the fourth hill the plain on the shore is a different width. The part that extends to the southwestern point of the hill is four hundred paces broad, whereas the part that extends to the northern point is no more than two hundred paces wide.

In short, the situation of the fourth hill is such that when you sail along the bay, you would take it to be an advanced part of the third valley. The top of this hill runs so far southward that its descents slope very modestly and seem almost level; whereas the top of the fifth hill, which is the same height, projects beyond the fourth directly northward. The descents on the back of the third hill, which lies southward, are very easy and agreeable until you come to the plain of the vale that divides the Promontory from the seventh hill; so that the back part of this hill shoots southward and is not bounded on either side by the third valley. This southern part is somewhat narrow, just beyond a little hill of the third, near a caravansaray built by the Sultan Mohamet; but behind the fifth hill, below the Columna Virginea, it is much more strait.


# XIV

# The Fifth Hill


THE BOTTOM OF THE FIFTH HILL, ON TOP OF WHICH stands the Tomb of Selim the Emperor is bounded partly by the bay and partly by an eastern and western valley. It is four thousand paces in circuit. The pitch of this hill hangs so far over the bay northward and the pitch of the fourth hill lies so low towards the same point that the fourth hill seems to be a kind of valley situated between the third and fifth hill. For the fifth hill does not join at the top and continue the ridge of the Promontory as other hills do, but, being equal in height with it, shoots a great distance beyond it, running as far northward as the foot of the fourth hill does. It has descending slopes on three sides. One is to the north, the steepness of which the reader may learn from this: that although it is very nearly the height of the fourth hill, which is over a thousand paces high, the highest ascent of this hill comes nearer the line of the lower ascent from the bottom than that of any other hill; for you ascend through a little valley no more than three hundred paces high to the top.

This valley is formed by two small hills adjoining the shore of the bay upon which, at about four hundred paces distance, you discover some stone steps belonging to a foundation of a caravansaray built by the Emperor Selim. This northern side of the hill has four small hills jutting out of it and three small valleys running between them.

These rise from the top of the hill and are situated at such a distance from the plain on the shore that two of them touch the wall that stands on it. The other two are a hundred paces from it. The plain on the shore is in no part narrower than at the foot of this hill; for to the distance of a thousand paces it does not exceed a hundred paces in breadth and in some places not fifty.

Two of these hills are very steep, so that the buildings you see on them are all underpropped as though they were in danger of falling, and the inhabitants have been obliged to cut windings in the rocks to moderate the descent. The other two are less precipitous; the valleys that enclose them do not lie so deep. The side of the hill that shoots eastward is 1400 paces long and two hundred wide, and its altitude is two hundred paces on the perpendicular. The height of the side that falls westward slopes to a different depth according to the way the valley sinks. Where it descends into a level plain, it advances to a height of five hundred paces. In other places it rises no higher than three hundred, with a very moderate ascent.

The side of the Promontory that points southward, situated behind the fifth hill, ends in the plain of the valley that divides the Promontory from the seventh hill. In other places it falls with a more confined and sometimes with a more expanded descent on a small squat hill that hangs over the fifth valley, as it does over the valley that separates the Promontory from the seventh hill. The back of the fifth hill also winds into a small valley that rises at the brow of the Promontory where the Columna Virginea still stood not long ago. From here the ridge of the Promontory bends somewhat over the top of the plain of the fifth hill, which in some places is six hundred and in others seven hundred paces broad. But beyond the ridge of the hill it widens for a great distance, as far as the plain of the fourth hill and shoots on with the plain of the

Promontory and falls down to the neck of the isthmus and so, extending itself further, still is at least 2000 paces in length.

# XV

# The Fifth Valley

THE FIFTH VALLEY, WHICH DIVIDES THE FIFTH FROM the sixth hill, winds from north to south. It is as long as the Promontory is broad; that is, about 1200 paces; the first eight hundred of which have no ascent. At its first entrance the valley is at least four hundred paces broad but afterwards straightens into half that breadth. Yet for a length of six hundred paces it is nowhere less than two hundred paces broad. Further on it is at least five hundred paces wide. Above this is the top of the valley, or the ridge of the Promontory, opening on a level width of two hundred paces. From the top of the Promontory, to the left side of it, there falls a valley with a gentle descent a distance of five hundred paces, where it descends into another valley, which divides the Promontory from the seventh hill. The fifth valley seems to cut through the ridge of the Promontory. This may easily be discerned by the right and left descent of the two hills that lie nearest to it; for there is a very easy ascent from the height of this valley to the top of either hill.

# XVI

## The Sixth Hill

THE SIXTH HILL IS JUST AS LONG AS THE PROMONTORY
is broad, which widens on this hill to the breadth of 2400
paces. The city walls shoot over the ridge and the north
side of it down to the sea shore. You descend gradually
from the top of it within the walls; outside the walls it lies
level and is joined to the Continent by a field in the
suburbs. The broadest part of it is not over eight hundred
paces, the most narrow only four hundred. It descends
with a triple declivity; one on the left hand of the
Promontory with an easy descent to the southeast; another
on the right falling to the bay northward that extends a
distance of 1500 paces. There are two lower hills
separated by a small valley that runs between them. At
the foot of the lower hill that stands nearest the city wall
there is an aqueduct.

Between this hill and the bay there formerly stood the
Church of the Blachernae, which has been recorded in the
writings of many historians. The foundation of this
church still existed when I first arrived at Constantinople.
From the foot of this hill, which stands above the church I
have mentioned, there rises a spring whose waters are
conveyed through arched subterranean passages into the
city. Appearing above ground there, they flow constantly
into a marble cistern.

The side of the sixth hill that lies eastward is as long as
the hill itself but does not fall with the same descent on all
sides. The descent varies depending on whether the
adjoining valley lies higher or lower. Where the valley
lies level the pitch of the hill rises to a height of six
hundred paces; where it does not lie so low, it is not over
five hundred paces high; where it rises higher, not over

four hundred. Nor does the side of the hill shoot only eastward. On the right side it also projects northward, and on the left side it extends fully southwest.

The plain on the shore, which lies between the foot of the hill and the bay, is not over eight hundred paces broad at the most narrow. I mean here the place where the Church of the Blachernae formerly stood, as did a Triclinium; but farther on it winds around into the third valley and widens much more.

# XVII

# The Valley
## That Divides the Promontory
## From the Seventh Hill

THE VALLEY THAT DIVIDES THE SEVENTH HILL FROM the six hills of the Promontory is an easy descent. It extends a distance of 4000 paces in length, if you include the plain on the sea shore. If you exclude that and take your dimensions from the winding of the seventh hill, it is not more than 3300 paces long. It lies so level that you cannot perceive that it has the least ascent by walking on it; yet you may discover by the eye that it perceptibly lengthens and widens into a greater breadth. It bounds the sides of the third and fifth valley and the lowest heights of the fifth and sixth hills. It is full of gardens and pleasant meadows. Here the soldiers sometimes act out their mock fights. There is a rivulet that runs through the middle of it, which is often dry in the summer.

# XVIII

# The Seventh Hill

THE SEVENTH HILL IS CALLED THE XEROLOPHON, ON which stands the Pillar of Arcadius. This hill is a little less than 12,000 paces in circumference and contains more than a third of the city. The other two parts are contained in the bounds of the Promontory, which is over 20,000 paces in circumference. By paces I would here mean the ordinary steps we take in walking, which I cannot exactly reduce to a just equivalent with the Roman pace because of the turnings and windings of the ways and the difference of paces, which are longer or shorter, according to the different ascents and descents of the ground we walk. This hill makes the third angle of the city, from which Constantinople is considered a triangle.

It lies sloping with a very moderate descent and has a double declivity. One of those falls gently into the valley that divides the seventh hill from the Promontory and is equal in length to the valley itself. The other descent, which partly lies to the southeast and partly to the south, falls into the Propontis and in some places is five hundred paces steep, in others four hundred, three hundred, a hundred, in fact even fifty until it comes to the point of the third angle of the city from which a large plain shoots out towards the sea that is a different width in different places. The entrance to this plain at the angle of the city just mentioned is very narrow; it afterwards widens, occasioned by the winding of one of its sides, from which it gently rises to the foot of a small hill where it is four hundred paces broad; later on it narrows to fifty, and afterwards widens to a breadth of only a hundred paces for a distance of a thousand paces. On the ridge of this hill there is a plain of some length and breadth. The hill itself is bounded by the land wall; and on the top of it is a cistern that is called Mocisia, which is wholly unroofed and stripped of its pillars. This cistern is nine hundred and seventy paces in circumference. Its walls, which are made of squared freestone, are still standing, and the ground where it stands is now turned into a garden.

I have thus laid before the reader a plan or description of the topography of the city of Constantinople, so that the topography of the wards of that city will be more easily discovered. I hope I shall not be thought to have dwelt too long on this subject, since its verbal delineation is the most concise way of coming to a knowledge of it. Although Constantinople offers a most agreeable prospect at the most remote distance because of the eminence of its site, to particularize the various parts of the city leads the reader to a more exact and expeditious insight into it than any other means of information.

# XIX

## The Walls of the City

THE WALLS OF CONSTANTINOPLE ARE BUILT WITH squared freestone in some places, in others with rough stone, and in many places with a mixture of brick and stone. The walls on the land side are double, secured by a large ditch twenty-five paces broad. One of the walls is carried somewhat farther than the length of the ditch and is very strongly fortified. These walls stand eighteen feet from each other. The inward wall is very lofty and more than twenty feet thick; upon it are built two hundred and fifty towers with steps facing the Continent. The outer wall is not more than half as big but has the same number of towers.

As to the nature of its fortification, the ground that takes up the distance between the ditch and the outer wall is higher than the adjoining side of the ditch; and the ground between the two walls is higher than that. The country opening up outside the walls is not encumbered with buildings and is partly hilly and partly level, but chiefly the latter, so that you have a delightful prospect over the fields before you and a very extensive view all around you. And there is no doubt that Constantinople might be made a terribly strong place.

The walls that run around the sea are not as high as the land walls. They are plainly built but very thick and well guarded with towers. On the side of Ceras Bay they are about fifty paces distant from the shore. On the side of the Bosporus and the Propontis they are built upon the shore except where they are discontinued by some port or landing place.

Zonaras relates that Emperor Theophilus not only repaired but raised these walls higher after they had been much damaged by time and the dashings of the sea. This is also confirmed to us down to the present age; for in many places along them I observed that the name of Emperor Theophilus was cut in very large characters. Emperor Nicephorus was hated by his people for levying a tax on them, which was called Diceraton, for repairing these walls. I learn from the *Constitutions* of Justinian that in his time the walls were commonly called the old and the new walls, where he decrees, "that a larger fee shall be paid the bearers and those who attend a corpse beyond the new walls of the city." What I would observe from this is that the old walls that were built by Constantine and the new walls that were built by Theodosius II were both standing in the reign of Justinian.

I have described the walls of old Byzantium in the beginning of this book. We may learn more fully the condition that they were in formerly from Herodian, who writes that Byzantium was enclosed with a very large and very strong wall made of square stones of a great size, so artfully cemented that it was considered one compact piece of work. This is also confirmed by the authority of Pausanias who tells us that he:

> never saw the walls of Babylon or of Memnon, nor ever heard of any person who had seen them. But the walls of Byzantium and Rhodes are accounted exceedingly strong; and yet the walls that enclose Messene are stronger than these.

It is recorded by some historians that the Athenians kept their treasury at Byzantium because it was a well fortified place. Whether those walls that the author of the *Ancient Description of the Wards* calls the double walls are the same that we see at Constantinople at present, or whether they were built by Theodosius, I leave it to the judgment of the reader. At this point I shall give my opinion that they do not seem to me to be entirely the same walls that the author describes, for he places the Church of the Apostles in a ward that is near the walls of the city and places the fourteenth ward outside the walls of the city. At present at least the best part, if not all, of it is within the walls. I would add that Theodosius II, who reigned before Justinian, does not place the Blachernae within the walls of the city, and yet I have the authority of Procopius that these were a part of the suburbs in the time of Justinian, although at present they are enclosed within the walls, as were the Seven Towers and the church that was built by Stadius, or rather Studius, who was afterwards consul.

# XX

## The Gates of Constantinople
## And the
## Seven Towers of Old Byzantium

THE WALLS ON THE LAND SIDE HAVE SIX GATES: ONE within the palace, another that is called the Adrianopolitan Gate, and a third on the brow of the seventh hill. Besides these there is the Porta Aurea or Golden Gate, the Gate of Selymbria or Rhegium and the Gate of the Seven Towers. On the side of Ceras Bay is the Gate of the Blachernae, at present called Xyloporta, situated near the third angle of the city. There are also the gates called Cynigos, or Porta Palatina, Phanaria, Agia, Porta Jubalica, Farinaria, Lignaria, Seminaria, Piscaria, the Gate of the Neorium, and the Gate of Demetrius, which stands on the ridge of the first hill.

On the side of the Propontis there are about five: every one of which has stairs or a landing place and a haven for ships, besides the gates of the Imperial Palace. There is also the Porta Stercoraria, Leonina, and Condescala, two of which stand at the foot of the seventh hill. Those principally noted by historians are the gates of Cynigos, Rhegium, and Xylocercon, the Gate of Eugenius, the Porta Aurea, that called Myriandros, the Porta Condescala, and the Porta Carsiana.

In old Byzantium there was the Thracian Gate. For we are told by Dion that the Seven Towers reached from the Thracian Gate to the sea, which Cedrinus tells us was Ceras Bay. If any one spoke anything in the first of these towers, it immediately flew to the second, and so through all the rest so that you might hear the voice distinctly repeated in every one of them. Pliny tells the very same story of Cyzicus. "In that city," he says, "near the

Thracian Gate there are Seven Towers that multiply the voice by repetition or reiteration more than seven times." This, he adds, was looked upon by the Greeks as somewhat miraculous and was called the Echo. I never found any mention made of the Thracian Gates in any historian but in Pliny, though it is not altogether improbable that there were such gates there. Apollonius, in the first book of his *Argonautics,* mentions the Thracian Haven in Cyzicus; and Plutarch expressly states that near this city there was a street called the Thracian Street. This is also attested not only by some more modern writers of Constantinople but also by Dion and Xenophon, the latter of whom writes that when Alcibiades appeared before the town the Byzantines opened the Thracian Gates to him of their own accord.

# XXI

# The Long Walls

THE SUBURBS AND ADJOINING FIELDS WERE ENCLOSED by walls of such an immoderate length that they extended from the city a distance of two days' journey. They were built by Emperor Anastasius to prevent incursions by the Scythians and Bulgarians. They reached from the Black Sea to the Propontis, were forty thousand paces from the city and twenty Roman feet wide. These walls were often taken and battered by the barbarous nations but repaired by Justinian. In order that the soldiers garrisoned there might defend themselves to their best advantage he ordered the passages from one tower to another to be stopped up. No entrance was allowed except for the door at the bottom of the steps by which it was ascended. By this means it was thus sufficiently guarded, even though the enemies forces were in the heart of the city. Evagrius, the sacred historian, tells us that Anastasius built the long wall, which was two hundred and eighty furlongs distant from the city, that it reached from sea to sea, was four hundred furlongs long, that it was a good security for those who sailed out of the Black Sea to the Propontis, and that it put a stop to the incursions of the barbarous nations.

\* \*
\*

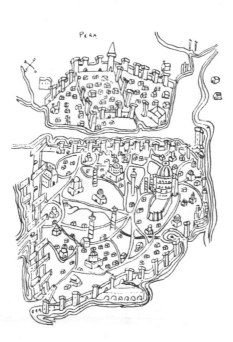

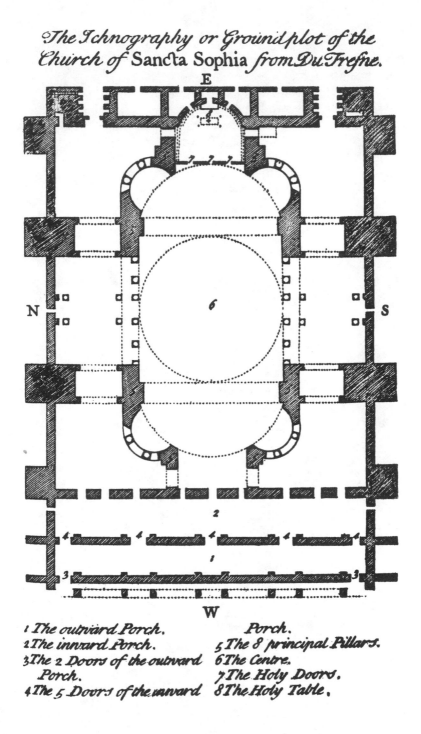

The Ichnography or Ground plot of the Church of Sancta Sophia from Du Fresne.

1 The outward Porch.
2 The inward Porch.
3 The 2 Doors of the outward Porch.
4 The 5 Doors of the inward Porch.
5 The 8 principal Pillars.
6 The Centre.
7 The Holy Doors.
8 The Holy Table.

# BOOK TWO

## I

## The Buildings and Monuments
## Of Old Byzantium and Constantinople,
## Called New Rome

NOW THAT I HAVE DESCRIBED THE SHAPE AND EXTENT
of the city and examined the situation of the seven hills in
detail, I shall proceed to consider what buildings and
monuments Constantinople had in ancient times or now
has, and into how many wards it was divided. For when I
accidentally fell upon this division of the city into wards
in an ancient manuscript written over one thousand years
ago by a gentleman more noble by his birth than his
writings, I hoped to be able to trace out the ancient city
with some ease, but the barbarous Mohametans have
either so demolished those venerable and truly heroic
ornaments that distinguished it, in order to adorn their
own paltry houses, or they have entirely buried them in
their own ruins, so that you shall see remains of an old
foundation in very few places.

I omit to mention the fires and other devastations
committed not only by the savages of other countries but
the great havoc lately made by the Turks themselves. For
the last hundred years they have incessantly endeavored to
deface and destroy entirely by building it in so different a
manner that those who have formerly seen some parts of
it scarcely know its ancient condition.

Consider further the profound ignorance of the Greeks at present. There is scarcely one of them who either knows or has so much as an inclination to know where their antiquities are. Indeed, their priests are so heedless and negligent in this respect that they will not make the least inquiry themselves about those places where only a few years ago very magnificent temples were standing; and they are so very censorious as to condemn those that do. However, so that I might not pass my time uselessly while I was expecting of remittances from my royal master for purchasing all the ancient manuscripts I could find, I made it my business to discover all the signs of antiquity I was capable of observing. In my description of the ancient monuments I shall observe the same method I did in the description of the hills. I shall consider them in order as the hills stand, or as I find them in the different wards of the city. This, like Old Rome, was divided into fourteen wards.

# II

# The Ancient Monuments of the First Hill, The First Ward of the City

THE FIRST HILL, WHICH PLINY SOMETIMES CALLS Chrysoceras and sometimes Auri Cornu — though this was a mistake as appears from what I have written concerning the Thracian Bosporus — and Dionysius of Byzantium calls the Promontory of the Bosporus. "There are two reasons," he says, "why it is called the Promontory of the Bosporus. The first is, as some say, because a cow stung by a gadfly forded it. Others report more fabulously that Io, the daughter of Inachus, after being changed into a cow, swam across it when she went to Asia." The same author, speaking of a place called Semystra, tells us that Byzantium would have been founded there had not a raven snatched out of the fire a part of the sacrifice they offered on their landing and carried it to the Promontory of the Bosporus. This they considered a token from the gods that they should found their city there.

The same writer speaks in another place of a promontory called Metopum, opposite the first hill of Constantinople. This promontory, he adds, faces the city and lies directly opposite the Promontory of the Bosporus. The same author informs us that a little above the Promontory of the Bosporus there was an altar erected to Minerva, who was called Ecbasia or Egressoria, because those who transplanted the colony here sallied out from there with a bravery equal to those who fight for their country. We might also call her Ecbateria, under which name, as Hesychius reports, Diana was worshipped in Siphnus.

He adds farther that on the same Promontory stood the old Temple of Neptune and that below it on the plain the Byzantine youth took exercise in horse racing, chariot driving, wrestling, and other martial sports; and lastly that at the foot of the Promontory stood a bay called Ceras, which had three havens, fortified with three citadels and high sand banks. Upon it stood the castle of Byzantium, which Xenophon notes when he tells us that after the men under his command had forced their way into town, the inhabitants feared that they would be put to the sword if their city was taken. Some therefore fled to the adjoining Promontory, others to the sea, and some of them, sailing a long time in a fishing boat, at last made a landing, got into a tower, from there made signals of distress and were assisted at last by the people of Chalcedon.

Not only was the castle of old Byzantium built on the first hill, but historians assure us that the emperors of Constantinople also maintained a fortress there when they tell us that to keep the enemy from entering the port they laid a boom across the river from the citadel to the Castle of Galata. In fact, even at this day, the Grand Seignor has a citadel there fortified with thick walls that enclose his spacious gardens on all sides. In old Byzantium there was a level place called the Thracian Field not encumbered with houses. It was on this plain that Xenophon drew up the Greek army in military order. He informs us in his book, *Helenici*, that this field was near the Thracian Gate. They opened, he says, the gates adjoining the Thracian Field. In Book VII of the *Expedition of Cyrus* he speaks of a place near the walls of Byzantium where he ranged his army in order of battle. He tells us that the most convenient place to draw up or muster an army is the Thracian Field, because, as he goes on, it is free of houses and on a plain.

I observed before that the Seven Towers of Byzantium reached from the Thracian Gate to the sea; Georgius Cedrinus asserts that they reached the northern sea, that is to the bay called Ceras. Herodotus asserts that in old Byzantium stood an altar erected to Diana Orthosia and a temple dedicated to Bacchus. He says:

> Darius, upon viewing the Black Sea, came back to the bridge and erected on the Bosporus two stone columns on which he ordered to be engraved the Assyrian and Greek alphabets. The Byzantines afterwards removed them to the city near the altar of Diana Orthosia. The Greek alphabet was what they retained and made use of. The column with the Assyrian characters they left near the Temple of Bacchus where they had set it.

Laurentius translates the Greek word *Orthosia, Erecta,* but he would have translated it more properly had he called it *Erectoria,* or *Erectrix,* because being the goddess of childbirth she raises up or recovers women in labor. This I deduce to be the true sense of the word not only from several authors but from Plutarch, who has this story in his *Book of Rivers:*

> Proud Teuthras, king of Mysia, with his retinue of spearmen chased a boar, which fled into the Temple of Diana Orthosia to implore her assistance. As they were all driving furiously into the temple, the boar cried out with an audible human voice, "Let your compassion, Royal Sir, be shown to one whom Diana brought into this world." Enraged at this, Teuthras slew the creatures. Resenting the affront, Diana threw the king into a frenzy and punished him with ulcerous sores. He could not bear the indignity of his punishment and so retired to the mountains. His mother Lysippa, with the prophet Polyidius, who informed her of the reason for her son's sufferings, immediately hastened in search of him and by sacrificing some oxen to Diana reconciled her to him. When she perceived that her son had returned to his senses, she erected an altar to Diana Orthosia and near it placed a golden boar with a man's head upon its shoulders.

Before the destruction of Byzantium by Severus both the altar and the boar were standing in the first valley of the first hill.

Since Constantine rebuilt the city the first hill included the first ward, which contained the House of Placidia Augusta, that of the most noble Marina, and the Baths of Arcadius. I learn this from the ancient division of the city into wards, though I must confess myself at a loss to know in what part of the city the first ward began; nor can I make any such discovery from the remains of any ancient buildings, which are now entirely destroyed. However, this much may be inferred from Procopius, who has it on record that when you sail from the Propontis to the eastern part of the city, there stand the public baths built by Arcadius. He says:

> In this place Justinian built a court, which was encompassed with so calm a sea that when you walked in the galleries you might discourse audibly with the sailors. It made a very beautiful, a very delightful, and most magnificent prospect. It was fanned by gentle breezes, supported with lofty columns, and laid with the most curious marble, which, like the sun, reflected a most amazing luster. It was also adorned with an abundance of marble and bronze statues finished to the finest perfection; a lovely scene to the spectators. The reader, had he or she seen it, would have taken it to be the work of Phidias, Lysippus, or Praxiteles. Upon a high pillar of porphyry marble, in the same place, stood the statue of Empress Theodora, as if addressing herself to him for building so noble a structure. The beauty of the column is exceedingly surprising, yet it by no means comes up to that inconceivable, inexpressible gracefulness and dignity you see in the statue.

From these words of Procopius I would observe, by the way, that that pillar, now standing on a descent lying east of the Grand Seignor's Palace, is not the same as that on which Theodora was erected, as some are of the opinion, because it is not a porphyry color and is too remote from the court.

So I would have the reader understand that the first ward contained the length of the first hill, which is bounded on three sides by the sea. I find not only in many historians but also in Suidas the Grammarian that the statue of Arcadia, the second wife of Zeno, stood in the Arcadian Baths near the places called the Bathra, from the stairs by which you ascend them. I find also in that place two statues of Verina, the wife of Leo the Great, one in the northern part of the city near the Church of St. Agathonicus beyond the Bathra, the other on the side of the city where the Church of St. Barbara stands. The first was erected by Leo in his lifetime, the second since his death when on the flight of Zeno, his son-in-law, his brother Basilicus was crowned emperor in his stead.

I have reason to believe when I consider the natural situation and order in which the wards stand, that part of the second ward was enclosed in the Palace. According to the ancient description of it, the first entrance for this ward stood on level ground. After some distance it rose by a gentle ascent and at last, with very deep precipices, fell into the sea. I am of the opinion that these precipices descended on that spot of ground where the kitchens and the baths of the Grand Seignor stand at present. But wherever they might have stood in ancient times, all steep places that were formerly enclosed within the Palace are now levelled where an old church commonly called Sophia the Less now stands.

Some of the most ancient inhabitants affirm it to be the Church of St. Eirene, which Socrates tells us was built by Constantine the Great. I take it to be the same church that the people of the second ward call the Old Church. I also have reason to believe that the other part of the second ward stood outside the Palace from the situation of the churches and baths that the second ward encloses. Zonaras and other historians assert that the church that formerly went by the name of the Great Church was afterwards called the Church of St. Sophia, which everybody knows stood outside the enclosure of the Palace. I also have reason to conjecture that the Palace of Maximinus formerly stood within the bounds of the court from the following inscription made in its commendation by Cyrus, once a consul and nobleman of Rome:

Great Maximinus raised this noble pile:
From hence to lengths unmeasurable I view
Unbounded prospects; for behind me stand
The city, and Bithynia's beauteous towns.
The swelling ocean rolls its waves before me;
When near my doors, it moves but slowly on,
Delighted to behold the lovely landscape
Of blooming trees, gay seats, and floating ships,
The city's rising towers, and pleasing site.

# III

# The Church of St. Sophia

MODERN GREEK WRITERS WILL HAVE IT THAT THE Church of St. Sophia was first built by the Emperor Constantius, the son of Constantine the Great, and was arched at top, not with brickwork but a wooden roof. In the time of Theodosius, when the second synod was held there, the Arians, rising in sedition, burnt it. It was later rebuilt by Theodosius the Great and beautified with arches of a cylindrical form. The same writer tells us that it was burnt a second time in the reign of Justinian; but Sozomen, an ancient and credible author, records that in the time of Theodosius II, when there were heated debates in the great church about expelling St. Chrysostom from the synod, all of a sudden it caught ablaze, while those who adhered to him threw fire into it with the intention of burning down the church and of destroying all who were in it.

Procopius would have it that it was first burnt down in the reign of Justinian, who rebuilt it in the same form as it stands at present; but he does not tell us whether it stands on the same site or not. It therefore remains doubtful from this author, who is not to be depended on too much, even though he has a catalog of the names of the persons from whom Justinian purchased the houses where it stood before the fire. An *Ancient Description of the City,* written before Justinian's time, seems to fix it in another place; for the author places the great church and the old church in the second ward, the Forum of Augustus in the fourth, which, I shall demonstrate, stood near the Church of St. Sophia.

Zonaras says that Justinian built it much larger than the old foundation; but it is very questionable whether Justinian purchased the neighboring houses for its enlargement. As to the Forum of Augustus and the great church's being placed in different wards, we cannot conclude from this that they did not stand near one another. When Justinian had enlarged and beautified it, and adorned it with a great variety of metalwork, when he had built the walls and roof with brick to strengthen them even more, he therefore reinforced them in many places with iron-work, using no rafters in the whole fabric for fear of fire.

Although it has hitherto escaped the flames, it has often been damaged and endangered by several accidents from the time of its rebuilding. Before it was finished the eastern arch bore its weight so hard on the pillars that in all probability it would have fallen had not the architect been very expeditious in finishing it. When bearing on its own curvature it laid less heavily on the pillars that supported it. The two northern and southern arches bore so heavily on the pillars and foundations that the tops of the pillars began to fly apart. They would have sunk if the workmen had not taken them down with the greatest skill and afterwards replaced them when the greenness and moisture of the building had abated somewhat. At the emperor's great expense and by the indefatigable industry of the workmen, the church was at last finished. Yet in his own time it was grievously shaken by an earthquake, by which, as Agathius writes, the tower above the roof was greatly shattered in the middle so that the emperor was obliged to repair and strengthen it, raising it much higher than it was before. This was done when Athemius, the first architect, was dead.

However, young Isidorus and some other architects who succeeded him, notwithstanding the errors committed in the former building, did not judge it necessary to take down the eastern and western arches but widened the north and south arches and so visibly enlarged them that the whole building seemed more regular and uniform. Thus it was evident to the eye of the spectator that the sides of the church, which terminated with their arches in the roof, were of an equal dimension and that the architects had so skillfully constructed the vast cavity of the body of the church into so narrow a compass at the top that the whole structure seemed very well proportioned and agreeable.

Above the arches, in the middle of the church, they raised a dome or cupola to a very great height. This was regular and not as round at the top as usual but more spiked and better contrived for the security of the building. Zonaras writes that:

> the great church being finished and consecrated, it happened that the eastern arch was thrown down by an earthquake that broke the pulpit and the communion table. It was afterwards rebuilt by Justinian, who raised it twenty-five feet higher than it was before.

The same report is given by Cedrinus almost word for word.

He also built other pillars proportionate to the weight of the arch that bore on them. On the outside of the church he built a pair of winding steps against the pillars near the church. Rising from the ground to the roofs, these support the pillars and the arches. Other writers of less note would have it that the roof of the church was thrown down by the above-mentioned earthquake, but that the arches stood secure, that the emperor rebuilt the roof, but lower than before by twenty-five feet.

I could, for my own part, bear with this version, if these historians would agree with me that the church was afterwards shaken by other earthquakes and then built lower than it stood before. For when Evagrius tells us that Justinian raised it to such a height that inside you could scarcely see the top and that the descent was so deep that it was dangerous to look from its height downwards, it was very probable that Justinian only raised it to its former height. Cedrinus relates that Emperor Basilius gave orders for repairing and strengthening the great western arch, which was very much shattered by an earthquake and likely to fall. Nicephorus inveighs bitterly against Empress Anna, who in the reign of Catacosmus sacrilegiously robbed the church of all its furniture and ornaments, and exclaims heavily that the tyranny and oppression and the different sects and opinions of those times were the chief occasion of the destruction of this church. For, as he adds, one midnight when the sky was very clear, one of the eastern arches fell to the ground and brought that part of the roof that it supported down after it. This broke down the pulpit and the images that adorned it and demolished the middle galleries. He adds further that it was the opinion of many in those times that if Emperor Andronicus had not built buttresses on the east side of the church it would have sunk completely into ruins.

Evagrius determines the length of the church in the following manner: from the arch where the bloodless sacrifice is offered to the gate opposite it is one hundred and ninety feet long. From north to south it is a hundred and fifteen feet broad; and from the pavement to the center of the roof it is a hundred and eighty feet high. It was dangerous for me to measure its length from east to west, so that I was obliged to have the dimensions taken for me by a Turk who made his report that the church was two hundred and thirteen feet in breadth, two hundred and forty in length and from the pavement to the highest curvature of the arches a hundred and forty-two feet in height. The fellow never measured the roof. If he had taken the height of it true he would have found only a small difference between his own account and that of Evagrius.

Should the reader desire to be informed at greater length of the dimensions and the architecture of this church as it stood in former times, let him consult Procopius, Agathius, Paulus Florus and Evagrius. What the architecture and dimensions of it are at present, I shall, as far as my observations have reached, describe more fully in the following chapter.

# IV

# A Description of the Church of St. Sophia As It Now Appears

THE WALLS AND ROOF OF THIS CHURCH ARE BUILT with brick. The inside of the walls of the church are encrusted with elegant marble of several kinds. All its materials are the most valuable productions of nature, so that viewing it employs the thoughts of the spectator with delight and admiration. Its roof is a surprising piece of gilded mosaic work, which reflects such a luster to the eye that even the barbarians who behold it are wonderfully taken with the sight of it. This roof is supported by eight pillars, four of the largest and tallest of which bear up the four arches that support the roof. Two of these arches, namely the northern and the southern, bear a thin wall full of windows at the bottom of their arch. This wall is strengthened by two ranges of pillars standing one above another. In the lower range stand eight pillars that rise from the pavement; the six above them support the thin wall. The eastern and western arches have neither a wall nor a pillar to support them but are so open that they make the body of the church appear larger. Projecting beyond the former, these arches bear four other arches, which are supported by two small and two large pillars. The four pillars not only bear up the four great arches, but each of them also supports two small arches, one of which extends lengthwise, the other across the church. By this means the church is lengthened and widened to a great distance; for on the east and west side there are two semidomes that are joined to the cupola in such a manner that they have the same roof inside the church although outside the roofs seem to be distinct.

These semidomes are a great ornament to the cupola, which rises very high above them. The breadth of the church is widened beyond the dome with arches and pillars and by the northern and southern walls, which form the three upper and lower galleries. These are encrusted with elegant marble of different kinds; their roof is covered with Moresco mosaic work, finely gilded.

Every arch that lies across the church bears on only one pillar, for one end of their curvatures is supported by the outer wall of the church, which bears on the large pillars from which there rise four arches, supported by the wall on both sides of the church. Two of these arches bear up the roof of the three lower galleries; and the other two support the roof of the the upper galleries, the sides of which bear on the wall, arches, and pillars.

Hence, if we consider the inside of the church by itself, enclosed by its pillars and columns, we discover it to have an oval plan; whereas if we view the whole place outside these pillars, it is a perfect square. For the upper and the lower galleries, which are the wings of the church, adjoin it in such a manner that if we measure it from the pavement to the bottom of the curvature of the upper galleries, it has a square plan; but if contracted within the enclosure of the four large and four smaller pillars as far as the curvature of the four arches of the dome, it is entirely an oval plan.

The plan of the galleries is as follows. On three sides they are built in a square manner. The fourth side, which looks into the church, is an oval plan, as is the church itself. The roofs of these galleries are supported by arches and columns. I shall give the reader a description of three of them, by which means he or she may easily form a judgment of the rest, for they all have one plan.

Those that I shall note are the three upper galleries on the north side of the church. The first of these galleries has two facades and looks both eastward and northward. The two sides of the gallery rise from the wall of the church and end in an arch. In the middle of each side there are three square columns five feet and nine inches in circumference, which form the jambs of the windows. These pillars support three other square pillars, which are all made of blue and white marble. The side that faces the body of the church is adorned with six pillars of green marble standing below the arch that supports an eastern semidome, whose shafts are seven feet and eight digits in circumference at the bottom.

Since the intercolumniations of these pillars is little less than seven feet and eleven digits wide, they are strengthened by marble closures four feet high, so that those who lean over them have a full view of all the upper and lower parts of the church. The side that separates the first and second gallery, reaching from the outward wall northward to the great pillar that supports the dome, is forty-four feet in length, part of which is adorned with pillars and an arch that supports the dome.

You pass through this into the second gallery, the breadth of which is twenty-four feet. It is made up of the arch of a pillar and a wall that is a part of one of the wings of the church and extends as far as the roof of the dome. This gallery is borne up by arches and walls at both ends. In the middle it is supported by four white pillars speckled with blue, the shafts of which are seven feet in circumference. It is on a square plan and, as I observed, bears on arches and walls. At one end these arches rise behind two of the larger pillars that support the dome; at the other end they bear on pillars that rise inside the walls and support the four large pillars. The outer side of this gallery is supported by eight square pillars, which are six feet in circumference. In the middle of them there rises a pillar of larger size. These pillars take the place of jambs for the windows; and above them there are other pillars that are also jambs to other windows. These windows, which are sixteen in number below and above, lighten up the second and middle gallery very much. The front of this gallery facing the church is beautified with six pillars of green marble. Their intercolumniations, like those of the first gallery, have marble closures at the bottom.

From this middle gallery you pass through an arch into the third gallery, which is much like the first in its length, windows, jambs, and pillars. Its roof is supported by four pillars and the side towards the church with six green pillars. There are also four green marble pillars that support one of the western semidomes, which stands between two other pillars. These pillars stand two and two together, and between them are raised two smaller pillars of the Ionic order.

At the western door of the church, instead of a vestibule, there are two porticos, the lower of which lies level with the church itself. The upper leads to the women's galleries. Both of them are as long as the width of the church and twenty-eight feet in breadth. The portico over it is situated between the pillars that support the western semidome and the windows. Both inside and outside it is supported by eight pillars, between which the windows, both on the upper and lower galleries, cast a great light into the church. Nothing parts this portico and the women's galleries, except the pillars that bear the roof of the portico, for the pavement of the portico lies on the same level as the pavement of the galleries. The inside of the lower portico is enclosed by walls that are lined with a delectable variety of marble. It is covered on top with curious Moresco mosaic work, very beautifully gilt.

On the eastern side of the portico there are doors that open into the church; on the west end you go out through five brass folding doors into a portico that stands outside the church; and from there you pass into a court, where there are several springs constantly running, to which there is a very steep descent by many steps. At the ends of these porticos there are two entrances to the church, one on the northern side and another with six folding doors on the south. These doors were formerly all of brass; at present only three of them are so, but curiously wrought. The church also has two folding doors on the east side. There are also some doors in the sides, which were formerly opened but are now kept shut.

The inside of the church is very light because of the multitude of windows all around it. The high wall between the great arches and the cupola has a circular plan, and lets in light from forty windows. The walls under the arches are lightened by twenty-six windows, the middle of the galleries with thirty-two, and the end with more than twenty. I shall take no notice of the lights in the two western and the four lower galleries, nor those of the two semidomes, nor those of the *Sanctum sanctorum*, and of the upper portico, which I omitted to count because of their great number.

The largest entrance into this church is on the west side. Here you do not ascend to the pavement as formerly, and as the Romans did to their Pantheon, nor do you descend into it by five steps. You go up to the top of the church by four pairs of winding stairs, not winding around like cockle shell, as Cedrinus reports, but turning more on the square and worked by the line. These stairs rise with a very easy ascent and are cut out of large marble tables. Every turning of these stairs is nineteen and a half feet high and five feet broad. Above these there is another pair of winding stairs that reach to the top of the church. You must ascend these when you go to the upper galleries and porticos.

If the reader will take the trouble to compare what I have said of the Church of St. Sophia with what has been written by Procopius and Agathius on that subject, he or she may easily discover that the ruins of what was built by Justinian have not been so great as the Turks pretend. They tell you that the church was formerly much larger and that several parts of it have been pulled down by the barbarians, and that scarcely a tenth of it remains today. This story would carry a face of probability if they meant that the palaces, the houses of the priests and the noblemen that were built around it had been demolished by fire and by the ravages of those people. Otherwise I am convinced it is a gross mistake; for I saw every part of the old church that was mentioned by Procopius as standing, except one portico.

Where Procopius writes that the church had two porticos at each end, there is none remaining at present, except that at the west end. It is very probable that the other was thrown down by an earthquake and that in place of it the inhabitants erected a large lump of a building of square stone that now stands to support the east end of the church. This lump of stone you would take to be a piece of craggy rock, although it does not seem, because of the earthquakes, to be the same height as it was when it was first built; yet it is nearly as high as Evagrius mentions it to be, since it is lengthened with four walls to fortify the bearing pillars.

These walls are more than twenty feet long and eight feet broad, rising to the height of the great pillars. To speak in terms of architecture, they seem to be wings of the church, or rather buttresses by which the north and south side are strengthened and supported.

Both ends of the church that project beyond the eight pillars, each extending into a semidome and rising at the top into an arched form, are still surviving. The same lower galleries for the men and the same upper galleries for the women, the whole roof, the same walls and pillars, the same dimensions of the church as originally beautified and adorned are still extant. There are indeed some flaws in the building occasioned by those who opposed the setting up of images in the church. In short, the whole, and every part of it, is to be seen at present; and it is despoiled of nothing except a little of the metalwork that appears in great abundance through the whole church.

The *Sanctum sanctorum,* formerly holy and unpolluted, into which only the priests were allowed to enter, is still standing, though nothing remains of the jewels and precious stones that adorned it, which were plundered by its sacrilegious enemies. That inimitable table, given to the church by its founder Justinian, made of the different materials of gold, silver, all kinds of wood, costly stones that either the sea or the whole world could produce, and which was embellished and enriched with infinite offerings of emperors, popes, princes, and ladies of the first quality, among whom was Pulcheria, the daughter of Arcadius and sister of Theodosius II, is at present despoiled of all its fine decorations. Sozomen tells is that this table was a very beautiful and surprising ornament to the church, which was endowed with very ample donations, of which the Mohametan priests are now in possession. They have eleven hundred shops and public houses situated in the best markets of the city, which pay them a constant revenue or rent for their maintenance and support without any deductions.

# V

# The Statues Discovered on One Side of the Church of St. Sophia

ON THE SIDE OF THE CHURCH OF ST. SOPHIA, SAYS Suidas, there were discovered more than seventy statues of the Greek deities, the figures of the twelve signs of the zodiac, and no less than eighty statues of Christian princes and emperors. Justinian commanded these to be placed in several parts of the city before he built the great church. I could give the reader an account of the names of these deities from an anonymous author who has written a treatise on Constantinople and the adjacent country, but I have found him faulty in so many of his narrations that I cannot depend on his authority.

# VI

# The Pharo on the Promontory Ceras And The Mangana

AMMIANUS MARCELLINUS WRITES THAT NEAR THE Promontory Ceras there was a high watchtower, which was called Pharos and was a guide to the ships at a great distance. The location of this Pharos, in all probability, was near the Church of St. Sophia. For from what part of the city could it spread a more convenient and diffusive light to those who sailed out of the Bosporus and the Propontis? Dionysius calls it the Bosphorian Promontory and tells us that Io the daughter of Inachus, provoked by Juno's resentment against her, passed from there to Asia.

The place called the Mangana was their armory where they kept their ordnance. It stood in the imperial precinct or by it near the cliffs of the Bosporus. Emperor Constantine, surnamed Monomachus, built a handsome and large monastery, which is also called Mangana in honor of the noble martyr St. George. Alexius Comnenus, when he was ill with the gout, was carried to the great palace that stands in the eastern part of the city; but when his physicians judged the air not to be so wholesome, he was removed to the Palace of Mangana.

# VII

# The Baths of Zeuxippus and its Statues

THESE BATHS WERE SO CALLED, AS CEDRINUS RELATES, because they were built in a place where the Temple of Jupiter had formerly stood. This is narrated by Eusebius, who writes that "there are some of the opinion that the fine bathing place at Constantinople took its name from the famous painter Zeuxes, whose pieces adorned it." I gather that it stood near the Church of St. Sophia not only from the treatise of the *Ancient Description of the City,* which places them both in the same ward, but also from the fire that occurred in the reign of Justinian and burnt down, as Procopius observed, the Church of St. Sophia and the adjacent buildings, such as the Baths of Zeuxippus and the entrance hall before the palace. Zonaras writes that Emperor Severus joined it to the Hippodrome and built it on the same ground where the Temple of Jupiter had formerly stood. Leontius, a more ancient and judi-

cious historian, does not join it to the Hippodrome but
makes it stand near it, as appears in his verses inscribed
over a door of a house situated between the Zeuxippum
and the Hippodrome.

Between Zeuxippus' cool refreshing baths,
And the famed Hippodrome's swift course I
    stand.
Let the spectator, where he baths himself
Or sees the struggling steed panting for breath
Pay a kind visit, to enhance his pleasures;
He'll find a hearty welcome at my table.
Or if more manly sports his mind affects,
Practice the rough diversions of the stadia.

Cedrinus relates that in this bath there was a pleasant
variety of views of surprising art, both in marble and
stonework, in statues of brass and figures of persons of
antiquity who seemed to want nothing but a soul to
animate and enliven them. Among these celebrated pieces
of the most exquisite workmanship was the statue of old
Homer in a thoughtful posture, just as he was, his hands
folded on his breast, his beard carelessly hanging down,
his hair very thin in front, his face wrinkled with age and
the cares of the world; his nose well proportioned, his
eyes fixed in their sockets, as is usual with blind persons,
which he was generally considered to be. Over his closed
coat hung a loose garment and under his feet, upon the
pedestal of the pillar, was a bridle in brass.

This place was also beautified with the bronze statues
of all those renowned personages who have been famous
for wisdom, poetry, oratory or courage throughout the
world, but these were all destroyed by fire. Among these
were the statues of Deiphobus, Aeschines, Demosthenes,
Aristotle, Euripides, Hesiod, Theocritus, Simonides
Anaximenes, Calchas, Pyrrhus, Amymone; of Sappho,
Apollo, Venus, Chrysa, of Julius Caesar, Plato,

Hermaphroditus, Herinna, Terpander, of Pericles, Pythagoras, Stesichorus, Democritus; of Hercules, Aurora, Aeneas, Creusa, Helenus, Andromachus, Menelaus, Helena, Ulysses, Hecuba, Cassandra, Polyxena, Ajax, Paris and his Oenone; of Milo, Dares and Entellus, Charidemus, Melampus, Panthous, Demogeron, Isocrates, Amphiaraus, Sarpedon, Achilles, Mercury, Apuleius, Diana, Pherecydes, Heraclitus, Cratinus, of Menander, Amphitryon, Thucydides, Herodotus, Pindar, Xenophon, Alcmaeon, Pompey and Virgil. There were also many other statues that have been described in verse by Christodorus, a poet of Thebes or, as others report, a native of Coptos in Egypt. Were it not a long-winded work I would explain it to the reader.

There stood near the Zeuxippum Bath a small bath noted by Leontius in the following lines:

Let not thy stately walls, O proud Zeuxippum,
Resent the meanness of this little bath.
In heaven's high tower, near the constellation
Of Ursa Major shines the Polar Star.

There is nothing of the Zeuxippum remaining at present, nor of many other fine baths; although we have many inscriptions relating to them, as, for example, that famous one celebrated by Agathius, in which Venus is said to have bathed herself; or another called Didymum, in which both sexes used to wash, described in verse by Paulus Silentiarius, and a third made memorable by an inscription of the learned Leontius. Besides these, there was another named Cupido, described by the ingenious Marianus; yet all of them are either entirely ruined or so defaced by the Mohametans that you cannot discover who built them or to whom they belonged.

# VIII

## The Hospitals of Sampson and Eubulus

AS PROCOPIUS SAYS:

> A hospital was built for the relief of poor and sick
> people. It was founded in ancient times by a holy
> man, whose name was Sampson. But it did not
> escape the flames set by a riotous mob who burned
> down that and the Church of St. Sophia. It was
> rebuilt by Julian, who beautified and enlarged it
> with a multitude of small handsome apartments,
> and afterwards endowed it with a yearly stipend for
> the support and comfort of the miserable and
> distressed. But, not being content with this oblation
> that he had made to God, the good emperor, with
> the assistance of his imperial consort, Theodora,
> built two other hospitals next to it on the same
> ground where the houses of Isidorus and Arcadius
> formerly stood.

From this I would observe that the Hospital of Sampson
was not far from the Church of St. Sophia; and I have
read in the history of an anonymous author that it stood
opposite it. I am confirmed in this opinion by the
authority of Zonaras, who tells us in the same manner that
there was a fire set by a faction that burned down the
great church, that of St. Eirene, the Hospital of Eubulus,
the Chalca, the Bath of Severus, called the Zeuxippum,
and many other buildings. This is further attested by
Cedrinus who, speaking of the same fire, tells us that:

> a great part of the city, the churches of St. Sophia
> and St. Eirene, the hospitals of Sampson and

Eubulus, with the sick people inhabiting them, as well as the Augustan gatehouse of the basilica, the Chalca, the two porticos as far as the Forum, the Octagon and the Bath of Zeuxippus, were destroyed by fire.

After I had taken the former quotation from the printed works of Procopius, I lighted by chance on a manuscript of him, in which I was informed that the Hospital of Sampson stood between the two churches of St. Sophia and St. Eirene.

## IX

## The Statue of Eudoxia Augusta, For Which St. Chrysostom Was Sent into Banishment

SOCRATES AND SOZOMEN, WRITERS OF SACRED HISTORY, tell us that a silver statue of Eudoxia Augusta was erected on a porphyry pillar on the south side of the Church of St. Sophia, though at some distance from it, near the Senate House. The people commonly paid their homage and acclamations to this statue. There were public entertainments of dancing and other mime acts played out before it, according to a custom that has long prevailed of paying adoration to the images of princes. Reflecting on this practice as contrary to the precepts of the Christian religion, St. Chrysostom publicly condemned it in a sermon. Believing herself to be struck closely in that discourse, Eudoxia banished him. Here I should take notice of the Miliarium and the Basilica as being near the

Church of St. Sophia, but then I would invert the outline I had proposed to observe.

# X

# The Parts of the City in the Third Ward

THE THIRD WARD IS DISCOVERED TO HAVE BEEN THAT area upon which stood the Hippodrome, the house of Ibraham Pasha, the Gate of Leo, and the haven that the inhabitants called the Caterga Limena, where the three-decked galleys used to anchor, and so on to the top of the second hill as far as the Forum of Constantine. I made this observation not only from the order the wards stand in but also from the treatise, *The Description of the Wards,* which says that the third ward is level ground at the entrance but in the most remote part it descends with too great a declivity into the sea and contains the tribunal of the Forum of Constantine, the Circus Maximus, the house of Pulcheria Augusta, the New Port, and the semicircular portico made in the form of an old Greek sigma.

# XI

## The Hippodrome,
## Its Obelisk, Statues, and Columns

MODERN HISTORIANS, SUCH AS ZONARAS AND OTHERS, write that the Hippodrome was built by Severus upon his reconciliation with the Byzantines. Zosimus, a more ancient writer, tells us that it was built and curiously beautified by Constantine the Great. He built part of it, the Temple of Castor and Pollux, whose images remained in the porticos of the Hippodrome down to his time; that is, until the reign of Theodosius II. In the middle of the Circus, which the Greeks call the Hippodrome, there stood an obelisk made of Theban stone. Since the *Ancient Description of the Wards* takes no notice of it, though it does of the square Theban obelisk in the fifth ward, I should be inclined to believe that the Obelisk I am speaking of was overturned by an earthquake and removed by Theodosius to the Hippodrome after that treatise was written had the author not taken notice of many of Theodosius' works and omitted some things in the wards that he afterwards mentioned in his *General View of the City*. It is probable that Constantinople had more obelisks than one.

As to that noted in the fifth ward, it is not now extant. When first I arrived at Constantinople I saw two of them, one in the Circus Maximus, another in the imperial precinct standing on the northern side of the first hill. This latter had a square shape and was erected near the houses of the Grand Seignor's glaziers. A little after I saw it lying prostrate outside the precinct and found it to be thirty feet in length.

Each of its sides, if I am not mistaken, was six feet broad, and the whole was eight yards in circumference. It was purchased by Antonius Priolus, a nobleman of Venice, who sent it there and placed it in St. Stephen's Market.

The other is standing in the Hippodrome to this day. It is supported by four square, broad pieces of brass, each a foot and a half high with a base and a pedestal of the same height. From the ground there rise two steps against the pedestal, the lowermost of which is a foot high and of the same breadth. The upper step is two feet high and projects four feet and four fingers breadth beyond the pedestal. The steps are not laid inside the pedestal but are joined to it outside, as appears from the cement. Upon the steps stands the pedestal, which is twelve feet broad on every side, four feet, eight digits in height, and projects beyond the base a foot and a half. A little above a foot higher it is more contracted and does not project beyond its base; for from the top of the pedestal there is a fluting on four sides of the Obelisk that is cut out of the same stone of which the pedestal is made and is a foot and thirteen digits high. The corners of the top of the pedestal are worn and defaced but are repaired by four stones of Theban porphyry marble, each of them a foot and a half high. All the fluted part of the pedestal that lies between these four angular stones, together with the upper part of it, support the base, which is seven feet and thirteen digits high and projects a foot and a half beyond the bottom of the shaft of the Obelisk to a width of nine feet and as many digits.

It is carved on all sides, as is the pedestal, which is covered with curious stones cut in bas relief. The sculptures on the north side stand in two ranges, the lowermost of which contains eighteen statues and two capstans that are turned with iron crows by four men. They wind ropes, which are drawn through pulleys around the capstan and so draw the Obelisk along the ground. In the same range the Obelisk is engraved in an upright posture, as it now stands, with three statues. One of these, as the inhabitants tell you, represents the master and the other the servant whom he intended to correct, if a third person had not interposed, because he had erected the Obelisk in his absence. In the upper range there are also the figures of the two capstans with the same number of men working them and laboring with those below them to drag the Obelisk. The wreaths of the ropes, in particular, are very nicely cut.

If the reader could understand the manner in which this cumbersome pillar was erected, I believe he or she would judge that it was done the way Marcellinus describes. There was nothing lacking, he says, but the erection of the Obelisk, the accomplishment of which could hardly be conceived without the greatest danger. You might see, he says, a vast wood scaffolding made of tall beams. At the top of these were fixed large and long ropes in the manner of threads on a weaver's loom, which darkened the air by their thickness and closeness to one another. At the bottom these ropes were fastened around the Obelisk, which was leisurely drawn into the air by many thousands working at the capstans and at last fixed on its base.

I believe there are at present in Constantinople people who could do the same thing. I am induced to think so by what I observed of a pillar on the side of the fifth hill that was almost equal in magnitude to this Obelisk. I saw this pillar taken off its base and laid upon the ground in the following manner. Around the pillar, though at some distance from it, they closely fixed large poles in the ground at an equal distance from each other that were much taller than the pillar. They laid others across the tops of these poles, fastened to them in the strongest manner, to which were affixed the pulleys through which the ropes slipped. These reached from the bottom of the shaft of the pillar to the top and were fastened to it. The ropes were so thick, both lengthwise and crosswise, that at some distance the scaffolding looked like a square tower. There were many capstans fixed in the ground on all sides, which were turned by infinite numbers of the strongest youth until they had moved it from its base and laid it prostrate on the earth. They afterwards laid it on strong carriages, the wheels of which were bound with thick iron, and brought it safely to the third hill and set it up as an ornament to the mosque of Süleiyman the Emperor.

But to return to the Obelisk. On the west side of the pedestal was the following inscription in Greek:

To raise this four-square pillar to its height
And fix it steady on its solid base,
Great Theodosius tried, but tried in vain.
In two and thirty days, by Proclus' skill,
The toilsome work, with great applause, was
    finished.

And on the other side was this inscription in Latin, which was somewhat defaced, but I could read it, and it is as follows:

Difficilis quondam dominis parere serenis
Jussus, & extinctis palmam portare Tyrannis.
Omnia Theodosio cedunt, sobolique perenni
Ter denis sic victus, duobusque diebus,
Judice sub Proclo, sublime elatus ad auras.

On its south side there are two ranges of statues, the lowermost of which has four chariots engraved on it, two of which are drawn by a pair, and the other by four horses with a driver for each of them. In the upper range are two equestrian statues, three footmen, the *togati,* two obelisks, and four square pillars. On the north side of the base are engraved four ranges of statues, which contain thirty-five figures in gowns. On the west side there are two ranges, the lowest of which has nine figures in a suppliant posture, giving presents to the emperor, who stands in the upper range with sixteen figures around him. The south side has two ranges. On the lowest are cut ten figures in gowns, in a petitioning pose; the upper contains twenty figures, all in gowns, except four in a fighting posture, armed with bucklers. The east side has three ranges on the lowest part. The lowest range contains sixteen statues of men and women dancing and playing on musical instruments, above which are two more ranges, in which appear little more than heads, which I consider to be the spectators. The highest range has twenty figures, six of which are divided from the rest by pillars. The middle figure holds a crown in his hand. These are placed in a quadrilateral plan, and the whole Obelisk bears on them. It is engraved from top to bottom with Egyptian characters.

# XII

## The Colossus

IN THE MIDDLE OF THE HIPPODROME STILL STANDS A Colossus made of square stones, which was formerly, as an injudicious author writes, encrusted with marble. But, as appears in an inscription carved on its base, it was covered with plates of brass secured together with iron, as appears not only from the holes made in the shaft but by those that still remain in the base where the iron pins were fastened and strengthened with melted lead. Having felt the effects of the avarice and rapine of the barbarians, it is now despoiled of its beautiful outward appearance and reveals only the workmanship of its interior.

This was also the fate of the Colossus of Rhodes, which was demolished by the Hagarens in the reign of Constans, nephew of Heraclius, thirteen hundred years after it was erected. It was purchased afterwards by a certain Emesenus, a Jew. The brass, when stripped off, was so heavy that it was carried off by nine hundred camels.

Upon the base of the Colossus at Constantinople are inscribed the following verses:

Famed Constantine, Romanus' princely son,
Who wore with Homer the Imperial Crown,
This lofty pile, by time decayed, repaired;
And joined fresh beauty to her builder's art.

This Colossus has three steps at the base. The lowest is two feet high, the next a foot and two digits, and the uppermost the same height. The base is a square marble, seven feet and three digits high, each side of which is ten feet and nine inches broad. This Colossus is taller then the Obelisk. One day, on the festival of the circumcision of the prince of Boldania, I saw an ingenious fellow of a mountebank climb to the top of it and come down safely. The same attempt was immediately made by another who made shift to reach the top, but the height so dazzled and confounded him that, despairing of getting down without injury, he threw himself with all his might as far as he could from the Colossus to avoid the danger of being dashed to pieces on the foundation. So falling down right upon his feet, he struck the earth and died upon the spot.

# XIII

## Some Other Columns in the Hippodrome

AROUND THE MIDDLE OF THE HIPPODROME, AMONG A

strait range of small obelisks, there stand seven pillars. One of which, made of Arabian marble, is seventeen feet and eight digits in circumference. The statue of Hercules was erected on the top of it by Ibraham Pasha. It was cast in brass and made of the spoils that he had taken in Hungary. But upon the death of Ibraham, Hercules, who was reported to have traveled in so many countries and tamed so many monsters, was at last forced to submit and be torn to pieces by the Turks, the most inveterate enemies of statuary and the whole Vitruvian art. They treated him in as barbarous a manner as he was by Diagoras. He went into an inn, and wanting wood to boil his lentils, found a well-finished wooden statue of Hercules, cut it to pieces and threw it into a fire, saying these words: "O Hercules, who has passed with so much courage through your twelve labors, see how you can struggle with the thirteenth."

In the same range of obelisks there stands another pillar. It is made of brass, not fluted, but wreathed around with the foldings of three serpents, like those we see in great ropes. The heads of these serpents are placed in a triangular pattern and rise very high upon the shaft of the pillar. There are many fabulous and trifling reports among the inhabitants concerning the erection of this pillar, which are occasioned by their ignorance of the history of their ancestors.

Zosimus, among other historians, writes that in the Hippodrome Constantine the Great placed the Tripod of Apollo that was brought from Delphi and which had the image of that god on it. Sozomen tells us that Constantine not only placed the Delphic Tripod in the Hippodrome, but also the celebrated tripod that Pausanias the Lacedaemonian general and the cities of Greece consecrated to Apollo upon the conclusion of the Persian War. Eusebius is more clear on this point and says that in some part of Constantinople Constantine set up an image of Sminthius Apollo, which was a title given to him; but that in the Hippodrome he placed the Pythian Tripod, around which was wreathed the figure of the serpent Python. It therefore seemed to me very probable that this was the same tripod that was placed on the brazen pillar I am speaking of at Constantinople. Herodotus writes that the golden tripod that was at Delphi was made out of a tenth part of the spoils taken from the Persians and erected on this pillar and adds further that when the Persians were routed at the battle of Plataea, there was found a golden tripod that was restored to Apollo and set on a brass pillar encircled with three entwined serpents near an altar.

It was a mistake of those who imagine that this pillar was formerly overlaid with gold but was plundered of it by the Turks, since Pausanias makes it plain that it was stripped of its gold long before the Turks took Constantinople. "After the battle of Plataea," he says, "the Greeks made a common offering to Apollo, which was a golden tripod supported by a brazen serpent." The brass, he tells us , remained intact in his time, but the gold was carried off by the Phocean generals.

There are five other pillars in the same range. In the front of the Hippodrome, facing the Propontis, there was a range of seventeen pillars of white marble standing when first I came to Constantinople. They stood on the southwest side of the Hippodrome. The pedestal of each of them is two feet and ten digits high. All of them are supported by arched foundations that lie level with the plain of the Hippodrome but rise above the ground to a height of fifty feet. They are all placed on a little wall, which projects two steps, or on square plinths, the lowermost of which is a foot and a digit high. The upper is a foot and six digits high and projects beyond the pedestal eight digits. Their pedestals are five feet square and seven inches high. Their lowest projections, which are placed there for tores and other modules, are six and a half digits high, the upper projections the same height; the plinth of the cornice is eleven digits thick; the lower tore seven and a half digits; the scotia four digits; the upper tore six digits; the stone that supports the shaft is five digits high; and the shafts themselves three feet, five digits in diameter and twenty-eight feet in height.

These pillars were recently taken down and their bases removed by order of Emperor Süleiyman to build a hospital. I was concerned to see them thus demolished, not so much for the use they were intended but because some of them were squared out for paving a bath. The capitals, made after the most exact plans of ancient architecture, were cut into rude and ill-shaped models for covering a bake-house, and the pedestals and all the entablature were hewn out, probably only to build a wall. The shafts of the pillars stood a distance of eleven feet apart. I observed that the capitals were impaired because of the great space of the intercolumniation. The capitals were finished in the Corinthian order, and the trabeation was beautifully wrought but was not adorned with an ovolo. There were iron rings fixed to the architraves, upon which were hung curtains. Beyond this was another range of pillars, which were extant some time after the taking of the city by the Turks.

Before it was taken by the Gauls and the Venetians, there was in the Hippodrome an abundance of figures of horses both in stone and bronze. There were four in particular of surprising skill, which were gilt, equal in beauty and workmanship to those that now stand in front of the Church of St. Mark's in Venice, which some say were brought there from Constantinople. I shall omit the statues of great numbers of emperors and princes that were set up in the circus. Among these stood the statue of Emperor Justinian, which has been celebrated in verse. There were also the statues of some eunuchs who were most in the interest and favor of their masters. Among others, there was the statue of Plato the Eunuch, the emperor's chamberlain, who was burnt to death in the reign of Basilicus. There was an inscription, according to

Suidas, fixed on the breast of this statue, which ran thus: "Whoever removes this statue to another place, let him be hanged." Yet it was taken out of the church of Procopius and carried to the Hippodrome.

I have no time to note the numberless statues of all the combatants, wrestlers, and charioteers formerly placed in the Hippodrome. Although there is nothing remaining of them at present, the memory of them is still preserved in a small poem of three hundred verses, in which some chariot racers are mentioned with particular honors, although no notice is taken there of a person named Thomas, a man of surprising agility and speed in that kind of exercise.

At Constantinople I have seen the fragment of a stone with this inscription: Θομᾶ Ἡνιόχου. This is probably the same person mentioned by Emperor Theoderic in a letter to Faustus, a Roman praetor, in the following words:

> Of our imperial bounty and consideration we have given and granted to Thomas, the famous chariot racer, a stipend to be continued to him until we have further experienced and been fully satisfied with his wonderful skill in that exercise. Having now received ample testimony of his superiority in that performance and, since he has left the country and has chosen voluntarily to settle within our dominions, out of our imperial munificence we have encouraged him with a monthly salary to remain among us. He has, by his frequent successes, received the repeated applause and stood high in the favor of the people whom he has sometimes, though unfortunately, vindicated, and at other times has eminently distinguished himself in the chariot race. Victory so often attended him that he was looked on as a sorcerer by a set of people, who would have considered it the highest commendation to have been thought so themselves

for the same reasons. It is no wonder that men should ascribe the excellence that they cannot arrive at to the power of sorcery and enchantment. The sight of a chariot race in ancient times was held in the highest honor and esteem, though at present it is little better than the occasion of buffoonery, an incentive to trifling disputes, an encouragement to roguery and sharping and the constant source of broils and quarrels.

Thus the emperor, from whose words I would observe that the chariot racer mentioned here, who had left Constantinople probably over some party quarrels among the chariot racers, who were therefore called "factions," was also in danger in Rome for the same reason. Not only have the commonwealths of Rome and Constantinople both been often harassed by such commotions, but the emperors themselves have often fallen into the greatest danger of losing their government because of them.

But all the diversions of the Circus have now ceased. I was concerned to see it despoiled of all its ornaments, though the Turks have begun to build there again of late. I was more concerned because, looking carefully at a medal I then had in my hand, it reminded me of Belisarius triumphing in the Hippodrome after his victory over the king of the Vandals, as well as of the disgrace and poverty — notwithstanding his bravery and courage — that he afterwards fell into through the jealousy of the emperor. On one side it was stamped with the triumphant reception of Belisarius, and on the other this image with this inscription:

GLORIA ROMANORUM BELISARIUS.

Procopius writes that there was a gate in the Hippodrome called the Cochlia, because it had winding stairs within it. There was also a passage through which they went to their burial ground. The same writer tells us that in the same place there was a portico called Venetia, from the companies or factions of chariot racers who used to assemble there and who distinguished themselves from other factions or companies by a sky-colored garment, which was named for the Venetians, a people that particularly used that color.

It is very probable that the Prasin Faction also had a portico here. These were another company of charioteers, who distinguished themselves with a green livery. The word "Prasina" is derived from πράσον in Greek, which means a leek. Nor is it unlikely that there were other companies with liveries of other colors who were not promiscuously crowded together but seated in their own apartments on the porticos to see the races.

# XIV

## The Church of Bacchus, the Court of Hormisda, And The House of Justinian

IT IS OBSERVABLE FROM THE SITUATION OF THE Church of Bacchus and Sergius, now standing on the plain between the Propontis and the Hippodrome, that the Imperial Palace and the house Justinian lived in before he was emperor stood near it. Procopius writes that Justinian built a church and dedicated it to St. Peter and St. Paul. It stood near the imperial court, where a palace built by Hormisda had stood formerly. Justinian made a mansion for himself so that the beauty and elegance of its building might be an ornament to the Palace.

After he had arrived at the imperial dignity, he built other fine palaces around it; and near it he built another church in honor of two illustrious saints, Sergius and Bacchus. These churches, which are both equally beautiful, stood on the same plot of ground, and there is no material difference between them. They shine alike with the most glossy marble; both are curiously gilded and with the richest offerings; nor is there anything in which they do not resemble each other except that one is built lengthways and the other in a semicircular manner. They are both wonderful of their kind and are a great ornament not only to the Palace, but to the whole city. Procopius adds a little further that Justinian changed the house that was called the House of Hormisda into a more magnificent form and joined it to the Palace.

I am of the opinion that this Hormisda, whom he dignifies with the title of prince, was the son of a king of Persia. As Marcellinus reports, when Constans, the son of Constantine, came to Rome, he boasted how far he would transcend Hormisda in his immoderate schemes for building, but unable to accomplish his designs, he was content, he said in a humble manner, only to have built another such house as the one that stood in the Forum of Trajan. This story later came to Hormisda's ear, and he replied in a jocular manner, "Let him try if he can build a stable for himself first."

Cedrinus explains at greater length how near the House of Justinian was to the Church of Bacchus:

Justinian built the Church of Sergius and Bacchus, which on its sea side is near the Palace, and also built another church near it on the same piece of ground on which his own house had stood. In building these two churches, and in founding a monastery that he filled with men of sound learning and exemplary conversation, he laid out his whole estate and all he was worth until he arrived at the imperial dignity.

There is nothing left at present of the Church of St. Peter and St. Paul; but the Church of Sergius and Bacchus is yet standing. It still goes under its ancient name, though the Turks have changed it into a mosque. It is covered at the top with a brick roof and bears on eight pillars of the Ionic order. In the lowest range there are sixteen pillars that bear on the pavement. Six of these pillars are of green marble and ten of white streaked with red veins. The upper range consists of eighteen pillars, eight of which are of green and ten of white marble and are veined as the others. The capitals of the lower are adorned with ovolos at the bottom. Their upper part is covered with a foliage. The volutae of the upper range of pillars project from the four angles of the capitals; but the ovolos project from their sides, which are also covered with a foliage of fine workmanship. The architraves over the capitals of the lower range are finished with the nicest art.

There is a noble piece of sculpture in this church. It was done by Zoophorus, who has carved around the church some Greek verses in the largest characters. The tops of the pilasters are shaded with a vineal foliage, intermixed with clustered grapes, which denote that the church was dedicated to Bacchus.

# XV

## The Port of Julian and Sophia,
## The Portico Named Sigma,
## The Palace of Sophia

NEAR THE CHURCH OF BACCHUS STOOD THE PORT OF

Julian. This is plain from the account we have of the fire that occurred in the reign of Leo the Great and, as Evagrius tells us, began on the north side of the city and destroyed all before it from the Bosphorian Port to the old Temple of Apollo. On the south side of the city it made the same havoc from the Port of Julian to the houses near the Temple of Concord. Zonaras, who describes the devastations of that fire, writes that it burned with great fury from the Bosporus to the Church of St. John the Calybite and on the south from the Church of St. Thomas to the church of the renowned martyrs, Sergius and Bacchus. The Church of St. Thomas stood near the Temple of Concord. The account that Cedrinus gives of this fire is that it took its course around the city all the way from the northern to the southern shore as far as the Church of Sergius and Bacchus.

Emperor Anastasius fortified the Port of Julian and secured it by a strong wall. It was afterwards called the Port of Sophia, according to Cedrinus, who writes that Justin, the nephew of Justinian, built a palace in the Port of Julian, which he ordered to be cleansed, and that he commanded his own and the statue of Sophia, his consort, to be erected there. From this he gave it the name of the Port of Sophia. The inscription of the statue of Justin placed here is as follows:

I, Theodorus, Prefect of the City,
Here, on the shore, erect this lofty statue;
It represents the Emperor Justinus.
May his kind presence guard and ever shed
Its peaceful influence over the neighboring ports.

Procopius writes that the Church of the Martyr Thecla stood near this port. Some modern historians tell us that Belisarius set sail from this port when he went to battle against the Vandals. But I cannot conceive why they have this idea, unless it comes from some words of Procopius, who says that Justinian commanded the ship in which the general sailed to be brought near the Palace, and that there Epiphanius, bishop of Constantinople, offered a prayer for his success, as was customary on such occasions, and that then Belisarius went off with his wife Antonina.

There were, indeed, some palaces near this port, but there were also other palaces near the bay, which was full of havens, a little distance from which stood the house of Belisarius. Suidas confirms that Anastasius fortified this harbor and made a pier there. Zonaras attests that Justin built some palaces there and called them the Palaces of Sophia, from the name of his consort, whom he passionately loved.

Many historians are of the opinion that these palaces stood near the Port of Sophia; but I am inclined to think, both from reason and the authority of learned men, that it was not so. For Zonaras, among others, writes that Justin built these palaces close to the city. Agathius Scholasticus, a much more ancient writer who was living at the time they were built, wrote the following inscription, which was fixed upon them. From it the reader may observe that they were not situated near the Propontis — to which the Port of Sophia adjoined — but were opposite the city near the shore of the Bosporus where the Continent is divided into two parts:

Where the straight sea divides the continents,
These gilded palaces the emperor built
For his dear consort, fair Sophia's use.
The wonders of thy beauty, potent Rome,
Europe, and Asia, half the extended world
With pleasure view and silently admire.

For the word that in the original inscription is δέρχεαι, Zonaras writes δέρχειν. It is easy to discover from these verses that the Palace of Sophia was not situated near the

Bosporus but outside the walls of the city, a fact attested to by Cedrinus and many other historians in their descriptions of the hard frost that occurred in the reign of Leo Copronymus, by which the Bosporus was frozen so hard that whoever wanted to pass over from the Palace of Sophia to the city or from Chrysopolis to the Church of St. Mamas or to repass to Galata on the shore of the Bosporus, might cross over the ice without the least danger.

Before it was called the Port of Julian, the Port of Sophia seems to me to be the same as that formerly called the Neorium and which the *Ancient Description of the Wards* places in the same ward as the Hippodrome. But whether it is one or either of these, it is now filled up. If it was the port that stands west of the Church of Bacchus, it is now almost demolished and enclosed by a wall. There is only a small part of it remaining. This is a pool of water where the women wash their linen.

The people tell you that they have seen some three-decked galleys that have been sunk there. It is now called Caterga Limena or the Port of the Three-Decked Galleys by the present inhabitants. I shall not determine whether it is the same port that is standing on the east of the Church of Bacchus near the gate of the city called the Porta Leonis. It took this name either from a lion carved in stone near it or from Emperor Leo who, they tell you, had a palace there.

Nicephorus, a modern historian, tells us that an emperor of Constantinople, when besieged by the people of Italy, summoned a multitude of smiths into the Morion, which ran round the Hippodrome. I never could discover in Constantinople the place that was called the Pyctacia; yet I cannot help but note from Cedrinus and other modern historians that in the place that they called the Pyctacia there was a pillar that supported the statue of Emperor Leo, the consort of Verina. This statue, as some write, was erected by his sister Euphemia, a lady of great wisdom and continence, near her own house where Leo used to pay her a visit every week. All persons who labored under afflictions of any kind laid their petitions to the emperor upon the steps of this pillar. The apparitors took them up; and when the emperor waited upon his sister, they presented them to him. Budé says that the Pyctacia or the Pystacia, as he calls them, were briefs; though I see no reason why they may not also be called petitions. For as the *Pyctium* signifies a book, I do not see why *Pyctacium* may not signify any smaller writing. The Greeks now generally call their letters *Pyctacia*. In a history written by an anonymous author, I have read that Eudoxia had set up her own statue, made of solid silver, in a place called the Pyctacium. If the author is not mistaken, I would take this to be the same statue that stood near the Church of St. Sophia near which — as I have shown before — the statue of Eudoxia stood.

I have seen a small treatise on Constantinople which says that Constantine the Great built a Church to St. Euphemia near the Hippodrome, which was afterward turned into an armory by Constantine Copronymus, a professed adversary of images in churches, who cast the relics of St. Euphemia into the sea. Suidas writes that the statue of Euphemia — the consort of Emperor Justin, who was a Thracian — was placed in the Church of St. Euphemia, which she herself had built.

Some modern writers say that in the time of Emperor Basilius there was a great earthquake that overturned the Church of St. Polyclete and killed all who were in it; and from that time it was called Sigma. I am more inclined to believe that it took its name from the portico so called many ages before this earthquake, because it was built in the shape of the letter Sigma and is placed in the *Ancient Description of Constantinople* in the same ward as the Hippodrome. Cedrinus seems to note this place. He says:

They dragged Emperor Michael in his monk's habit by the heels out of the monastery of Studius through the market; and leading him beyond the monastery called Periblepton, in a place called Sigma, they put out both his eyes.

The same author tells us that Emperor Basilius, a native of Macedon, rebuilt from the foundations a church in honor of the Blessed Virgin, which was called Sigma. Chrysaphius Zomas, a eunuch, set up the statue of Theodosius II in a place called Sigma. Some writers affirm that Constantine the Great built a church to St. Stephen in a place called Sigma. The Sigma therefore here intended must necessarily be another place in the city, distinct from the one that I observed was in the third ward. It ought to be written with the letter "e," as "Segma," because, as I hinted just now, the fall of the Church of St. Polyclete from an earthquake crushed to death all who were in it.

# XVI

## The Fourth Ward

IF THE MILIARIUM AUREUM EXISTED NOW, OR THE people of Constantinople had preserved the memory of its location, we might easily discover from the *Ancient Description of the Wards,* which tells us that the fourth ward extended with hills rising on the right and left from the Miliarium Aureum to a level plain, that it was in the first valley, or on the ridge of the hill that rises just above it. Nor could we have failed to make the same discovery from the remains of the Augustaeum, the Basilica, the Nymphaeum and other fine buildings, had they not been entirely buried in their own ruins. But since no observations can be made that way at present, I was in suspense as to whether or not the valley where the fourth ward stood was the same valley that I had described at first; because it is common to other vales to have hills rising to the left and right.

When I had sufficiently researched the learned writings and histories as to what ancient monuments had formerly been in the fourth ward and where they had stood, I was soon convinced that the fourth ward stood in the first valley on its slopes and on the hill near the Church of St. Sophia, as the reader will perceive from the following history.

# XVII

## The Forum Called the Augustaeum, The Pillar of Theodosius, That of Justinian, And The Senate House

PROCOPIUS WRITES THAT THE FORUM THAT WAS formerly called the Augustaeum was surrounded by pillars and was situated before the Imperial Palace. Not only is the forum quite defaced at present, but its very name is lost, and the whole ground where it stood is built upon. The palace is entirely in ruins, yet I gather from the pedestal of a Pillar of Justinian recently standing but now removed by the Turks — which Procopius says was built by Justinian in the Augustaeum and Zonaras in the court before the Church of Sophia — that the Augustaeum stood where a fountain is now at the west end of the

Church of St. Sophia. Suidas says that Justinian cleansed
the court after he had built the church of St. Sophia and
paved it with marble and that it was formerly called the
Forum Augustaeum. He adds that he erected his own
statue there. Procopius writes that:

> there was a certain forum facing the Senate House,
> which was called the Augustaeum by the citizens.
> Here there are seven stones so cemented together in
> a quadrangle and so closely set, the upper within
> the lower stone, that a man may conveniently sit
> down on every one of their projections.

I was more induced to give this account of the pedestal
from Procopius because I do not find it in his printed
works. On the top of it, he says, there is erected a large
pillar composed of many stones covered with brass,
which at once both strengthened and adorned them. The
plates of brass did not reflect as strong a luster as pure
gold, yet it was little inferior to silver in value. On the
top of the statue was set a large horse in brass facing east
that afforded a noble aspect indeed. He seemed to be in
marching posture and struggling for speed. His near foot
was curved in front as though he would paw the ground;
his far foot was fixed to the pedestal; and his hind feet
were contracted as though he was prepared to gallop off.

Upon the horse was placed the statue of the emperor.
It was made of brass, large like a colossus, dressed in a
warlike costume like Achilles, with sandals on his feet and
armed with a coat of mail and a shining helmet. He
looked eastward and seemed to be marching against the
Persians. In his left hand he bore a globe devised to
signify his universal power over the whole world. On top
of it was fixed a cross, to which he attributed all his
successes in war and his accession to the imperial dignity.
His right hand was stretched to the east, and by pointing

with his fingers he seemed to forbid the barbarous nations
to approach nearer but to stand off at their peril.

Tzetzes, in his *Various History*, described what kind of
helmet he had on his head. He says:

> The Persians generally wore a turban on their
> heads. When the Romans obtained any victory
> over them they plundered them of these turbans,
> which they placed on their own heads. They are of
> the same shape as that with which the statue of
> Justinian, erected on a large pillar, is crowned.

Cedrinus relates that Justinian held the globe in his silver
hand. Zonaras writes that Justinian set up this pillar in the
seventeenth year of his reign in the same place where
another pillar of Theodosius the Great had formerly
stood. This bore his statue in silver, which weighed seven
thousand, four hundred pounds and was made at the
expense of his son Arcadius.

When Justinian had demolished the statue and the
pillar, he stripped it of a vast quantity of lead from which
he made pipes for aqueducts that brought the water into
the city. This ill treatment of Theodosius by Justinian was
revenged on him by the barbarians; for they used his
pillar in the same manner and stripped it of the statue, the
horse, and the brass with which it was covered, so that it
was only a bare column for some years. About thirty
years ago the whole shaft was taken down to the pedestal,
and that was demolished down to the base about a year
ago. From it I observed a spring sprouting up with pipes
into a large cistern. At present there stands in the same
place a water house, and the pipes are enlarged. I recently
saw the equestrian statue of Justinian erected on the pillar
that stood here and which had been preserved a long time
in the imperial precinct, carried into the melting houses
where they cast their ordnance. Among the fragments
were the leg of Justinian, which exceeded my height, and

his nose, which was over nine inches long. I dared not publicly measure the horses legs as they lay on the ground but privately measured one of the hoofs and found it to be nine inches in height.

Suidas and some modern historians assure us that it was called the Forum Augustaeum because the Curatores and Sebastrophori used to dance in the market place there on the fifteenth day of October in honor of Augustus or because the statues of Constantine and his mother, Helena, were set up in an arched gallery that stood here.

Zosimus, a more ancient historian than Procopius, asserts that Constantine built a round market with four porticos, two in a row above each other; and that he roofed them with Preconnesian marble, so that you might pass from them to the Portico of Severus and from there beyond the bounds of the ancient city. He adds that this market stood in a place to which there was a passage through an adjacent land gate. This is the same market meant by the anonymous author of the *History of Constantinople*, where he tells us that Constantine built a market in a circular manner.

The same author tells us in another place that when he was in Constantinople, Constantine had surrounded the great Forum with four porticos and placed two statues at both ends of one of them, which you ascend by many steps. At one end was placed the statue of Rhea, the mother of the gods. This is the same statue as those who sailed with Jason placed on Mount Didymus, rising above the city of Cyzicus. They tell you that for her neglect in paying divine worship to the gods the statue was defaced and that her hands, which previously held the reins of two lions that stood before her, were changed into a petitioning posture. This statue faced and adorned the city at the same time.

At the other end of the portico he placed the Fortune of the City, though Suidas relates that the Fortune of the City stood in a niche of the Miliarium. If this statue were set up here by Constantine, I should think that both the markets mentioned by Zosimus are one and the same. But to me they seem to be different, because Zosimus tells us in one place that Constantine built a market with two porticos around it and afterwards that he built a market with four porticos around it, unless he takes into account the porticos of Severus and Constantine, from which there was a free entrance into other porticos.

Procopius writes that on the east side of the Forum Augustaeum Justinian built a large court where the Senate used to assemble and celebrate an anniversary festival every year. Before the Senate House stand six columns, two of which support the middle of the western wall. The other four stand a little distance from it. These pillars are all of white marble, and I consider them to be the largest in the world. The other six support a portico that runs around the top of a large building. The upper part of the portico is adorned with marble elegantly variegated and equal to that of the columns. It is furnished with an infinite variety of curious statues.

I am of the opinion that Justinian did not build this Senate House but that he rebuilt the old Senate House, which was burnt down by the fire that consumed the Church of St. Sophia and the Baths of Zeuxippus. For Sozomen writes that Constantine the Great built the Great Council Hall, which was called the Senate House, and ordered it to be held in equal dignity and honored it with the same public celebration of the feast of the calends as that of ancient Rome. He tells us where great court stood, when he writes that the silver statue of Eudoxia Augusta was placed upon a porphyry pillar on the south side of the Church of St. Sophia, beyond the high pulpit, which faces the Senate House. Socrates tells us that it was neither erected near nor at any considerable distance from the Church of St. Sophia, but beyond the broad way, as Suidas observes, that runs between them both. "In the Tribunal of the Palace," he says, "stood the Pillar of Eudoxia, the wife of Theodosius."

The *Treatise of the Ancient Description of the Wards* places the Senate House, the Tribunal with porphyry steps, and the Basilica all in the same ward. Sozomen clearly points out the location of the Senate House when he says that when a tumult arose concerning the expulsion of St. Chrysostom, the great church was all of a sudden in a blaze, which burned down the buildings on the walks and the great Senate House, lying to the south of them. There are some remains of the walls of the Senate House still standing south of the Church of St. Sophia, beyond the way that leads from the imperial gate to the Forum of Constantine.

# XVIII

## The Imperial Palace, The Basilica, The Palace of Constantine, and The Entrance House Named Chalca

NOT FAR FROM THE FORUM AUGUSTAEUM, AS Procopius writes, stood a palace, the stateliness and magnificence of which the reader may easily guess from the description he gives of the vestibulum or the entrance house to it:

This vestibulum is called the Chalca, which is constructed in this manner: there are four straight walls carried up to a great height in a quadrangular form, from each angle of which there projects a stone building curiously finished, which rises with the wall from top to bottom, in no way interrupting the beautiful view before you, but seeming rather to add to its pleasure and agreeableness. Above this building are raised eight arches supporting the roof, which rises in a high dome most beautifully adorned. Its roof is not furnished with fine paintings but shines with mosaic work of all sorts of colors, with various figures of humans and of other kinds of creatures.

This historian has described at length the designs, which are scenes of war, of battles, and the surrender of many towns both in Africa and Italy. Among other curiosities are described the victories of Justinian under his general, Belisarius, and his triumphant return to the emperor. The courage and cheerfulness of his army is expressed in a lively manner. The general is represented in a humble posture, as if making an offering to him of all the kings, the kingdoms, and other rich spoils he had taken from the enemy.

In the middle of the work is represented the emperor and his empress, Theodora, in a pleasant, gay humor, celebrating a festival in honor of his victory over the Goths and Vandals, and bringing great numbers of captives before him. The whole Senate is depicted around them, joining in the celebration. They all look cheerful and merry, smiling and highly pleased with the honor they have in attending the emperor on so important an occasion.

I would observe here that, just as Papinius calls the Basilica of Paulus the Palace of Paulus in his *Sylvae,* so the house that Procopius calls Βασιλεῖον went by the name of both the Basilica and the Palace. I am confirmed in this opinion by Cedrinus, who says that the fire that broke out in the reign of Justinian burned down the porch, or entrance house, to the Basilica, the Basilica itself, the bronze covering of the palace of Constantine the Great, which from that time to this day is called the Chalca because it is covered with plates of gilt brass. What Cedrinus calls the Basilica, Procopius calls τὰ Βασιλεῖα in his book *De Aedif. Justiniani.* When speaking of the above-mentioned fire he tells us that it consumed the gate houses, two basilicas, and the one in particular that was called Chalca. The same writer adds a little below that the emperor commanded Belisarius to go to the Chalca and other entrance houses situated near it. From these words it is observable that Procopius seems to believe that there were other entrance houses into the palace, though in the beginning of this chapter he mentions only the Chalca.

It is my opinion that the house where the emperor dwelt was first called the Basilica; that afterwards, when the great houses where the merchants assembled for trade and commerce were called basilica, the emperor's house was called βασιλεῖον; and, at last, the Palace. If there were any difference between the Basilica and the Palace, the Basilica was either a part of the Palace or built near it, as the reader may see in the *Ancient Description of the Wards,* which places the Augustaeum and the Basilica in the same ward. As this treatise takes no notice in this ward either of a palace or a court, but only of a basilica, it seems to intimate that the Basilica was the Palace itself. But whether the Basilica was within or outside the Palace, it is certain that it was near it, because they were both destroyed in the fire due to their proximity to one another. The rules of architecture prescribe that it be built near a market, which is always near the palace; and that it be built warmly so that the merchants may manage their business there in winter time without any molestation from the severity of the weather.

Julius Pollux is of the same opinion. He says that the Stadia, the Hippodrome, the Senate House, the Forum, the Court, the Imperial Portico, and the Tribunal ought to stand near the Theater. Cedrinus writes that the beautiful structure of the Chalca was built by a certain Aetherius, a famous architect, at the command of the wife of Emperor Anastasius, as appears from a Greek inscription on it that runs like this:

I am the palace of famed Anastasius
The scourge of tyrants; none surpasses me,
In beauty, and in wonderful contrivance.
When the surveyors viewed my mighty bulk,
My height, my length, and my extensive breadth;
'Twas thought beyond the reach of human power
To roof at top my widely gaping walls.
But young Aetherius, ancient in his art,
This building finished, and an offering made
To our good Emperor.
Not Italy, with all its glory shows
A structure so magnificent and great;
Not the proud Capitol of ancient Rome
With all its gilded roofs can rival me.
The costly galleries of Pergamus,
Ruffinus' walks, and stately porticos
Crowded with art, and marbled images
Submit to my superior workmanship.
Not the famed temple, which at Cyzico,
By Adrian built, stands on a lofty rock,
Nor Egypt's costly pyramids, not at Rhodes
The mighty Colosse equal me in greatness.
When my good Emperor, in hostile manner,
Quelled the Isaurian faction, thus he raised me
In honor of Aurora, and the winds.

Some modern historians would have it that Constantine the Great first built the Palace of Chalca. I would be inclined to disbelieve them, but I am induced to think that it was so since I observed the bronze tiles gilt with gold, resembling those of the Capitol and a forum of Old Rome, whose buildings Constantine was proud to imitate as closely as he could. I could never learn who it was who removed the tiles of the Chalca; though it is not improbable that they were spoiled by the fire. It is related by Procopius that Genseric plundered half the Roman Capitol of the gilt plates of brass that covered it, and that Constantine III, the nephew of Heraclius, carried off the silver plates that were laid over the Pantheon.

On the southwest side of the Church of St. Sophia, a small distance from the water pipes of an aqueduct running from a conduit situated in the Forum Augustaeum where the Pillar of Justinian was erected, seven Corinthian pillars still remain. On the shaft of one of them is cut the name of Constantine with the sign of the Cross he saw in the heavens with this inscription: 'εν τούτῳ νίκα.

The base and shaft of these pillars are buried under ground a depth of six feet, which I discovered when I casually fell into the foundation of the walls that were built between them. I could not see the plinth of the base of any of them, because it was covered with earth; yet I perceived the lowermost tore, which was eight digits thick and seven high. The stone at the bottom of the shaft was nine inches wide. Every pillar is thirty feet and six digits high. In short, the whole pillar, capital, and pedestal is about forty-six and a half feet high. The bottom of the shaft, which I measured just above the stone it bears on, is eighteen feet in circumference. The pillars stand a distance of twenty feet and ten digits from each other.

The inhabitants say that these pillars stood inside the Palace of Constantine; others say that they formerly supported a bridge over which you passed as you went from the Palace to the Church of St. Sophia. But there is no truth in either of these opinions; for it is plain from what I observed before that they stood in the Forum Augustaeum. I am therefore inclined to believe that they supported the arches of the porticos in which the statues of Constantine the Great, his mother Helena, and other statues were placed.

From what I have said the reader may trace the beauty and grandeur of the palaces at Constantinople. In addition, Zosimus says that Constantine built some palaces at Constantinople little inferior to those of Rome. Eusebius reports that he illustrated and adorned New Rome and the Imperial Palace in other respects beside those I have mentioned, but that in the finest buildings of his palace and in the middle of all his gilt roofs he fixed a cross set with several kinds of the richest jewels, shining with heavy gold. He therefore intimated that he looked upon the Cross as the defense and bulwark of his government. St. Jerome tells us that "he stripped almost every city of its curiosities and ornaments to adorn his New Rome." Eusebius also mentions the statues of the Muses that he caused to be set up in his palace. Sozomen writes that at the command of Constantine all that was valuable in the temples of the ancients under his government, and all the bronze statues of the nicest workmanship, were brought to Constantinople to beautify the city. These, he tells us, remained in the public ways, in the Hippodrome and in the Palace down to his time.

Not only Constantine the Great but many other emperors of Constantinople ravaged the whole world for the decoration of this city. Among these was Constantine III, the nephew of Heraclius, who plundered ancient Rome of all its bronze and marble statues, shipped off all the costly furniture of the temples, and made more havoc there in the space of seven days than the barbarous nations did in the space of the two hundred and fifty years during which the Roman Empire was in decline before that general pillage. Jordanes, no indifferent writer of the *Getic History,* reports that Theoderic, Prefect of Constantinople, was adopted and made consul by Emperor Zeno, who honored him with an equestrian statue that was erected in front of the Palace. Tzetzes, in his *Various History,* tells us that even in his time the head of Apollo made by Phidias in the likeness of the Sun remained in the Palace. Suidas relates that the statue of Pulcheria, the daughter of Arcadius, was placed in the Chalca near the Walks of Ariadne, the first wife of Zeno, and that the statues of Zeno himself were set up in the imperial gate house of Chalca; as were two other statues on foot, erected on a small pillar with elegies inscribed on them composed by Secundus the Philosopher.

I have seen it in the history of no credible author — though it is well known to the people of Constantinople — that on the left side of the Chalca Justinian erected seven statues in honor of his relatives, some in brass and some in marble, and that he also set up two horses in the niche in front of the Chalca, as well as some gilt heads of women in the frightful likeness of Medusa. I could mention others, but for these I do not depend much on the authority of history. Suidas says that in the Tribunal of the Palace there stood until the time of Heraclius the statues of Eudoxia and her Emperor Theodosius, of Marcian and Constantine.

# XIX

## The Basilica and the Imperial Walks

AS I OBSERVED BEFORE, THE BASILICA THAT STOOD IN the Forum Augustaeum had four arches, as appears from the following ancient inscriptions on them:

Great Theodore, who beautified the city
With four extensive arches, highly merits
The government of four imperial cities.

And on another part of the same arch:

You, Theodorus, with surprizing art,
Once Consul, and thrice Prefect of the City,
Adorned this shining fane with lofty pillars,
Sacred to Fortune, goddess of the city.

Calliades, general of the Byzantine army, placed the statues of Byzas and Phidalia in the Basilica with this inscription on them:

Calliades erected here the statues
Of Byzas, and his loved Phidalia.

And on the statue of Phidalia:

This is the Statue of the fair Phidalia
Young Byzas' wife, the work of Bupalus.

Pliny, among other guides to sculpture, mentions Anthermus of Chios and his sons Biopalus and Anthermus. Dionysius of Byzantium writes that Byzas, from whom Byzantium took its name, was the husband of Phidalia, from whom the port of the Bosporus took the name of the Port of Phidalia, of which I have written more extensively in my *Treatise on the Bosporus*. Suidas and some modern writers say that in the Basilica, behind the Miliarium Aureum, there was a gilt statue in the likeness of a man. Here also was the Exammon of Heraclius and the statue of Emperor Justin in a kneeling posture. Terbelis is said to have preached in the same place.

Here was also placed the figure of a large elephant by order of Severus on the following occasion. An elephant was stabled near it; and the house of a silversmith who worked in plate was robbed. He suspected the keeper of the elephant to be the thief and threatened him with death unless he would move his work place. The fellow defied him, so he slew him and threw him to the elephant. At this the beast was enraged and killed his keeper's murderer. Learning of the event, Severus offered sacrifices to the elephant and commanded him and his keeper to be cast in brass and set up here.

Here also, as Suidas relates, was the statue of Hercules to which the Byzantines paid divine adoration and offered sacrifice. Afterward, in the consulship of Julian, it was moved to the Hippodrome; but it was originally brought from Old Rome with ten other statues, partly by sea, and partly by land carriage. So it was that Hercules, living and dead, traveled the major portion of the world.

Suidas writes that in the Imperial Walks there were placed the equestrian statues of Trajan, Theodosius, Valentinian, Gibbus, and Firmillianus the Buffoon. There were many other statues of emperors and eunuchs set up in this place, the most famous of which was the statue of Eutropius, who was chamberlain of Emperor Arcadius. The honor and opulence of this eunuch appeared in numberless gilt statues erected to him in every part of the city and in the magnificence and superiority of the houses he built on almost every street. This so far encouraged and increased the number of the eunuchs that even the boys pretended to be so, so that they might become as rich and as honorable as Eutropius. The Basilica was so near the Miliarium and the Augustaeum that Cedrinus places the clock made at the command of Emperor Justin in the Miliarium, others in the Forum Augustaeum, and others in the Basilica, as is evident from the following inscription on the base of the dial over the arch in the Basilica:

This dial was erected at the cost
Of Prince Justinus, and the fair Sophia.
The scourge of execrable tyrants he,

She the bright patroness of liberty.
Behold the gnomon vast in shining brass,
The certain index of the flying hours.
This was the invention of the learned Julian
An honest, upright, and imperial lawyer.

# XX

# The Imperial Library and Portico,
# The Imperial Cistern

THE IMPERIAL PALACE, SAYS ZONARAS, STOOD NEAR the Basilica, right by the Braziers' Shops. The Basilica was furnished with many volumes of both human and divine learning. It was formerly the mansion of some person of distinguished knowledge, whom they called the "President" or "Master." He had twelve assistants under him, excellently skilled in the art of reasoning, who were maintained at the public expense. Each of them had several pupils under him who were instructed in the methods of argumentation and were held in such high esteem that the emperors summoned them to council on all important affairs of state.

In the reign of Basilicus a great fire broke out in Constantinople. It began at, and consumed, the Braziers' Shops with all the adjoining buildings, burned down whole streets, and — among other fine edifices — destroyed the famous Basilica that contained a library of six hundred thousand volumes. Among other curiosities of this place was the gut of a dragon one hundred and twenty feet long, on which was inscribed in golden characters the *Iliad* and *Odyssey* of Homer.

Malchus, a learned Byzantine, wrote the *History of Constantinople,* which he brought down from the reign of

Constantine to the time of Emperor Anastasius, in which he passionately laments the burning of the public library and the statues of the Forum Augustaeum. Speaking of the same library, Cedrinus gives the same account of it as Zonaras, almost word for word, and adds that "this library contained the histories of the achievements of the greatest heroes of the various ages of the world."

Many years after this Basilica was burned down the students vigorously opposed the heresy of Emperor Leo Conon, who ordered the palace set on fire and burned them, and the library. This was later rebuilt and furnished with a most curious collection of the best authors. The basilicae of Old Rome were the places where they used to plead, to hold their councils and Senates, and to carry on the business of merchandise and commerce. At Constantinople they were used as libraries and schools of learning, as appears from what I have already observed and also from the following inscription on the public school of Byzantium:

> This place was built for all the unlettered youth
> Whose genius leads them to the Roman Law.
> In pleading skilled, and fraught with eloquence,
> They leave these walls and plead their country's
>  cause.

Modern writers tell us that the place where the library stood has an octagonal shape; here there were arched porticos and a large room, where the headmaster used to converse with his assistants. Cedrinus affirms that the great church, the Hospital of Sampson, the gate house of the Basilica, the Augustaeum, the Chalca, the two long porticos as far as the Forum of Constantine, the Octagon, and the Baths of Zeuxippus were destroyed by a fire that broke out in the reign of Justinian. I would observe from this passage that there must necessarily be two octagons near one another. For if, as Cedrinus reports, the

Octagon had been the same as that where the Library stood, he would not have omitted to note that the Library was also burned down in the reign of Justinian. It is my opinion that the place where the Library stood had a quadrangular shape and seems to be the same building that Procopius says was surrounded by pillars erected in a square manner. Zonaras mentions nothing of the form of the Basilica that contained the Library but says only that it adjoined the Chalcopratia, or Braziers' Shops. Cedrinus calls the Basilica *Cisterna*, which some writers erroneously tell us was built by Constantine the Great. I am confirmed in this opinion by Procopius, who says that near the Imperial Portico where the lawyers used to plead there was a spacious building of great length and breadth surrounded by pillars on a quadrangular plan, situated on rocky ground, which was built by Justinian to a great height for preserving the water that was brought into it by subterranean pipes in summer and in the winter from the aqueducts for the use of the poor.

Menander, surnamed the Protector, says that it was against his inclination to enter into legal litigations in the Imperial Portico and, by force of pleading, to attempt to reconcile the jarrings and contentions of men. Agathius plays handsomely on a certain Uranius, a native of Syria, who set himself up as a physician, although he was entirely ignorant of the Aristotelian discipline. This fellow was blustering, noisy, an impudent pretender to infallible cures, and very talkative in the Imperial Portico, among other places. Speaking of himself, he tells us that he has often read over many law books and discourses on trade and commerce from morning to night in the Imperial Porticos. From these passages it is observable that the Imperial Portico and the Imperial Cistern stood in the same place.

The Imperial Portico is not to be seen, though the Cistern remains. Through the inhabitants' carelessness and contempt for everything that is curious it was never discovered except by me, who was a stranger among them, after a long and diligent search for it. The whole area was built over, which made it less suspected that there was a cistern there. The people had not the least suspicion of it, although they daily drew their water out of the wells that were sunk into it. By chance I went into a house where there was a way down to it and went aboard a little skiff. I discovered it after the master of the house lit some torches and rowed me here and there across through the pillars, which lay very deep in water. He was very intent upon catching his fish, with which the Cistern abounds, and speared some of them by the light of the torches. There is also a small light that descends from the mouth of the well and reflects on the water, where the fish usually come for air.

This Cistern is three hundred and thirty-six feet long, a hundred and eighty-two feet broad, and two hundred and twenty-four Roman paces in circumference. The roof, arches, and sides are all brickwork covered with terracotta, which is not the least impaired by time. The roof is supported by three hundred and thirty-six marble pillars. The space of the intercolumniation is twelve feet. Each pillar is over forty feet, nine inches high. They stand lengthwise in twelve ranges, broadways in twenty-eight. Their capitals are partly finished in the Corinthian style, and part of them are unfinished. Over the abacus of every pillar is placed a large stone, which seems to be another abacus that supports four arches.

There is an abundance of wells that empty into the Cistern. When it was filling in the winter time I saw a large stream of water falling from a great pipe with a mighty noise until the pillars were covered with water up to the middle of the capitals. This Cistern stands west of the Church of St. Sophia a distance of eighty Roman paces.

# XXI

## The Chalcopratia

IT IS PLAIN FROM WHAT HAS BEEN OBSERVED THAT THE
Chalcopratia, or places where they worked their brass,
stood near the Basilica. Cedrinus reports that Theodosius
II built the Church of the Chalcopratia and dedicated it to
the Virgin Mary. Others say that the Jews, who had lived
there from the time of Constantine the Great, had obliged
Theodosius II to retire from there and built the church.
Afterwards, when it had been shattered by an earthquake,
it was rebuilt by Justin Curopalatos, although Zonaras is
of another opinion:

> When Theodosius the Great had marched into the
> western regions, the Jews took the opportunity and
> made Honoratus, their friend, Prefect of the City
> and obtained from him the freedom to build a
> synagogue in the Chalcopratia. The people were
> enraged at this, set it on fire, and burned it down.
> When Theodosius was acquainted with the fact, he
> imposed a fine on those who were involved in it and
> gave them a fresh license to build another. St.
> Ambrose, who was then bishop of Milan, was
> informed of the matter and laid before Theodosius
> the greatness of the crime in allowing the Jews to
> build a synagogue in the very center of the Queen
> of Cities, upon which he remitted the fine and
> stopped their proceedings.

There are no Braziers' Shops in this place at present;
they have been removed to another part of the city,
although I was informed by some of the inhabitants that
not too many years ago they followed their trade near the

Chalcopratia. The anonymous author of the *History of Constantinople,* in describing the boundaries of Old Byzantium, tells us that the Chalcopratia "were not far from the Miliarium." Others say that they were near the Church of St. Sophia. Strabo, speaking of the Palace of Alexandria, relates that in conformity to this the one at Constantinople had a library, a portico, a convocation house, or place of assembly for public affairs, and a large public foundation for the encouragement of persons of literature and science.

# XXII

# The Porticos
# Situated Between the Palace
# And the Forum of Constantine

BESIDES THE IMPERIAL PORTICO, WHICH STOOD NEAR the Library, there were also other porticos a little distance from it, which reached from the Palace to the Forum of Constantine. The first fire that occurred in the reign of Justinian consumed the Palace and the Church of St. Sophia and both the long porticos as far as the Forum of Constantine. Cedrinus says that besides these, it also destroyed the Chalca and the Augustaeum. The fire that occurred afterwards in the reign of Basilicus began at the Chalcopratia, burned down the two adjoining porticos, all the neighboring buildings, the Basilica in which the Library was, two porticos that stood between the palaces, and all the fine ornaments of the Lausus.

These porticos have often been burnt and as often rebuilt; first of all by Justinian, then by others, and last by Domninus. This is confirmed by a modern historian, who says that when Constantinople was taken by the Gauls and the Venetians, the covered porticos of Domninus that reached on both sides of the road from the Miliarium to the Forum of Constantine were burnt to the ground. Some say that in the time of Constantine the Great, Eubulus built four double porticos that were arched at the top and reached from the Palace to the Land Wall of the city. One of them stretched as far as the Church of St. Anthony, at the end of the city, another from the Port of Sophia to the church named Rabdon; the other two extended from the Chalca and Miliarium to the Forum of Constantine, the street called Taurus, and the Brazen Bull. All of them were paved with square marble and adorned with an infinite number of statues.

Although these accounts come from anonymous authors who, as I have sometimes observed, have not so strictly adhered to the truth, they do seem to carry a good face of probability, since it is evident from historians of greater veracity how industrious Constantine was in adorning the city. It is no less evident from the *Treatise of the Ancient Description of the Wards* that in the reigns of Arcadius and Honorius Constantinople had no less than fifty-two public porticos, five of which the author places in the fourth ward, in which stood the Basilica, the Imperial Portico, and the Portico of Fannio. Besides this, he places four large porticos in the sixth ward. In the same ward he places another large portico. He adds that the seventh ward abounds with porticos and that the eighth ward had six more porticos. In the ninth ward were two large porticos. The tenth had six, the eleventh four. From this it is credible that the porticos stood very thick from the Chalca to the Land Wall, but I cannot say they were contiguous beyond the Taurus.

# XXIII

## The Miliarium Aureum and its Statues, The Fortune of the City and Her Statue

THE MILIARIUM AUREUM WAS A GILDED PILLAR FROM which they used to adjust the measure of their miles and the distances from the city. Pliny tells us that it was set up at Rome on the highest ground of the public forum; but whether the Miliarium at Constantinople was like that at Rome, the Greek historians have been so far from declaring their opinions concerning it that in all their writings they have not so much as mentioned its name. Yet it seems very probable to me that it was like it and was also situated in the Forum, or near it. The *Ancient Description of the Wards* places it in the ward where the Forum Augustaeum and the Basilica stood, on which it adjoined.

The authors of the *History of the Achievements of Emperor Alexius Comnenus* tell us that at break of day the forces of Alexius marched out of the great palace under the command of Sebatius, their general, and entered the Church of St. John the Divine; and when they had gotten to the top of the church they expressed themselves in a provocative manner, so that a battle began about three in the morning. Many people in the Forum who fought from the roof of the Miliarium and the top of St. John's Church were wounded. The inhabitants say that this was the church where the elephants of the Grand Seignor are now stabled. It is near the Hippodrome and the Forum Cupedinis, famous for niceties, situated near the Church of St. Sophia, and was formerly called the Forum Augustaeum. But to come closer to the point: Suidas says that in the Basilica, behind the Miliarium, there "was placed a gilt statue of a man and of an elephant and his keeper." Others, with more probability, say that these statues were erected behind the Basilica, near the Miliarium. Suidas adds that the statue of Theodosius was placed in the Miliarium and that upon setting it up, he distributed large donations of grain among the people. On the equestrian statue of Theodosius, no longer extant, were inscribed these verses:

Not the bright sun, which gilds the eastern sky,
With greater luster shines, than Theodosius.
See how he sits aloft in radiant arms,
And with mild aspect views his loving people!
The fiery steed, pleased with the royal burden,
In warlike posture seems to move, and live.

Suidas proceeds further and tells us that the statues of Sophia, the consort of Justin the Thracian, of his daughter Arabia, and his niece Helena, as well as the equestrian statues of Arcadius and Theodosius, his son, were placed in the Miliarium near the statue of Theodosius the Great. Cedrinus writes that two statues stood above the niche of the Miliarium, one of Constantine the Great, the other of his mother Helena, with a cross between them. Behind them was placed the statue of Trajan on horseback, and near him was placed the statue of Aelius Hadrianus. Suidas adds that the cross that was placed between Constantine and Helena had this inscription:

Una sancta, & duo cleres cursores.

From this it is evident that the Forum, the Miliarium, and the Basilica stood so close together that they are not only placed in different places by different authors but sometimes by one and the same historian. The same writer says that in the Miliarium there was also a great piece from antiquity. This was a chariot drawn by four fallow horses, supported by two square pillars. It was in the place where Constantine was received by his army with joyful congratulations after he had conquered Azotium, but originally because Byzas, the founder of Byzantium, had been highly applauded by the people there.

The Chariot of the Sun in which a small statue made at the order of Constantine was seated was taken to the Hippodrome. This statue was the Fortune of the City, which on great festivals and the day of the celebration of the foundation of the city was set up with a cross on her head in the Senate House. Julian the Apostate demolished it in the same place where Arius died in a miserable way, which was a small distance from the Senate House. In the same place the pious Emperor Theodosius had ordered the statues of Arius, Macedonius, Sabellius, and Eunomius, which were cut in marble, to be placed in a sitting posture on the ground to be polluted with the excrements and receive the curses of the people as a sign of their flagrant perfidy.

Other historians say that the statue of the Fortune of the City was brought from Rome to Constantinople by Constantine the Great and placed in a niche in the Palace. Zosimus writes that Constantine placed the Fortune of Rome on the side of one of the four porticos that surrounded the Great Forum. It is very probable that the people of Constantinople celebrated a festival in her honor, as was customary in Old Rome both by natives and foreigners on the same day on which the Palilia — the Festival of Pales — were celebrated.

Socrates tells us that Julian was publicly sacrificing to the Fortune of Constantinople in the Basilica where her statue was set up. Mares, the bishop of Chalcedon, was led there by the hand, for he was blind with age, and he sharply reprimanded him and called him an apostate from the Christian religion. Julian, in return, called him a blind old man, adding this question sarcastically: "Is your god, the Galilean, able to cure you?" For this is what he used to call Our Lord contemptuously. Upon which the good old bishop replied, "I thank my God, who has taken my sight from me, so that I cannot behold the man who has fallen into such great apostasy." At this Julian fell silent.

Zonaras and some historians who lived before him have recorded that in the time of Anastasius the statue of Fortune, made of brass, stood with one foot on a bronze ship and was placed in some part of the city. When this ship began to decay with age, however, or some parts of it were stolen or shattered by treachery, it happened that no cargo ships came into the port of Constantinople as they approached the city even without a storm preventing their arrival into the harbor. If their cargo was taken aboard the longboats and brought into the city, they tell you it was soon consumed because of the famine that then prevailed.

Upon this the Curatores of the City were obliged to inquire into the reason for it. When the Magistrates of the City were informed, they began to suspect the cause. Upon inquiry, they found the fragments of the ship. These were fitted in their proper places; and all of a sudden navigation was open and free, and the sea became constantly full of vessels sailing into the port. In order to fully discover the real cause of this calamity, they repeated the experiment by stripping the ship again of some of its pieces. The ships coming into harbor were prevented as before; so they repaired the bronze vessel she stood in and took particular care of it.

Eunapius, who wrote the *History of the Lives of the Philosophers and Wise Men,* says that in the reign of Constantine the inhabitants attributed this difficulty of coming into harbor to another cause:

There was no entering the port at Constantinople unless the wind stood full south. When this had frequently happened, the people, oppressed by famine and enraged at Constantine, assembled in the theater. The chief of the courtiers had conceived a resentment for Sopatrus the Philosopher, brought him before the emperor, and accused him in the following manner: "This Sopatrus, sir, who is so high in your favor, has chained up the winds by his excessive wisdom, for which you so much admire him as to admit him to your Imperial Person." Believing the allegations, Constantine ordered him to be beheaded.

# XXIV

## The Temple of Neptune,
## The Church of St. Mina,
## The Stadia,
## And the Stairs of Timasius

I CANNOT OMIT NOTING THE CHURCH OF ST. MINA, because it shows what part of the city the fourth ward stood in. This contained the Basilica, the Augustaeum and the Church of St. Mina. The history of an anonymous author reports that Byzas formerly built a Temple of Neptune near the Acropolis by the sea. Here, he says, the Church of St. Mina the Martyr stood in his time. Nevertheless, he seems to contradict himself when he says that the Church of St. Mina was formerly the Temple of Jupiter, and that its roof, which was arched with marble, was supported by two large pillars. I can therefore conclude nothing from the uncertainty of this writer except that it seems more probable to me that the Church of St. Mina stood in those parts of the Acropolis in which the Temple of Neptune formerly stood, as appears from Dionysius the Byzantine, who says that a little above the

Promontory of the Bosporus an altar to Minerva Egressoria and the Temple of Neptune were erected, and that below the Temple of Neptune were the Stadia and the Gymnasia where they diverted themselves with martial sports and exercises, as I have shown at greater length in my *Treatise on the Bosporus.*

I am confirmed in this opinion from the information of some of the present inhabitants, who told me that within the Imperial Precinct, formerly called the Acropolis, stood the Church of St. Mina. The *Ancient Description of the Wards of the City* tells us that the Church of St. Mina stood in the same ward as the Stadia and the Stairs of Timasius. Procopius writes that "at the place called the Stadium, near the sea, where they exercised in martial sports, Emperor Justinian and his Empress Theodora built some large inns for the entertainment of strangers."

# XXV

## The Lausus and its Statues:
## Venus of Cnidos, Juno of Samos,
## Minerva of Lindia, A Winged Cupid,
## Jupiter Olympius, Saturn,
## Unicorns, Tigers, Vultures,
## Beasts That Are Half Panthers,
## The Cistern of the Hospital Called
## Philoxenos,
## And the Chrysotriclinium

THE LAUSUS IS A PLACE CELEBRATED IN THE WRITINGS of many historians, some of whom write that it was the house of Lausus, a patrician who held many offices in the reign of Arcadius, the son of Theodosius the Great, and that he adorned his house with many famous monuments of antiquity. There is a book still extant, under the title of *Lausaicus,* which was written by Heraclidas, bishop of Cappadocia, and inscribed to Lausus.

No author mentions what part of the city this place was in, but it is very probable that it was between the Palace and the Forum of Constantine on the authority of both Zonaras and Cedrinus. After describing the runs of the fire that broke out in the reign of Leo both on the north and south side of the city, they tell us that in the middle of the city it burned from the Lausus to the street called Taurus. Evagrius, speaking of the same fire, says that it destroyed all the buildings from the Forum of Constantine to the Taurus. The reader may observe from this that the Lausus was not far from the Forum of Constantine. In his description of the fire that happened in the reign of Basilicus, Cedrinus also makes it plain that it stood in the east between the Palace and the Forum of Constantine. The fire, he says, consumed the Chalcopratia, the most beautiful part of the city, the Basilica, with its eminent library and all the surprising ornaments of the Lausus up to the Forum of Constantine.

In the Lausus, our historian continues, there was an infinite number of statues, the most remarkable of which was the statue of Minerva of Lindia, which was four cubits long and made of emerald stone. It was cut by Scyllis and Dipoenus, two eminent sculptors, and presented by Sesostris, king of Egypt, to Cleobulus, king of Lindia, a prince of incomparable wisdom. It is probable that the place is called Lausus from this, for Minerva sometimes goes under the name of Laossos.

Theophrastus writes that the Egyptian commentators mention that the king of Babylon made a present of an emerald to their king that was four cubits long and three in breadth. If Sesostris, Scyllis, and Dipoenus were living at the same time, Pliny should have called it the Emerald of Minerva instead. But these sculptors were no less ancient than eminent, born on the island of Crete under the rule of the Medes, before Cyrus was king of Persia, that is, about the fifteenth Olympiad. They carved the statues of Apollo, Diana, Hercules, as well as of Minerva, which was blasted by lightning.

Pliny notes that Ambracia, Argos, and Cleone were full of statues made by Dipoenus, although he says nothing of the statue of Minerva of Lindia. Cedrinus adds that the statue of Venus of Cnidos was placed in the Lausus and considered everywhere a celebrated piece of sculpture. It was finished by Praxiteles, is made of white marble, and appears in a naked pose. There is also a Juno of Samos, the workmanship of Lysippus and Bupalus, and a winged cupid with his quiver. This statue was brought from Myndus. There was also a Jupiter riding on an elephant, which was carved by Phidias and placed in his temple by Pericles.

There was also another statue made by Lysippus, which was bald in the back, though not in front, which was taken for the statue of Saturn. There were also many statues of unicorns, tigers, beasts that were half bulls and half harts, besides several statues of vultures erected there. The anonymous author of the *History of Constantinople* says that in his time there were some eagles standing in the Lausus that were cut in stone. I am inclined to think that there were some figures of birds standing there at that time, but I believe that they were the vultures mentioned by Cedrinus. This author tells us that there stood in the Lausus several fine buildings, some hospitals, and a place for the entertainment of strangers, which had very good spring water and was called Philoxenon. Some writers affirm that the Philoxenon was a cistern built by someone of that name. I took it to be the same cistern that was situated between the Triclinium and the Lausiacum and was filled up by the order of Heraclius. Menander, surnamed the Protector, tells us that Philip of Macedon cleaned most of the cisterns of the city that Heraclius commanded to be refilled with earth.

If that prince gave orders for the cleansing of that cistern, among others, it is the same one that lies underground on the north side of Ibraham Pasha's house, between the Lausiacum and the Triclinium. Its roof was supported by four hundred and twenty-four marble pillars, two hundred and twelve supporting the same number of pillars above them. I measured one of them, for they all seem to be the same size, and I found it to be six feet, nine inches in circumference. There is another cistern on the west side of the same house, whose arches are supported with thirty-two Corinthian pillars, standing in four ranges, each range consisting of eight pillars, whose shafts are nine feet in circumference.

As to the Triclinium, between which and the Lausus the Philoxenon was built, I suppose it to be the same one that Justinian III built near the palace and called by his own name, the Triclinium of Justinian. It is reported by Cedrinus that this Triclinium was finely decorated by Emperor Tiberius. The western gate of the Triclinium is noted by Leo V when he foretold that the head of the man that should be cut off in the Hippodrome for his tyranny should be brought before him through the western gate of the Triclinium.

Frequent mention is made of this Chrysotriclinium by historians who wrote just before the taking of Constantinople by the Turks. All the inhabitants knew both the name and the place where it stood. But the people have since fallen into such an aversion to learning and dislike for what is ingenious and polite that they rather choose to embrace a voluntary ignorance and treat everything that is curious with indignity and contempt.

* *
*

# BOOK III

## I

## Several Places in the Fifth Ward, The Second Hill, The Neorium, The Port Named the Bosporium, The Strategium, The Forum of Theodosius

IT WAS IMPOSSIBLE FOR ME TO DISCOVER FROM THE *Ancient Description of the Wards* that the fifth ward stood on the north side of the second hill, in a plain at the bottom of it, and that it descended together with the fourth ward from the side of the Promontory to the bay called Ceras, although the author notes that a great part of it fell down in winding descents into the middle of a plain. But this description is no less suited to other wards. Nor could I find out its situation from any buildings remaining in it or from the information of the most ancient inhabitants.

All the light I could get was from the location of the Phosphorian or, as some call it, the Bosphorian Port and the Stairs of Chalcedon. These do not take that name because they are built in the eastern part of the city facing Chalcedon, for they stand full north. It is, therefore, called the Bosphorian Port not from the sea of Bosporus but from a depraved custom of the people who pronounce it so; whereas, according to the authorities or Stephanus and Eustathius, they ought to call it the Phosphorian Port. These writers assert that it took its name from this: namely, that when Philip of Macedon besieged Byzantium and his soldiers were digging a passage underground into the town, the moon, which is called Phosphora, shone in its full brightness and revealed the stratagem. Once the siege was raised, the Byzantines therefore called it the Phosphorium.

Although they gave some reason why it may be considered the same haven, though under different names, they are silent as to its location, whether it stood on the eastern, northern, or southern side of the city. It is reasonable to believe, however, if we do not consider the location of the Stairs of Chalcedon — which the *Ancient Description of the Wards* places in the same ward as the Bosphorian Port — that it stood on the south side of the city and not on the east side, although it directly faces Chalcedon. For the force and speed of the Bosporus made it very difficult to sail from Chalcedon to the eastern and southern parts of Constantinople; but it is an easy passage for those who sail between that and Chalcedon to go in and out of port on the north side of the city. It is observable, further, that the *Ancient Description of the Wards* mentions no stairs that face Chalcedon. Even if the author had taken notice of any, he placed them in the first or second ward opposite Chalcedon or in the third ward, which stands southward where the Neorium or the New Dock stood, as I observed before.

But it would be of little significance to expand on this matter since I shall be very particular in naming and producing authorities who would make it evident that the Bosphorian Port and the Stairs of Chalcedon were not only situated on the north side of the city, but I shall also mention the very place where they stood. The first historian I shall quote is Dionysius, a native of the city, who places the walls of Old Byzantium just outside the Temple of Tellus on the bay of the Bosporus and a little below the

Temple of Ceres and Proserpina. He does not call her
Proserpina but simply κόρη, the Virgin. Yet by the situation of the place we may easily understand that virgin to
be Hecate, whose tripod Cedrinus mentions to have been
in the Strategium. Here, or at least not far from it, stood
the Temple of Proserpina, as appears from the same
author.

Evagrius is more clear on this point. He tells us that in
the reign of Leo a great fire broke out on the north side of
the city where the dock stood. It consumed all before it
from the Bosphorian Port to the old Temple of Apollo; on
the south side from the Port of Julian to the Temple of
Concord; in the middle of the city from the Forum of
Constantine to the Taurus. Zonaras adds that the same
fire destroyed all the buildings between the north and the
south sea. Cedrinus reports that the same fire began at the
dock and burned down all before it as far as the Church of
St. John.

From this I observe that the Bosphorian Port and the
dock were near one another, although the author of the
*Description of the Wards* places the former in the fifth
and the latter in the sixth ward. For since both these
wards adjoined and descended from the ridge of the
Promontory down to the sea, it is not possible that they
should stand at any great distance from one another.
Zosimus, an ancient historian, points out the very place
where the dock was built in his *Description of Old
Byzantium*. He tells us that it was on a hill that made up
part of the isthmus that was enclosed by the Propontis and
the bay called Ceras. He adds that the wall of Byzantium
stretched over a hill from the western side of the city to
the Temple of Venus and the sea facing Chrysopolis and
that it descended on the north side of the city to the
Neorion or New Haven. This I take to stand near the gate
that the Greeks call Ὡραῖα and, by a corruption of
language, Porta Neoria, or at least not far from it.

There is at present between the seas and the Porta Neoria a broad piece of land, a market of merchandise and sea goods, which the Turks call Siphont or Tsiphont because the Jews inhabit it. It adjoins the stairs or landing place of Chalcedon, from which they daily sail to Scutarieum or Scutaricum, called Chrysopolis in antiquity, a market town and a port of Chalcedon. Near the stairs of Chalcedon is the ferry from which you cross the water to Galata. It was formerly called the Sycaene Ferry and is placed near the Bosphorian Haven or Dock in the *Description of the Wards*.

But the location of these places seems to be somewhat changed because of some granaries built there — which are now removed farther into the city — or because of the enlargement of the precinct of the Seraglio, or because they are fallen into decay and filled up with earth. For at the time when Philip of Macedon undermined the town it is very probable that there was no port built in the place that was later called the Phosphorion by the Byzantines. No haven could be built there because of the rising of the springs, but the Bosphorian Haven was built afterwards in another place. This is no more than what is said of the dock or the Neorium that they tell you was enclosed by Constans and made a market of merchandise and other naval items. This market was afterwards kept near the Port of Julian. Some historians write that Emperor Leontius, who reigned after Justin, ordered the dock to be cleansed.

Others write that the figure of a large ox in brass, which much resembled the Brazen Bull, was erected at the Neorium. This figure was set up in the eleventh ward and, as some modern writers would persuade you, it bellowed once a year, an event that portended great mischief and detriment to the city. But I take this to be a fable taken out of Callimachus and Pindar, who tell you that on the Mountain of Artabyris in Rhodes there are brazen bulls that used to bellow upon any impending calamity for the city. Nothing presently remains of this haven where the dock was.

I gather from the location of the Bosphorian Port and the Stairs of Chalcedon that the fifth ward stood on the side of the second hill and on a plain below it. Here also were the Baths of Honorius, the Prytaneum, the Baths of Eudoxia, the Granaries of Valentinian and Constantius, the Theban Obelisk, the Bosphorian Port, the Stairs of Chalcedon, the Cistern of Theodosius, and the Strategium, in which the Forum of Theodosius was.

Justinian notes the Bath of Achilles in a letter in his *Constitutions:*

> Our imperial will and pleasure is that the lead pipes conducting the water to the Achillean Baths, contrived by your wisdom and purchased by your munificence, be under the same regulation and management as has been appointed by Theodosius and Valentinian in the same case. The said pipes shall only supply such baths and nymphaea as your excellency shall think fit, granting at the same time full power, license, and authority to the apparitors of your excellency to enter without fear or molestation such houses and baths in the suburbs, as they shall judge convenient, to inquire into all evasions of this order and to prevent stoppage of the water to the detriment of the public.

The law by which Constantine the Great decreed that Constantinople should be called New Rome is inscribed on a public pillar near his own equestrian statue in the Strategium. I find in the *Ancient Description of the Wards* that there were three fora in the city that took their name from Theodosius. One was in the fifth ward and stood, as I just observed, in the Strategium; another stood in the sixth ward, and a third in the twelfth. The two last were provision markets, the first was the Forum

Praetorianum, a court of public justice, where the praetors presided and which was called Praetorium by both the Latins and the Greeks. This I gather from the *Treatise* just mentioned. I am not certain, though it seems very probable to me, that this great Praetorium was beautifully finished at the expense and care of Emperor Justin and Domninus, as will appear from the following verses of Paulus Silentiarius. I shall add them in order to prove that the word *Praetorium* was used by the Greeks, as were also very many other Latin words:

> When great Justinus had reformed the world,
> This noble structure consecrate to Themis
> He then repaired with fresh increase of beauty;
> And yet some share of praise to thee is due,
> Domninus, skillful architect, whose head
> Long labored nightly in the great design.

# II

# The Sixth Ward
# And the Remaining Ancient Buildings
# Of the Second Hill

IT WOULD HAVE BEEN VERY DIFFICULT TO DISCOVER, either from the location of the Forum of Constantine or the pillar of Constantine still standing at Constantinople, or the *Description of the Wards* — although it notes the Pillar of Constantine and tells us that the sixth ward enters on a short plain and that it is afterwards lengthened by a long descent — whether the sixth ward was on the north or the south side of the city. However, the author added that it reached from the Forum of Constantine down to stairs from which you sail over the Sycaene Ferry. It was originally called the Sycaene Ferry from Sycae but is now called the Galata or Pera, as will appear more fully when I come to speak of it in the thirteenth ward.

That the fifth and sixth wards adjoined I observed earlier from the closeness of the dock, the Stairs of Chalcedon, the Sycaene Stairs, and the Bosphorian Port to each other. Having therefore discovered the situation of Sycae, I take it for granted that the dock stood near a plain on the sea shore that was below the foot of the second hill, and that the ferry place from which you passed over to Sycae is the same as that from which you sail at present to Galata, and that the Porphyry Pillar now standing is the same as that mentioned by the author of the *Description* and placed by him in the sixth ward. Nevertheless, he takes no notice in his description of the sixth ward where he places the Senate House or of how near it stood to the Forum or Pillar of Constantine. But in what follows I shall make it plain to the reader from other historians that the Senate House stood on the north side of the Forum of Constantine and that this ward stood partly on the ridge of the second hill where the Porphyry Pillar now stands, as does the Poultry Market, which the Turks call Taubasor or Taouck Baser, the dyers shops, the house of Aenobarbus, a Turkish admiral, and the Mosque of Ali Pasha. Part of it also spreads over the right side of the second valley, and part of it covers a plain near the sea below the valley and the foot of the second hill, which is densely inhabited by the Jews.

# III

# The Porphyry Pillar,
# The Forum of Constantine,
# And the Palladium

THOSE HISTORIANS WHO HAVE TREATED THE ACTIONS of Constantine the Great report that he brought the round Porphyry Pillar from Rome. This pillar was bound at the joints with circular wreaths of laurel made of brass and was placed in the Forum called the Placoton, because it was paved with smooth, broad stones, which the Greeks call *placae*. They add further that there was erected on this pillar a curious statue of brass, surprising both for its workmanship and size. It was an ancient piece of statuary, exquisitely finished and lifelike. They tell you that it was originally the image of Apollo of Troy and that the emperor gave it his own name and commanded to be fixed in its head some of those nails that fastened our Savior to the cross.

Upon the statue was cut the following inscription:

To thee, O Savior, Lord of the Universe,
Who rules the immeasurable globe
With deepest knowledge, I this people offer.
May they be thine, I conquered them for thee.
I lay my imperial scepter at thy feet,
With all the united force and power of Rome,
Let thy good providence, with watchful eye,
Look down, and guard the city from all ills.

Cedrinus relates that at the bottom of the pillar were carved the twelve baskets full of the fragments that were left after the Miracle of the Loaves and Fishes.

This pillar has no winding stairs but is all solid marble. Fulvius, otherwise a good antiquarian, is therefore visibly in error when he tells us that it had an ascent within it. Zonaras says that the statue of Constantine was standing on the pillar in his time and that in the spring, in the reign of Alexius Comnenus, among other buildings that were thrown down by a violent windstorm, the statue of Constantine the Great was blown down and demolished, and that by its fall several people who were passing by were dashed to pieces. The author who has written the *History of Alexius Comnenus* tells us that not only was the statue struck down by lightning, but also that three of the tores, or round circles of the pillar, were also removed.

The pillar is still standing on the top of the second hill; it is somewhat damaged, not so much by time — although it is very ancient — as by fires, earthquakes, and tempests. The statue and the three upper wreaths are gone, and in place of them there is a plain round superstructure, almost of the same thickness and size as the other part of the shaft. Its pedestal is made of squared marble and is eleven feet, nine inches broad on every side and eighteen feet high. Upon this is placed a cornice in Doric style, consisting of a plinth, an upper and a lower tore, and a scotia in between them. Upon the cornice stands the shaft of the pillar, which is about eleven yards in circumference. It consists of eight large pieces of marble, each of which is encircled at the joints with a wreath of laurel work, which covers the cement of the fissures.

If it had not been injured by time, it would look like one entire piece of marble and has therefore been thought so by some historians who have handed it down to posterity that it consisted of only one piece of marble. They also ridicule the ignorance and injudiciousness of those who, they tell you, have been impressed by the wreaths of brass, which were only added for the sake of ornament. There is nothing of these bronze wreaths or tores to be seen at present. To prevent its falling to pieces, the pillar is bound round with iron hoops. At the top of the pillar is carved the name of the emperor who, after the statue was thrown down, laid its uppermost stone

This pillar bore some resemblance to those mentioned by Athenaeus, who writes that there were some tall, round pillars erected in Egypt made in the same manner. They were covered at the fissures with circular wreaths, alternately white and black, one below another. Their capitals were also round, around which were fine sculptures of roses just opening. There were no flutings on these pillars, nor any coarse foliage in the Greek style that enfolded it. Instead, it was adorned with dates and the fruit of young lotus trees and sculpture of all kinds of flowers. Below these is a representation of Egyptian beans mixed with flowers and foliage that projects beyond the fissure of the capital. Thus the Egyptians make and adorn their pillars. In building their walls it is their constant practice to lay alternately a row of white over a row of black bricks. I have seen the same method in building their walls among the Persians and Syrians. The finest of these they built with bricks or stones naturally variegated; the inferior sort they colored several ways with paintings and other inventions of art.

The wreaths or tores mentioned before that were fixed to the Pillar of Constantine were carved, as some writers tell us, to signify how many years Constantine would live and the many victories he would win over his enemies. I believe the design of the sculptor was only to express that the laurel was sacred to Apollo and that this ancient pillar supported his image made in a stupendous size. However that may be, it is certain that Constantine ordered it to be called his own statue, whether on account of his many victories or whether he was better pleased with the heathen notion of that god than any other. When he demolished the heathen idols he therefore commanded the statue of a Delphic Apollo and his tripod to be set up in the Hippodrome, as is observed by a German orator who addressed a panegyric to Constantine in the following manner:

> When your Imperial Majesty turned down to the Temple of Apollo, the most stately, the most beautiful building in the world, you saw your favorite God offering his crowns to you, a happy presage of length of days and a life extended beyond that of Nestor. You saw him, you gazed on his features, and beheld your own likeness in him who, as the ancient prophets have sung, deserved the empire of the world. That auspicious period of time seems to have now come, since you, like that god, are gay and youthful, like him salutary, like him a personable and a beautiful prince.

If the Turk, whom I employed to climb the pedestal, had followed my directions — while I was obliged to appear a mere accidental tourist — and held his perch steady, I would have discovered the lowest stone of the shaft — from a notch he had cut in it — to have been nine feet and four digits high, and the tore that projected six digits beyond it to have been a foot and a half broad. I mean the tore at the foot of the shaft, so that every stone was ten feet, nine inches high. The height of all the eight stones was therefore about eighty-six feet and nine inches. The whole pillar was lengthened even more with an abacus placed on the uppermost stone and below with a pedestal and its cornice and four marble steps at the bottom. The lowermost of these steps is a foot and six digits high; the second is the same height; the third and fourth each a foot and a half.

No discovery can be made from what has been said where this prodigious columns or rather where this Colossus, stood. For since neither Procopius nor any other historian of those times takes any notice of the Forum called Πλαχίτον, where Zonaras and other modern writers say it was erected, I was uncertain whether or not this was the same as the Forum of Constantine. For it seemed very probable to me here that Constantine had here followed the example of Trajan in setting up his statue in the Forum that went by his own name. But I was soon cleared of this difficulty by the authority of Socrates, the author of the *Dissensions Among Christians*. He writes that they are one and the same place. He also writes that Arius, when he came near where the Forum of Constantine stood, expired with the falling of the guts. But this is no less evident if it is considered where the Palladium of Minerva stood. This, as Zonaras says, was conveyed by the command of Constantine from Troy to the Placotum and, as Procopius adds, into the Forum of Constantine.

He says:

> The Hirpines report that Diomedes met Aeneas coming out of Troy and that, in conformity to the answer of the oracle, he gave him the image of Minerva that he, with the assistance of Ulysses, had formerly brought from Troy, when they went there to consult the oracle as to how Troy might be taken. They add further that Diomedes was indisposed and consulted the oracle concerning his recovery. It foretold that he would never be well until he had given that image to Aeneas.

The Romans pretend that they know nothing of this image at present, yet they show you an image cut in stone that to this day stands in the eastern part of the Temple of Fortune before the statue of Minerva. The statue is carved in a warlike posture, brandishing a spear as in battle, dressed in a long garment representing the image of Minerva, not as she is rendered by the Greeks, but as described by the Egyptians. The inhabitants tell you that

Constantine ordered this statue, which was placed in the Forum named after him, to be buried underground.

The authorities who claim that the Placoton and the Forum of Constantine are the same place ought to be followed because it is impossible to come to a knowledge of four of the wards without them. For the third ward contains the tribunal of the Forum of Constantine; the sixth reaches from the Forum of Constantine to the stairs opposite Sycae where the Pillar of Constantine is erected. The seventh extends with continual porticos from the right-hand side of the Pillar of Constantine to the Forum of Theodosius; and the eighth contains part of the Forum of Constantine. When I was asked by some gentlemen who were curious as to how Constantine came by that Palladium, I answered that I was uncertain about it. For Zonaras' account of its being brought from Troy did not seem very probable, since Troy was destroyed so many ages before it, and Strabo is hard put to trace out its location. The story of its being brought from ancient Rome seems very probable, since it was often destroyed by fire, and the inhabitants were entirely ignorant of where it originally stood. Yet the Latin historians tell us that Diomedes presented it to Aeneas, that it was kept for some time at Lavinium, and that it was afterwards moved to Rome and set up in the Temple of Vesta. The Greek historians are of another opinion. Among these, Pausanias, who wrote in the time of Hadrian, tells us that it was considered the most sacred of anything in Athens, that it fell down from heaven, that it was consecrated by the advice of all the Senators and placed in the citadel of Athens.

There has been some dispute whether it was made of wood or brass, and whether it was a figure or a shield. Some say that it was a sacred shield, such as they had at Rome. Dion and Diodorus think otherwise and tell us that it was an image made of wood, three cubits high, that it fell from heaven into Pessinus, a city of Phrygia, holding in her right hand a spear, in her left a spindle and a distaff.

To me it seems to have been the image of Pallas, whose statue was called the Palladium wherever it was placed. Procopius asserts that the statue that the Romans show in the Temple of Minerva is not cut in the Greek style. For they carve her, as was mentioned before, in a fighting posture with a spear in her hand, denoting her courage by the spear, and her wisdom by her shield, which repels attacks. She is covered with a helmet to intimate that the height of wisdom is not to be seen and discovered. She bears an olive tree as affording matter of light; and upon her breast is cut a Medusa to illustrate the quickness of thought and the surprising agility of the mind. She also had a breast plate, on which was the figure of a night owl and a Gorgon. The night owl was an emblem of the depth of prudence and conduct; for wisdom dives into the secrets and darkness of nature.

I wish the divine Palladium may guard all those who shall in future times attempt the same travels as I have done, and pray that they may be defended, as I have been, by that good providence and by that heavenly wisdom, the wisdom of the Father, which amidst all the treacheries and insults of a barbarous people and the almost incredible dangers of a long voyage not only supported and strengthened, but also animated, enlivened and refreshed me.

# IV

## The Senate House, The Nymphaeum, The Statues of the Forum of Constantine, The Philadelphium, the Museum, The Labarum and Syparum, The Death of Arius, The Temples of Tellus, Ceres, Persephone, Juno and Pluto

THE PORPHYRY PILLAR AND THE SENATE HOUSE ARE placed by the author of the *Ancient Description of the Wards* in the sixth ward and the Nymphaeum in the fifth; but he does not tell us how near they stood in relation to one another. That they stood very little distant is evident both from Zonaras and Cedrinus, who write that the fire that broke out in the reign of Leo burnt down the Senate House on the north side of the Forum of Constantine, which was adorned with statues of brass and porphyry marble and in which was placed the Porta of Diana of the Ephesians, a present from Trajan taken from the Scythians, containing a description of the wars of the giants, a Jupiter armed with thunder, Neptune with his trident, Apollo with his darts and quiver. In the lower part of the Porta were represented the giants attacking the dragons, tossing large clods of earth and looking in a fierce and a stern manner.

It was here that the principal men of the city usually convened freely to debate the important affairs of the government, here also the emperor himself came in procession when he received the consular robes. It was a very noble and magnificent building. The same authors mention another spacious edifice situated opposite it that was consumed by the same fire and was called the

Nymphaeum because the marriage rites were performed in this place, being spacious enough to hold the numerous assemblies that attended those solemnities.

They add further that on the west side of the same forum a statue of Minerva of Lindia was placed. She had a helmet on her head and a shield in her hand, on which was figured Medusa with snakes and adders entwined around her neck; for in this manner the ancient sculptors usually carved Minerva.

On the east side of it was placed the statue of an amphitrite, one of the Sirens, her temples encircled with crab claws. The anonymous author of the *History of Constantinople* says that on the same side of the Forum were placed the statues of several Sirens, which were called seahorses by some; three of which, he tells you, were extant in his time at a place in the suburbs called St. Mamas.

On the north side of the Forum a figure of the cross that Constantine saw in the heavens was erected on a lofty pillar. This is confirmed by the authority of most historians, but principally by Eusebius. Although he is not explicit as to his setting it in the Forum of Constantine, since his authority is not to be disputed when he asserts that he set it up in Old Rome in the heart of the city, it is reasonable to believe that he did so at Constantinople, since the same writer assures us that Constantine set up a true representation of the same cross in all his finest buildings and in the most remarkable places of Constantinople.

In memory of this, as Sozomen writes, Constantine changed the most famous and most honorable warlike standard among the Romans — which was always borne before the princes and to which the soldiers were obliged to pay divine adoration — into the ensign of the Cross to wean them from their heathen rites and idolatrous worship. Prudentius has the following lines upon this occasion:

Christ's radiant form upon the standard rose,
Embossed with sparkling gems and burnished
    gold,
Which over the purple ground-work cast a light.
No dreadful shields hung on the blazoned flag;
Christ's awful name alone was there inscribed,
While on its top, sure sign of victory,
The Cross triumphant blazed in costly stones.

Eusebius writes that he saw the same interpretation of
the Christian standard in his time:

There was a tall spear that was crossed near the top
with a short piece of wood in the shape of a cross, at
the top of which was a crown made of precious
stones and curiously wrought with gold, in the
middle of which were embroidered the two initial
letters of Jesus Christ with the Greek letter X in the
form of a cross. The ensign or standard was fixed
to the transverse part of the spear.

From this description of Eusebius the difference between
what was then called the Labarum and Syparum seems to
be this: that the Labarum signifies only the longer piece of
wood crossed near the top with a short piece; and that the
Syparum is the veil or flag that falls down from the
transverse part. The religion of the old Romans was
purely military, they worshipped their standards and
swore by them. This custom was abolished with the
introduction of the Christian standard.

    I hope the reader will pardon me here if I go a little
out of my way to vindicate the story of Constantine's
seeing the Cross on the heavens from the charge of fiction
and imposture. There is scarcely any miracle in my
opinion that seems to be better attested than this, or which
is capable if being confirmed by more eyewitnesses.

Eusebius, who lived in those times, writes that it was not only seen by Constantine himself but also by his whole army, and that too in the middle of the day. He adds that the truth of the fact was not only believed by the Christians but by those who were enemies of the Cross of Christ.

So prevalent was the report of this miracle that the inhabitants testify in the triumphal arch that they dedicated to Constantine that he conquered Maxentius by the immediate direction and assistance of the divinity, although only a little before many of them were of Maxentius' party and enemies of the Christian name. They did not therefore change the form of the Cross into that of our Savior's in that triumphal arch made in honor of Constantine but ordered it to be represented with such sculpture and expressions as were carved on the arches of Trajan, Severus and other Roman emperors, as appears on such monuments of antiquity as are to be seen at Rome at present.

I cannot conclude with so much certainty that Nazarius was a Christian because his daughter Euphemia was such, as I can from his panegyrical address to Constantine:

> It is the general discourse among the Gauls that there was an angelic host seen in the air and that they were sent by God; and although things of a celestial nature are imperceptible by human sight, because a simple and uncompounded substance is not properly the object of our senses; yet these — your auxiliary forces of heaven who are clothed with visible appearances — attended you as witnesses to the great merits and then withdrew to their ethereal mansions. But of what species of creation were these exalted spirits? Of what firmness and vigor of body, of what largeness of limbs. Their glittering shields blazed in an awful manner, and the splendor of their celestial armor

was terrible. They marched in such formidable array that they seemed to wait on you as your guards. This was the language that was heard among them: "We are flying to the assistance of Constantine." Beings of a heavenly nature may be allowed to triumph, and that is an ambition that becomes them. This noble army of spirits who descended from above were sent down by omnipotence itself and gloried that they fought for you.

But I shall add nothing further of our author and shall only observe that some historians note that this large cross was placed on a gilded column in the Philadelphium, which was the Poets' College and was built near the Porphyry Pillar, as the following inscription shows:

On the Porphyry Pillar in the Philadelphium

Muselius' public acts aloud proclaim,
A firm attachment to the Emperor's service.
This famed Museum, sacred seat of learning
He raised and placed his Prince's picture here.

And thus another:

This building is an honor to the learned,
One of the city's brightest ornaments,
A spur to laudable and virtuous actions,
A great encouragement to virtuous men.
And again:

The good Muselius, steadily believing
The heavenly λόγος to be truly God,
This structure made an offering to his service.

Julian, the Prefect of the City, set up a gilded statue of Anastasius before the College of the Poets, on which was inscribed a couple of elegant verses, yet no mention is made in them in what part of the city this college was built.

When a report was made to Emperor Manuel that from ancient times, on the west side of the Forum of Constantine, there had stood in the niche of the wall two female statues made of brass, one a Roman, the other a Hungarian woman; and that the statue of the Roman woman projected — because of this craziness — beyond its base, and that the statue of the Hungarian woman stood fixed in its position, he sent some workmen to erect the Roman and demolish the Hungarian statue. He thought by this means that the affairs of New Rome would take a new turn toward prosperity and success.

In the same forum, among other elegant statues of famous men, was the statue of Longinus, who had been Prefect of the City, on which was cut the following inscription made by Arabius:

Iberia, Persia, and the distant Nile,
The Solymaeans, Indians, and Armenians,
With all the extended regions of the West,
The Colchi, bordering near to Caucasus,
Which hides its towering head among the clouds,
And all the flowery plains of fair Arabia,
Longinus' expedition can attest;
With what dispatch he flew to treat of peace,
And with what speed successfully returned.

I shall take no notice of the statue of Themistius the Philosopher, placed near the Forum of Constantine, whom Valentinian had dignified with the title of Prefect of the City and to whom Emperor Valens had done more honor by his writings than any statue or high station whatever.

Socrates gives us the following account of the death of Arius, the ring-leader of the sect of the Arians. When

Arius had made his appearance before Constantine the Great, he came out of the palace with his bodyguards, of whom Eusebius was commander, and passed through the city, gazed at by the crowds of people. When he came near the Porphyry Pillar in the Forum of Constantine, he was informed, upon inquiring, where there was a privy. He went there under a strange terror and mental despondency. There, oppressed with an uncommon falling of the bowels, his straight gut fell from him. This was followed by a large effusion of blood, which brought away his small guts, his liver, and his spleen, so that he died instantly. The same author adds that this privy was standing in his time. There is nothing however remaining at present in the Forum of Constantine but the Porphyry Pillar, for its grounds are wholly built over.

Near the pillar there stands a caravansaray, or a place built for the entertainment of strangers; and near that a Turkish mosque, built by Ali Pasha, the vestibule or porch of which is large, made of marble, and adorned with six shining pillars, four of white and two of Theban marble. The shafts of these measure seven feet and four digits in circumference at the bottom. Though they are very tall columns, each of these have two bases, according to the Turkish style; the lowermost of which is marble, and the other brass. They learned this way of building from the Greeks, who generally raised their pedestals with a very high cornice.

Not far from this mosque there stands a school or college inhabited by the professors of the Mohametan divinity. There is a quadrangular portico that runs around it, which is supported by eighteen pillars, part of which consist of green and part of white marble. A little below that of Ali Pasha stands another mosque. It is sited in the highest eminence of the second valley and has a marble vestibule adorned with six columns; two of which are made of variegated porphyry marble, two of white marble with sky-colored streaks, and two of a dark green marble stained with white.

From some things that, as I remarked before, stood on the second hill you discover the location of part of the third ward, in which was built the tribunal of the Forum of Constantine, and almost all the fifth and sixth ward.

I would also observe here that Dionysius places the temples of Tellus, Ceres, Proserpina, Juno and Pluto partly on the eminences of the second hill and partly on the plain on the seashore below it. He places the Temple of Tellus in particular beyond the bay outside the walls of Old Byzantium. He tells us that:

> This temple is open at the top to show the freedom of the earth in her productions, and its walls are built of a fine polished stone. Above the Temple of Tellus stood the temples of Ceres and Proserpina, which were beautified with a large collection of fine paintings, the curious relics of preceding times, and with statues in no way inferior to them, finished in the most elaborate manner. The temples of Juno and Pluto were situated where the sea winds off from the Continent. Nothing remained of them in my time, but only their names. In return for the preparations made against him by the Byzantines in his expedition against the Scythians, Cyrus burned down the Temple of Juno. Philip of Macedon, when he was carrying on the siege of Byzantium and wanted some materials for that purpose, demolished the Temple of Pluto. The names of each of these temples still continue: for the Temple of Pluto was called Arca Plutonis, as the Temple of Juno was called Arca Heraea. In these temples the youth constantly offered their sacrifices at the beginning and end of each year.

It will appear more probable that these *arcae* were sited on some eminences of the second hill rather than on the plain below it, because there is not the least appearance of either of them in that place. So that when Dionysius records that these *arcae* of Pluto and Juno were situated very near the seashore, he must mean only that they were only the points of some dock or haven. If this is not his meaning, the *arcae* mentioned here ought to be interpreted as the seashores. But I have enlarged more fully on this matter in my *Treatise on the Bosporus*.

# V

# The Seventh Ward

THE *ANCIENT DESCRIPTION OF THE WARDS* TELLS US that the site of the seventh ward is more level in comparison with the sixth, although at the extremity of one of its sides it falls into the sea with a greater decline. From this I concluded that there would be little difficulty in discovering where this ward stood. But this description is not peculiar to it but also common to other wards. The author adds, namely, that this ward stretches with very long porticos from the right hand of the Pillar of Constantine to the Forum of Theodosius; as it also extended in the same manner on the side down to the seashore. I could make no more observations from this account than I could from the buildings that are mentioned contained in it, since the very memory of them is entirely lost.

I therefore considered what the author might probably be understood to mean "by the right hand of the Pillar of Constantine." For this problem I had recourse to Livy, who says that Romulus has determined all the wards that reach from east to west to be the right-hand wards, and all the wards that extended from south to north to be left-hand wards. But I could not explain away the problem this way, for by this means I have made this ward stretch south, whereas I shall show plainly in another place that it extended to the north.

Nor could the geographical method give me any light on this matter, for when these gentlemen take the altitude of the pole, they look fully north so that the east lies directly on their right hand. Varro, who has defined the four parts of the heavens exactly, following the astrological scheme, has given me some insight into this matter. He tells us that the south lies directly before us and the north behind us so that the east lies on the left hand and the west on the right. By this division of the heavens into four parts, I judged that the seventh ward was situated west of the Pillar of Constantine. Yet I was in doubt as to whether the author of the *Description* followed the division of Romulus or that of the astrologers. I was therefore in greater doubt than I was before until, after diligent inquiry, I made a discovery as to where the Column of Theodosius stood and of some steps of the churches of Anastasia and Eirene. I therefore realized that the seventh ward descended from the top of the Promontory down to the bay, and that this author would have described its location more distinctly had he told us that as you go from east to west the seventh ward extends on the right hand from the Pillar of Constantine to the Forum of Theodosius.

In this ward several fine buildings were erected in antiquity. These stood on the same ground where that most famous place of merchandise in the city, called Bezestan or the Exchange by the Turks, stands at present, and where the most valuable goods of all kinds are kept, as they were in the reigns of the Christian emperors, in the building called the Lampterum, which I believe formerly stood in another place. I am persuaded of this opinion when I consider the ruins left by the fire that broke out in the reign of Justinian and which, as Cedrinus relates, destroyed — among other edifices — the Church of St. Sophia, the place where they kept the records of it, the Octagon, the Baths of Zeuxippus, and the famous structure of the Lampterum, so called because of the lights burning there every night.

This building was roofed with wood. Here the most costly commodities, such as silks, velvets and the richest brocades, were deposited. In short, this fire consumed everything that the former fire had spared. I might not improperly have called it λαμπτῆρρες, which in Latin means *Lucernae,* as is confirmed by the authority of Livy and Pliny.

# VI

## The Street Called Taurus,
## The Forum of Theodosius,
## The Pillar of Theodosius
## With Winding Stairs,
## The Tetrapylum,
## The Pyramidical Engine of the Winds,
## The Statues of Arcadius and Honorius,
## The Churches of Eirene and Anastasia,
## And
## The Rocks Called Scironides

WHEN I WAS QUITE DISHEARTENED OVER DISCOVERING the seventh ward and the Taurus, without which no discovery could be made of the eighth ward, I made the best enquiry I could about some other buildings that might lead me to a knowledge of them. After I had searched for the location of the Pillar of Theodosius for a considerable time, I was informed by some elderly persons that it stood on the top of the Promontory where the plain of the third hill extends, which is near the new bath built by Emperor Beyazit, who had demolished that pillar over forty years before I came to Byzantium so that he might build his bath with more convenience. Beyond the bath northward there is a broad way where there are three booksellers shops and an ancient cistern. More towards the south is the Seraglio. This broad way widens eastward into a large area, at the farther end of which is the Sepulcher of Emperor Bejazit, with a mosque and a caravansaray.

Cedrinus relates that this Pillar of Theodosius is, in all parts, like the one erected by Arcadius and is still standing in the Xerolophon, which I shall have occasion to describe later. Zonaras writes that the pillar in the Taurus was erected at the expense of Theodosius. On it were depicted the trophies he took and his well-fought battles with the Scythians and barbarous nations. It was thrown down by an earthquake, along with his own statue on top, the same year that Old Rome was taken.

Emperor Anastasius ordered many curious pieces of brasswork to be demolished and then newly cast into his own statue. Among these was a famous statue of Constantine the Great that, with other statues, made a large equestrian group, was gilt, dignified with his own name and title, and placed on the same pillar where the statue of Theodosius had stood. I would observe here, by the way, that the street called the Taurus was the same place where the Pillar of Theodosius stood. From this I would observe further that the seventh ward stood on the top and sides of the third hill. Although the seventh ward does not contain the Forum of Theodosius, it is not improbable that it was only a small distance from it, if we consider how exactly Constantinople emulated Old Rome. We may also depend on the authority of Evagrius, who asserts that the fire that broke out in the reign of Leo burned down all the edifices from the Forum of Constantine to the Forum of Taurus:

An ancient native of Constantinople informed me that in his time the Forum of Taurus and the Pillar of Theodosius stood in the same place, and that it was like the Hippodrome, full of wild and uncultivated trees. Because it was only a shelter for thieves and robbers, Emperor Mohamet, who took the city, voluntarily bestowed the ground on those who would build on it.

I conjecture from Zonaras that the Forum Pistorium, or Bread Market, stood on part of the grounds of the Forum of Theodosius, or at least was very near it. Zonaras says that as Emperor Nicephorus Phocas was coming out of his palace, situated at the Golden Fountain and near the Porta Aurea, the people pursued him angrily with screams and shouts from the Forum Pistorium as far as the Pillar of Constantine. The anonymous author of the *History of Constantinople* is of the same opinion as to the position of the Taurus and the pillar and tells us that "the pillar stood in a paved court near the Forum Pistorium." He adds that "in the same place there was a square building with four gates and four porticos around it, which is called the Tetrapylum, which before was called the Quatrivium."

Cedrinus places the Tetrapylum not far from the Forum of Taurus, when he tells us that the fire in Leo's time destroyed two large churches adorned with all kinds of curious stones; one not far from the Tetrapylum, the other adjoining the Forum of Taurus. Speaking of another fire that broke out in the same emperor's reign, the same author writes that it consumed all the buildings from the Tetrapylum, covered with plates of brass, to the church. The author of the *Description of the Wards* writes that in Constantinople there was one gilt Tetrapylum but does not mention in what ward it stood.

Johannes the Rhetorician, so cited by Evagrius, tells us that in the reign of Emperor Zeno a certain Mamianus, an eminent senator, built some handsome porticos at Constantinople, and that between two of them he built a Tetrapylum as a boundary to both. He splendidly adorned this with brass and marble pillars. He adds that in his time the porticos bore the name of some emperor and that large stones of Preconnesian marble, relics of their ancient beauty and magnificence, lay on the ground, but that there was not the least sign remaining of the Tetrapylum.

The anonymous author mentioned above says that in this Tetrapylum there was a chamber over the pillars where the empress and the relations of the deceased emperor received the news of his death. Their faces veiled, they bewailed his departure until six in the evening, then meeting the passing corpse, they attended it to the Church of the Apostles where they usually buried their emperors. The Tetrapylum seems to me to have formerly been the Temple of Janus Quadrifons, which stood near the Capitol. It had, like that of Old Rome, four doors denoting the four seasons of the year. For Janus takes his name *ab eundo,* and therefore all passages are said to be sacred to him, and the doors of all temples are called *Januae.*

Some authors tell us that in the Forum Pistorium there was a quadrilateral pyramid. Cedrinus defines this Tetrasceles to be a quadrilateral engine invented to show in what point of the compass the wind stood. He adds that Theodosius the Great erected a machine in the shape of a pyramid, adorned with several figures of animals, plants, fruits, gilt bunches of pomegranates, and naked cupids in bas relief. Some of these cupids were cut in a gay, smiling humor. Some of the uppermost were wanton, playing their little tricks on those who were below them; while others were dancing.

On it was carved a set of young fellows playing on brass pipes. On top of the pyramid was a vane or weathercock that showed in what corner the wind sat. The statues of Arcadius and Honorius were placed near the statue of Theodosius, their father; that of Arcadius in an eastern and that of Honorius in a western niche.

Socrates, who has written the *History of the Christians,* tells us that Emperor Valens built a large aqueduct out of the ruins of Chalcedon, which he brought into the city and which supplied a cistern of a very large capacity, which was built by Clearchus, who was Prefect of Constantinople. In his time this was called the Cistern or, as the original word in Socrates seems more properly to mean, the "lake" of Theodosius. Zonaras and Cedrinus call this lake a nymphaeum and add to the authority of Socrates that the Prefect of the City celebrated a great festival there and very splendidly entertained all the people. I would remark from these citations that the place that Socrates calls the Forum of Theodosius is called the Taurus by Zonaras and Cedrinus, and that they are both the same forum and that the nymphaeum mentioned here is different from the nymphaeum that is situated near the Forum of Constantine, opposite the Senate House and where they usually solemnize their weddings, as has been observed before.

The author of the *Ancient Description* writes that the Carosian Baths were so named from Carosia, the daughter of Emperor Valens; but he does not tell us in what part of the third hill they stood, nor could I discover when I was in Constantinople whether or not they are entirely in ruins and others built in their place, since there are now very large ones built on the top and sides of the third hill by the Turks.

The same author places the churches of St. Eirene and Anastasia in the seventh ward but does not mention what part of it. Nor is it possible to find out their location except from the historical accounts we have received of it. They say that when the city was taken by the Franks and the Venetians a fire began at the Synagogue of the Saracens in the part of the city that declines toward the sea northward, very near the Church of St. Eirene. I was first informed by some elderly people of the city that this church stood within the precinct of the Seraglio. I afterwards noticed a lofty tower that stood outside the precinct of the Seraglio, which was situated on the east side of the third hill. It was a square building and is still called Eirene by the vulgar, but whether it was the Church of St. Eirene or of the Empress Eirene, I cannot tell.

I find among the monuments of ancient learning that there were three churches in Constantinople dedicated to St. Eirene. The first was called the Old Church of St. Eirene, which, as Socrates writes, was built by Constantine the Great and stood near the Church of St. Sophia. The second church I am now speaking of stood on the third hill; and the third, as Procopius says, was built by Justinian at the mouth of the bay called Ceras, or Cornu, and was called the Church of St. Eirene the Martyr.

Some authors write that the Church of Anastasia was built where the new Bezestan, or new Basilica, now stands. Others say that it was situated near the Cistern, supported by an abundance of marble pillars and stood between the basilicas of the forum and the tomb and caravansaray of Emperor Bejazit. Sozomen writes that when St. Gregory went from Nazianzum to Constantinople, he preached in a small church built by his followers. This was afterwards very much enlarged by succeeding emperors and was also beautified and adorned in the most expensive manner and was called the Church of St. Anastasia. I shall not determine whether it was so called because St. Gregory's sermons preached in this church revived the constitutions and decrees of the Council of Nicea or whether, as he adds, it went by that name because a woman big with child fell from the upper gallery and died on the spot but was restored to life again by the joint prayers of the congregation then present. However, it is plain from this passage of Sozomen that those historians are grievously in the wrong who say that this church was built in memory of St. Anastasia, a Roman saint.

In my *Treatise on the Thracian Bosporus* I have shown that on the north side of the third hill some rocks rise from its lowermost level. These were called Scironides by those who first transplanted a colony from Megara and Corinth to Byzantium. These rocks were so called because of their resemblance to the Scironides that rise between Corinth and Megara.

I shall take the freedom here just to mention what is worth observing on the third hill. On top stands the tomb of Emperor Beyazit near a caravansaray and a large mosque that was built by him in the likeness of the Church of St. Sophia. It is roofed with brickwork and covered with lead. It has a large porch or vestibule paved with white marble and is surrounded by four porticos that are supported by columns of the choicest marble. In the middle of it is a fine fountain that falls into a large basin and that emits the falling water through several little cocks. The mosque and vestibule is surrounded on three sides by a large area that is enclosed partly with walls and partly with a caravansaray. On the fourth side it is encompassed by an adjoining garden, in the middle of which is the tomb of Beyazit in a small edifice built in a cylindrical form.

On the top of the third hill stands the Seraglio, where the emperor's concubines constantly reside. It is enclosed by a high wall that, at my first arrival at Constantinople, was more than two miles in compass. The present Emperor Süleiyman has taken up residence in the middle of this precinct, where he is laying a foundation for a caravansaray and his future sepulcher. These are now being built with the most elegant marble, brought from several parts of the Turkish dominions, so that you may see infinite varieties of it lying around the building, not lately dug out of the quarry, but ones that for many ages have been used in the palaces of several princes and emperors, not only at Byzantium but in Greece and in Egypt.

In the seventh ward I saw three ancient cisterns not noted in the *Description of the Wards*. One in the Forum of Taurus, another between the Tomb of Beyazit and the Bezestan, both of which are supported by marble pillars. The third was built on a cliff of the third hill that faced north. Of these there still remain six Corinthian pillars, very large and tall, made of Arabian marble and curiously wrought. Below the pedestal's base was laid an earthen pipe that conveyed water into a cistern made of brick, whose roof, which is brickwork, is also supported with twenty square brick pillars.

A little above the cistern there was formerly a court belonging to a Christian church that the Turks demolished to repair and beautify their own houses. On the side of the hill that extends westward there stands a mosque whose vestibule is supported by twelve pillars, six of which are of Arabian marble. Above this mosque there stands another, which is also supported by pillars and was formerly a church dedicated to St. Theodorus. This, however, is not the same church that Procopius says Justinian built in a place called Rhessium. There is another Christian church, now a mosque, standing between the Seraglio and the tomb, that the Emperor Süleiyman built for his son Mohamet, which is encrusted with several kinds of marble, curiously variegated.

# VII

# The Eighth Ward,
# The Back of the Third Hill

IN THE *ANCIENT DESCRIPTION OF THE WARDS* I CAN
not find that the eighth ward was situated on the south side
of the third hill, though it says that the eighth ward is not
bounded by the sea on the side of the Taurus and may be
considered more a narrow than a broad piece of ground,
though this defect is sufficiently emended by its great
length. By this description I am left altogether in doubt as
to whether it lies north or south. But I discovered the
location of the eighth ward from this: the author of the
*Description* tells us that it contained part of the Forum of
Constantine and a portico on the left side as far as the
Taurus, and that the seventh ward stretched from the
right hand of the Pillar of Constantine to the Forum of
Theodosius.

I observe from these authorities that part of the
Promontory that reaches from sea to sea, situated between
the Porphyry Pillar and the Taurus, was divided into the
north and south side, and that the porticos in the right and
left extended from the Pillar of Constantine to the Taurus
and separated the seventh and eighth ward. The former
contained the right-hand porticos and the latter the left.
There is nothing to be seen of these porticos now except
the broad way that runs from the Church of St. Sophia to
the Land Wall.

This ward also contains the Capitol and the Basilica of
Theodosius, both of which, it is very probable, stood near
the Pillar and Forum of Theodosius. It is no less evident
from Zonaras and Cedrinus that the fire in Leo's time
consumed the Senate House built for the dispatch of public
business by the great council of the empire and for the

convenience of the emperor to preside over them as Consul. This Senate House, as the same authors add, had twelve pillars curiously variegated, made of Trojan marble, which were twenty-five feet high; the roof was supported by four arches. This house, according to these writers, was about two hundred and forty feet long and a hundred and fifty feet broad. I am inclined to believe, from what I have mentioned on this occasion, that it was either the Capitol or the Basilica of Theodosius. For it is plain from modern historians that these two structures, by whomever they were rebuilt, lost their names after the fire. They also tell us that in the Taurus there was a palace and a place for the entertainment of strangers. These authorities are strengthened by some elderly people of Constantinople who attest that in their memory, near the Mint House where they now coin their money, there stood a spacious palace inhabited, as some say, by the Mohamet who took the city before he built the great enclosed palace that stands on the first hill. Some of the sultans have since beautified their palaces out of the ruins of the former.

The place of entertainment, or rather the church that stood to the southwest of the Taurus, I saw entirely demolished and its pillars carried off to build a caravansaray that Emperor Süleiyman erected in memory of his son, whom he dearly loved. I leave it to the Greek priests to inquire whether this was the same as the Church of St. Paul that stood in the seventh ward, though I have yet to meet one of them who could give me a straight answer on this matter.

# VIII

## The Ninth Ward,
## The Temple of Concord,
## The Granaries of Alexandria
## And Theodosius,
## The Baths of Anastasia,
## The House of Craterus, The Modius and
## The Temple of the Sun and Moon

I AM CONVINCED THAT THE NINTH WARD WAS LOCATED behind the third hill, partly on the cliffs that lie under its ridge and partly on those that lie at the bottom, and partly on the shore of the Propontis, extending as far as the gardens called Blanchae. Among other authorities, it is principally the author of the *Description* who says that the ninth ward is all on a slope and is bounded by the sea. From the account he gives of the eighth ward, since it is not terminated on the side of Taurus by any part of the sea, I am convinced that it included the plain on the top of the third hill but not the descents below it; and that the ninth ward lies partly under the eighth on the side that extends from the Taurus south towards the sea of the Propontis. It was also partly situated on the two declines; one of which descends from the Taurus south-southwest; the other from the houses of the Janissaries to the south.

You may also discover where the ninth ward stood from the location of the Temple of Concord. Although it is not expressly declared by the author of the *Description*, reason and the authority of other writers will lead us to that discovery. Evagrius, describing the fire that broke out in Leo's time, says that it raged in a frightful manner on the north side of the city from the Bosphorian Haven to the old Temple of Apollo; on the south from the Port of Julian to the houses located a small distance from the

Temple of Concord; and in the middle part of the city from the Forum of Constantine to the Taurus; and farther that it extended a distance of five furlongs. From this it is discoverable that the fire destroyed all that part of the ninth ward through which you may draw a straight line from the Taurus to the Propontis. And this would evidently appear to anyone who would walk the five furlongs from the Forum of Constantine to the Forum of Taurus and there fix a mark, and afterward walk west from the Port of Julian through the plain on the seashore a distance of five more furlongs and there fix another mark and compare that mark with another fixed at the Taurus. He would vary very little as to the location of the Temple of Concord. But that and the Church of St. Thomas the Apostle are now entirely in ruins.

If we consider the rules generally observed in architecture, it is reasonable to believe that the granaries of Theodosius stood near the Port of Theodosius, which was situated in the gardens now called Blanchae. There was no port either in the eighth or ninth ward; but in that part of the twelfth ward that adjoins the ninth is the Port of Theodosius, of which I shall speak at greater length later.

Above the Blanchae to the north there stands a temple on an eminence called Myreleos; inside of which was a cistern, the roof of which is supported with about sixty marble pillars. On the site of this cistern there was formerly a granary that Suidas, though very improperly, calls Horeium. The statue of Maimus, who marched his army against the Scythians, he says, stood in the Horeium, which was in front of the house of Craterus, now of Myreleus, near the Modius and the Brazen Hands. This Modius, or Bushel, was a set measure, or standard, according to which they bought and sold their corn. Emperor Valentinian made a law that twelve bushels should be sold at such a sum; a certain seafaring man, acting in violation of this law, forfeited his right hand.

This, they tell you, was the reason why Valentinian ordered the two Brazen Hands to be set up in a niche somewhere in the Amastrianum and the Brazen Bushel to be placed between them. Others say that Valentinian commanded that this bushel should not be sold by the strike, but in full measure. A certain offender lost both his hands for not observing this order. Cedrinus writes that some places here were called the Amastrianum from a sorry abandoned fellow, a native of Amastrum. Laying under the deepest scandal for cursing the Paphlagonians, and in order to escape the punishment for homicide, he fled for shelter to Constantinople.

The same author writes that in the same place there was a very large Temple of the Sun and Moon. Here were carved, at the order of Phidalia, the Sun riding in a white chariot and the Moon as his spouse sitting by him. Below these figures, near the ground, was cut a powerful prince prescribing the rules of obedience to his people. Near his throne was carved a Jupiter in a recumbent posture, which was the work of Phidias. If the house mentioned before was the house of the learned Craterus, the Sophist, this is the spot where his Suggestum, or desk, was erected. This has been celebrated in verse by Julian the Egyptian. Besides such curiosities, the ninth ward also contained the famous Baths of Anastasia, which took their name, as Marcellinus says, from Anastasia, the sister of Constantine. Sozomen writes that Marcian the Grammarian was tutor to the two daughters of Emperor Valens, Anastasia and Carosia, and that the baths that went by their names were standing in Constantinople in his time.

# IX

## The Third Valley and the Tenth Ward, The House of Placidia and her Palace, The Aqueduct of Valentinian, The Baths of Constantine and The Nymphaeum

THE TENTH WARD EXTENDED TOWARD THE NORTH, AND it was situated in the third valley on the east side of it; and on the top of the Promontory rising above the third valley. This is evident from the author of the *Description of the Wards,* who writes that the tenth ward is divided from the ninth by a broad way; that it lies much more level; that it is in no part uneven, except near the seashore; that it is of a proportionate length and breadth; and that it contains the Church of St. Achatius, the Baths of Constantine, the House of Placidia Augusta, and many other fine buildings.

But after the most vigorous search and inquiry, I could not find the location of any of them; so I was obliged to have recourse to the authority of historians who had written on these matters. In consulting them, I could not help notice a mistake by the author of the *Description,* who says that this ward contained the Baths of Constantine, whereas I cannot find that Constantine ever had any baths at Constantinople, but that Constantius had.

Sozomen, speaking of these people who, favoring St. Chrysostom and his doctrine, were expelled from the city, says that "perceiving the people to be furiously enraged against them, they did not assemble the next day in the great church but celebrated Holy Communion in a bath that was called the Baths of Constantius." Suidas reports that "Elladius Alexandrinus wrote a *Description*

*of the Baths of Constantius* in the time of Theodosius II."
Socrates relates that "Emperor Valens commanded the
walls of Chalcedon to be taken down and the stone carried
to Constantinople to build a bath, which was called the
Baths of Constantius." He adds that "in one of these stones
was cut a prophecy that had been hidden for many ages
but was then explained, that is that when the city abounded
with water a wall would be of some service to a bath and
that numberless nations of the barbarians should invade
the territories of the Romans and make great devastations
there, but at last should be overcome." The prophecy, as
described by Socrates, is as follows:

When tender virgins shall in circles dance
Around the public cistern, and with flowers
Dress the capacious vessel, when the streets
Shall be with fragrant sweets and garlands
    crowned,
When rising waters shall overflow its top,
And a stone basin made to catch them in,
A mighty host, in shining armor clad,
A wild and warlike race, shall come from far
And pass the rapid Danube's silver streams:
Scythia, and Maesia's lands unmeasurable
Shall be despoiled by their all-conquering sword:
All Thrace shall fear, the fatal period is come.

Zonaras and Cedrinus write this prophecy the same
way but differ in the Greek from Socrates, and exchange
'ιερὴν for δροσερὴν, for λουτρόιο, λουτρόιοι; for ἄγρια,
μαρμαίροντα, ἄγρα μαργαίνοντα; for καλλιρόοιο,
κιμμερίοιο. This prophecy is so interpreted by Socrates,
who tells is that it was fully accomplished  when Valens
built an aqueduct that supplied the city with plenty of
water, when the barbarous nations invaded the territories
of New Rome.

However, it is capable of being interpreted in another manner. For after Valens had brought the aqueduct into Constantinople, Clearchus, the Prefect of the City, built a large cistern in the Forum of Theodosius, into which the aqueduct emptied and the people were there entertained at a jovial feast. Therefore it was called the Plentiful Cistern, which they tell you was foretold by the prophet in the above lines.

But some part of this prophecy was not fulfilled until some time after, when the wall of Chalcedon was being pulled down by the order of Valens. At this time the people of Nicomedia, of Nicea, and Bithynia petitioned the emperor against it. Being highly displeased with them for it, he could hardly be prevailed upon to comply with their petition. Therefore to disengage himself from an oath he had made to demolish the wall, he ordered other stones to be put in their place as fast as the old ones were taken down. You may therefore see at present what a mean superstructure is raised on the remains of the old wall, which consisted of stones of the largest and most wonderful size.

Zonaras and Cedrinus also record that to express his resentment against the people of Chalcedon for giving protection to his enemy Procopius, Valens commanded the walls of their city to be demolished and an aqueduct to be made of their stones. The former historian sometimes calls this the Aqueduct of Valens and the latter sometimes the Aqueduct of Valentinian. The latter adds, among other passages of the history mentioned above, that according to the prophecy, the barbarous nations made their incursions into Thrace but were afterwards defeated.

The Aqueduct of Valentinian, which is highly arched passing through the tenth ward, reaches from the sides of the fourth to the side of the third hill. I would be greatly surprised that the author of the *Description of the Wards*, who has taken notice of the granaries of Valentinian, had not mentioned it. But I am aware that he had omitted many other monuments of antiquity that existed in his time.

In the reign of Constantine, the son of Emperor Leo, who was a declared enemy of images in churches, and in the year of our Lord 759, there was so great a drought at Constantinople that the dew ceased to fall from heaven; and all the cisterns, baths and fountains of the city were dried up. Observing this, the emperor began to repair the Aqueduct of Valentinian, which continued in good order until the reign of Heraclius, when it was demolished by the Avars. Upon this he sent for workmen from many places to rebuild it; from Asia and Pontus he had a thousand builders and two hundred whitewashers; from Greece five hundred brickmakers; and from Thrace a thousand day laborers, over whom there presided a nobleman and some of the principal men of the city as surveyors of the works. When the aqueduct was finished, the city was again supplied with water, which was conveyed into the town through a passage lying between the ninth and the tenth ward.

There are many subterranean aqueducts that run through six of the hills, but the Aqueduct of Valentinian had its course above the ground. The historians who have written of the *Deeds of Andronicus* tell you that this passed through the Great Forum, that its water was clear and pleasant, that it was repaired and enlarged by Andronicus himself, and that he increased its current with the Hydrales River. At the springhead from which this aqueduct rose he built a tower and a palace, where he used to divert himself in the summer. He also brought the water from the same river into the Blachernae, which is part of the suburbs. The town was ruined by Isaac, his successor, in pure resentment of his memory.

We are told by Procopius that Justinian repaired the Church of Achatius, when injured by time; that he placed white marble pillars around it, and that he paved and encrusted the side of it with the same kind of marble so that the whole building was beautifully white. There were two porticos adjoining the church; one opened onto the forum and was encompassed by pillars. This passage is not inserted into the printed edition of Procopius, which induced me to make note of it here even more.

Cedrinus writes that the Church of St. Achatius stood in a place called the Heptascalum. Others say that it stood in the Scala; but nobody at present knows where that place was. However, if anyone hereafter should have the curiosity to inquire where this church stood, I would advise him to take the following direction along. Let him inquire where the great house that the historians call the Carya stands. On its grounds there is a nut tree, upon which, they tell you, Achatius was put to death. Upon that occasion a church was built in memory of him. Some think that this was situated in the Neorium, because they have seen in some authors that the image of St. Achatius, made with glass stones and inlaid with gold, was placed in the Church of the Neorium. But the person of whom this is said was another Achatius who—as many historians, as well as Suidas the Grammarian, tell us —was not only the bishop of Constantinople but also a man so proud and haughty that he commanded many of his pictures to be placed in churches while he was still alive. From this he was called Doxomanes.

The House of Placidia, I have observed before, stood in the first ward, so that it may be asked whether it ought to be read *Domus Placidiae,* or *Placillae,* or *Placidae.* Agathius notes the Palaces of Placidae or Placidi in the following inscription on a picture in the Palace of Placidia, set up by the gentlemen of the Wardrobe or New Chancery:

> The learned sages of the law have placed
> At their expense, great Thomas' picture here,
> Near that which represents his royal mistress.
> This mighty honor he is entitled to,

In that he served his prince with faithfulness,
And was the constant guardian of his throne:
His prudence filled the royal treasury,
And raised the imperial family, yet higher.
To celebrate his worth for times to come
His picture shines amongst our emperors.

Beyond the rocks called Scironides, Dionysius mentions a long shore on a plain of the third valley and the
fourth hill. This is considered a remarkable place for
fishing for it is a very deep and very still body of water,
which was called Cycla in antiquity because the Greeks
had formerly hemmed the barbarians in there. In the
same place there is also an altar dedicated to Minerva
Dissipatoria that was erected in memory of that action.

Beyond the Cycla is a creek called Melias, another
famous place for fishing, which is enclosed by several
rocks and a ridge of the Promontory hanging over the
sea. There is no creek in this valley at present. Time has
filled it up, as we learn from Strabo, who writes that this
creek was called Ceras because it had many inlets into the
shore in the form of a deer's antler. There is hardly any
sign of them at present.

Zosimus, who wrote his history in the reign of
Arcadius and Honorius, tells us that Constantinople was
then so crowded with inhabitants that the emperors not
only enlarged the walls beyond those of Constantine but
that they also built timber foundations over the sea. This
method of building, it is probable, very much contributed
in time to encumber and stop up these inlets of the creek.
At the end of the creek called Melias is a place that goes by
the name of Κῆπος, because it is very good garden
ground. Beyond the garden is a place named Aspasius,
but of this I have spoken in my *Treatise on the Bosporus*.

\* \*
\*

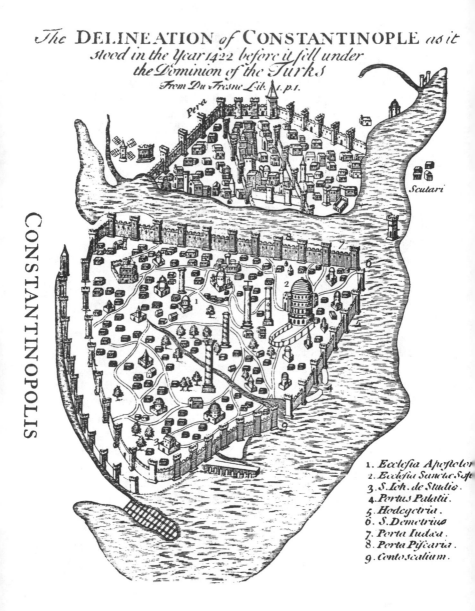

*The* DELINEATION *of* CONSTANTINOPLE *as it*
*stood in the Year 1422 before it fell under*
*the Dominion of the Turks*
*From Du Fresne Lib. 1. p. 1.*

Pera

Scutari

CONSTANTINOPOLIS

1. Ecclesia Apostolor
2. Ecclesia Sanctæ Sop
3. S. Ioh. de Studio.
4. Portus Palatii.
5. Hodegetria.
6. S. Demetrius
7. Porta Iudæa.
8. Porta Piscaria.
9. Contoscalium.

# BOOK IV

## I

## The Eleventh Ward,
## The Fourth and Fifth Hills

I HAD BEEN AT A LOSS TO DISCOVER THE ELEVENTH ward, though the *Ancient Description of the Wards* mentions it to have been wider in compass than the tenth and in no part bounded by the sea. It also says that it partly consisted of level and partly of rising ground. The author added, however, that it also contained the Church of the Apostles. Though nothing now remains of that church, I was informed by some elderly people of Constantinople who told me that they remembered that it stood on the back of the fourth hill, which fell on a hill of the third valley near the Saddlers Shops and the sepulcher of Emperor Mohamet. I observe from this that the eleventh ward was partly on the top of the same hill and partly on its north side.

I shall show by what follows that this ward reached the Land Wall of the city, which divided the eleventh from the fourteenth ward, and which was also itself divided from the city by an intermediate space of land. I shall convince the reader presently that this ward was situated on the sixth hill outside the walls of the city and was afterward walled around by Theodosius II.

The walls built by Constantine are said to have reached as far as the churches of St. Anthony and St. Mary, who was called Rabdos, and from there to have risen to a land wall called the Exacionion. This took its name from the fact that outside the land wall there stood a pillar, on which was erected the statue of Constantine the Great. Some modern writers would contend that he built a church that he dedicated to the Holy Trinity on a place called the Exacionion, now called the Church of the Apostles. If I am not mistaken, the walls of Constantine were built on the borders of the fourth and fifth hill near the Exacionion. Cedrinus writes that the walls of the city, the beautiful churches, the fine houses situated in the Exacionion were thrown down by a dreadful earthquake. They tell us in other places — though not consistently among themselves — that there were porticos that reached from the Miliarium to the street called Taurus and to the gates of St. John the Baptist's Church near the Hippodrome, which are more than a thousand Roman paces from the Church of the Apostles and as far from the walls of the city that were built by Constantine.

This may be gathered from the following passage of Sozomen. "Theodosius," says this author, "leading his army against Eugenius, went a mile out of the city to the Church of St. John, which he had built in the Hepdomum." This Hepdomum was a part of the city's suburbs; but it is now enclosed within the walls, as will appear when I come to speak of it. If the pillar from which the Exacionion took its name was the same as that high pillar that stood on top of the fifth hill and was seen not long ago at a great distance from the city above all the houses, we might easily determine that the walls built by Constantine did not reach beyond this pillar, which stood about half a mile from the Church of the Apostles.

I saw this pillar cut into pieces and removed for building a mosque by order of Emperor Süleiyman. The base, the pedestal, and the foundation stone alone was so high that I could not climb it without a ladder. The pedestal was four feet and nine digits high and the plinth one foot and six digits. The Greeks and the Turks, each in their dialect, called it the Pillar of the Virgin, which I take to be the one celebrated by our modern writers, which they say was erected on a hill and supported the statue of Venus carved in stone. When the *Ancient Description of the Wards* tells us that the eleventh ward is in no way bounded by the sea, it must be understood to mean that the plain situated between the Bay of Ceras and the foot of the fourth hill was not within the walls. The same treatise mentions that the city was six thousand, one hundred and fifty feet broad; that is, a mile and two hundred and thirty paces; for the latitude of the isthmus that stretches over the fourth and seventh hill, through which the old wall extended, exceeds the above-mentioned breadth. But Zosimus, an ancient historian, says that Constantine the Great so wholly surrounded the city with a wall that it cut off the isthmus from sea to sea. Upon the whole, therefore, there is a necessity to place the plain situated between the bay and the bottom of the fourth hill in the tenth ward.

# II

# The Church of the Apostles, The Sepulcher of Constantine the Great, The Cistern of Arcadius and Modestus, The Palace of Placilla, and The Brazen Bull

EUSEBIUS ATTESTS THAT CONSTANTINE THE GREAT built the Church of the Apostles to a great height; that he encrusted it with all sorts of variegated marble, which cast a beautiful luster from top to bottom; that he adorned it with small gilt roofs and covered it with plates of brass deeply gilt, which cast a blazing reflection a great distance. The upper part of this venerable structure was curiously wrought all around with brass and gold and was lightened with an abundance of lattices and windows. Around the church there was a fine court lying open to the air. The porticos that enclosed it stood on a quadrangle. Near the porticos stood the palace, the baths, the cloisters and many other houses and buildings belonging to the ecclesiastics and other ministers of the church. The pious emperor has handed these beautiful benefactions down to posterity in memory of the Apostles of the blessed Savior of mankind, to whom also he consecrated twelve purses of gold.

The coffin in which he intended himself to be buried after he was dead was placed by his order in the body of the church and guarded with effigies of the twelve Apostles. Socrates adds that the body of Constantine, lying in a golden coffin, was brought into the city by his intimate friends and buried in the Church of the Apostles. I am inclined to believe that Zonaras never read Eusebius when he tells us that it was buried in the cloister of the Church of the Apostles. This, he says, was built by Constantius for the interment of his father.

Near the broad way that stretches along the top of the Promontory from the Church of St. Sophia to the Gate of Adrianople, right next to the place where the Church of the Apostles stood, there is shown to this day a coffin made of porphyry marble, empty, and without a cover, ten feet long, and five and a half broad, which the Greeks and the Turks say was the coffin of Constantine the Great. I cannot vouch for the truth of it. The authority of Socrates and Eusebius seems to be somewhat doubtful, however. They tell us that he was buried in a golden coffin unless, perhaps, the golden coffin was enclosed in that of porphyry marble.

Zonaras is of the opinion that Theodora, the wife of Justinian, built the Church of the Apostles and adds that there was formerly in the same place a Church of the Apostles but much inferior in beauty and magnificence to that which stands on the same ground at present. Procopius says that for some time there had been a church at Constantinople that was much damaged by time and likely to fall. Justinian ordered it to be taken down, rebuilt and enlarged, and made in the shape of a cross with the body of the church pointing east and west, and the part crossing it north and south.

This church is well walled and adorned inside the ranges of the pillars standing one above another. Evagrius therefore seems to be mistaken in attributing the building of this church to Justinian, when it is evident that it was built by Constantine the Great. Procopius too grossly flatters Justinian in ascribing to him the building of many fine structures, whereas, in reality, he only repaired them when they were old or rebuilt them when they fell too much into decay or were destroyed by fire.

Nothing remains of this church at present. No, not even its foundation. You see only the ruins of an old cistern that supplied the church and the clergy with water. There are now standing on the same spot of ground over two hundred saddlers shops and workhouses, where they make and sell not only all kinds of horse gear but also leather buckets, quivers, and trunks.

A little above this cistern stands a mosque with a caravansaray adjoining it, situated on a plain. This was built with square stone on the plan of the Church of St. Sophia out of the ruins and sacrilege of the Church of the Apostles and other Christian churches by Mohamet, who took the city. The roof is on a semicircular plan, made of brickwork, and covered with lead, as are all the public buildings of the Turks. It is beautified with a very elegant, square porch as broad as the church itself, paved with the finest marble, and adorned with square porticos. Their arches, which bear up the roof, are supported with very large pillars of marble, curiously variegated. In the middle of it is a fountain with nine pipes whose waters fall into a great basin. Around the mosque is a spacious court, part of which is enclosed with walls, and part with long kinds of houses, some of which are inhabited by priests and schoolmasters. In the eastern part of this court there is a garden, in the middle of which stands the Sepulcher of Mohamet, built in a cylindrical form of the whitest marble. It is covered with lead, lighted with windows, and has an entrance door into it.

In the middle of this structure is the coffin of Mohamet, covered with velvet, placed on the ground on a rich carpet. The ground is wholly covered with the most costly carpets, where the priests continually sit and guard the body night and day. A little outside the court are several large caravansarays also built with square stone, which have courtyards in the middle and porticos surrounded by marble pillars. These caravansarays have large gardens adjoining them.

In short, this mosque, with the adjacent buildings around the court with the caravansarays and gardens, takes up an area six furlongs in compass. Mohamet, the same emperor, built in this place the largest baths in all the city where the old cistern of Arcadius or Modestus had formerly been. These baths are of two kinds, some for men and some for women. They adjoin each other but have different entries without any passage out of one into the other.

I shall only describe the men's baths, because the women's are like them. The first place you enter is the room where they undress. From here you pass into the hot and from there into the cold bath. They all stand on one range and are only separated from each other by walls. The room where they undress is a square structure, built of square stone up to the roof, which is arched and built of brick. The inside, measuring two hundred and fifty feet in compass, is surrounded by a stone stair over six feet wide and three feet high. The wall of this room, from the pavement to the bottom of the arched roof, is thirty-seven feet high. In the middle of the floor, which is paved with marble, there is a large marble basin, which is thirty-seven feet in diameter, and three feet deep, which is always supplied from a fountain of spring water. There are two doors out of the stripping room into the hot bath. This apartment is a hundred feet in compass inside and is supplied by four arches, which bear up a dome at the top. It contains eight cells or bathing rooms; one of which, not more than half as large as the rest, has some privies behind it that are cleansed by an efflux of all the waters that are turned out of the bath. Six of these cells have a bathing cistern and are built in such a manner that two of these arches hang over one bathing room.

From here you may pass, on the right and on the left, into another. The cells under the other two arches are so formed that the arch that is nearest the doors that lead out of the stripping room into the hot bath hangs over a very large bathing room. It is paved with marble; and the Turks wash their linen in this place. A plain wall arched at top parts the hot from the cold bath. In the middle of the hot bath there is a basin with a fountain playing. There is only one door that leads out of the hot into the cold bath. This apartment has eight arches that support its dome and contains eight bathing places that project beyond the sphere of its dome and encircle the whole bath, which is about ninety feet in compass. Its whole pavement is laid with marble, and in the middle is built a staircase in the form of an octagon, which is fifty-seven feet and nine inches in circumference and two feet and four digits high. Around the octagon there runs a channel of water, which is of the same depth as the height of the octagon.

The four inward bathing rooms are situated in four angles and are eleven feet and three digits broad in each direction. There are called the hot houses or sweating baths. The dimension of the two bathing rooms that are situated outside the two arches is the same. The other six bathing rooms are of a semicircular shape and stand under six arches within the circle of the dome of the hot bath. At the bottom of the pillars that support the arches they are eleven feet in length and five feet, nine inches in breadth. Every one of these bathing rooms has a marble cistern wherein they bathe, and in one of them, above the rest, there is erected a stately marble throne. There are no lights in the walls either of the hot or cold baths, although their domes are wholly illuminated with glass windows.

The stoke hole, which is two and a half feet in diameter, and of the same height, is built outside the baths. They keep a constant fire in it, which heats a bronze vessel, from which it emits its warm steams through pipes laid in a strait and oblique manner, by that means heating the bottom of the cisterns in which they bathe. There is a rivulet in a field in the suburbs, about six feet in breadth, which runs near the stoke heat. There are pipes laid in this brook that convey the water through the walls of these baths to all their parts. Upon turning a cock, one of these pipes, which passes through a heated earthen vessel, supplies the cisterns with hot water. Upon turning another cock the other pipe, which rises higher, tempers the hot water according to the pleasure of the person who bathes in it. But I shall deal with the use of bathing and the way of building baths among the Turks in another place.

I return now to the eleventh ward, which Procopius notes when he tells us that Theodora, the consort of Justinian, addressed herself to him in the following manner:

> We have, may it please your Imperial Majesty, other palaces still remaining, which are called the Palaces of Helena, as we also have those of Placilla, the wife of Theodosius the Great. For as Justinus

honored his empress with several noble palaces that were called the Palaces of Sophia after her, so it is highly probable the Theodosius did Placilla the same honor in building a palace for her, which was called the Palace of Placilla. I am induced to believe this, because he passionately loved her and because of that strong resentment he bore to the people of Antioch, whom he subjected to the dominion of the Laodenses for demolishing the statues of Placilla, placed in his own forum because, he laid an additional tribute on them.

This palace may not improperly also be called the Palace of Flacilla of whom Claudian speaks in the following lines.

'Tis Spain alone, subject to potent Rome,
Which pays her tribute in her emperors.
Provision, taxes and confederate bands,
Rome by her arms in every nation raises,
Which bows its head to her superior greatness.
Spain only furnishes a race of princes,
Wise, bold, and warlike, formed for empire,
And fit to rule the mistress of the world.
Nor pleased alone to send her valiant sons,
Unless a second offering she made,
Of princely mothers, noble empresses,
Flacilla, Maria, pious, humble, good,
And fair Serena, full of blooming charms.

The Brazen Bull was placed in the eleventh ward; where in that ward might be easily conjectured from a large cistern that the modern historians write was built near it by Nicetas the Eunuch in the reign of Emperor Theophilus, if that cistern were now in existence. If the bull itself remained in the forum where it stood I would have heard something of it. Tzetzes writes in his *History* that the Forum Bovis was so called from the Brazen Bull. This bull is more particularly described by Zonaras, who says that "the body of the unhappy tyrant Phocas was burnt at a place called Bos, where there was a stove or fireplace set up in the form of a bull, which was brought from Troy."

Cedrinus related that Antypas the Martyr was burned to death in this bull. It is a plain instance of the cruelty and tyranny of some of the emperors of Constantinople that they used to punish malefactors with a death so tormenting. We have a similar example of barbarity in Perillus, or rather Perilaus, a brazier of Attica, who made a brazen bull for the execution of Phalaris but first suffered in it himself. This piece of workmanship, says Pliny, was preserved a long time so that those who saw it might curse the hand that made it.

I am more inclined to believe that this bull was brought from Sicily or Italy. I inquired about it but could learn nothing, although the inhabitants are not ignorant that there was formerly such a bull at Constantinople and are used to boasting of a prophecy that had been handed down to them from their ancestors concerning such a bull. Lastly, they believe their own interpretation of it to be more in agreement with the truth than that of Tzetzes, who explained it over three hundred and seventy years ago in the following manner:

> There was mighty talk of a prophecy at Constantinople some time ago, which ran in these words: βοῦς βοήσει τε καὶ ταῦρος ἡ θρηνήσει, *bos mugiet, taurus lugebit.*

The people conjecture from this, he says, that great calamities should befall the city, that they should be perplexed with amazing fears, that an innumerable army of Germans and other nations should come against the town; and that they should be all terrified and frightened with strange dreams of the plundering and destruction of their city. Upon this, the wife of the Grand Hetaeriarch was in great consternation; and her fears and fancies were increased by some fabulous verses made on the occasion. She imagined she dreamed of all that had been the talk of the town for some time before. She dreamed that Constantinople was walled around with brick, that near the Forum Bovis, or the place called Bos, she saw infinite numbers of armed forced drawn up in battle array, and that right next to the street called Taurus she saw a man in a melancholy posture expelling his grief in a mournful tone and beating his breast. The credulous woman, believing the destruction was at hand, told her dream to Tzetzes, who interpreted it thus:

The brick walls that you saw denote great plenty of provisions to Constantinople. You are aware, gentleman (he said, speaking to those who stood by him) how wonderfully that part of the prophecy was accomplished at that time. As to the clause that mentions that an abundance of armed forces shall stand around the bull and that a man in a disconsolate and forlorn condition shall sit down by the bull, which is principally intended by the prophecy, though not yet fulfilled. This may prove beneficial and advantageous to every citizen of us. Therefore hear, O Constantinople, and tell it to others that this is the interpretation of Tzetzes. The same word that among us Greeks signifies a bull, signifies also a cow, and sometimes a heifer, and by the word *Taurus* or bull, the Latins call the Italian bull. Our cow, therefore, which is the famous city of Constantine, and which was built by three Roman bulls of Italy, full of arms, abounding with forces and plenty of provision, shall sound an alarm against our enemies; and the Italian bull, which is the army of the Latins, shall look pale with fear and mourn.

Tzetzes, without question, was a very learned man; and this interpretation of the prophecy was cunning enough; besides that, it was a fine compliment to the empress. At the same time the historian pleased his own humor in interpreting the prophecy according to his own wishes. See how ingenious is the weakness of man to impose upon himself!

But at that time there was another interpretation of this prophecy that, after the event, was much closer to the truth, although Tzetzes took a great deal of pains to confute and expose it. It was the general opinion of the people of Constantinople that the army of the Latins would besiege the city, as happened a little time after, ravaging, burning, destroying everywhere; throwing some of the ringleaders of an arbitrary party from the top of Theodosius' pillar into the street called Taurus and burning others to death in the Brazen Bull.

The same author is no less mistaken in the interpretation of another prophecy, which is as follows: "Woe be to thee, O Constantinople, seated on seven hills, thou shall not continue a thousand years." His explanation of it is this:

Although it is not your fate, O Constantinople, to endure a thousand years, but to be totally demolished, this ought to be no occasion for grief to you, but the cause for joy, for you shall rise again from your ruins more beautiful and more enlarged. For you shall be destroyed even to the advantage of those who shall destroy you.

This interpretation is a downright flattery of the principal leaders of several factions, or companies of charioteers, when they were struggling for the government. But take this interpretation whatever way you will, it seems to be a very wild one. For whether the city was demolished by its own inhabitants or any foreign power, neither way could be any reasonable cause for joy to them. This prediction of the oracle was seconded by another prediction of the astronomers to the same effect. Some historians have attested, as is confirmed by Suidas, that after he had finished the city, Constantine the Great sent for a certain Valens, an astronomer of great skill, and commanded him to inquire what star had the ascendancy at the birth of the city and by that means to inform him of its duration. Valens predicted that the city would continue six hundred and ninety years; but that time is past and gone. Zonaras, therefore, says :

> I must conclude that this prophecy of Valens was erroneous, and that one can hardly depend on the rules of astronomy, or otherwise that Valens only meant the time of her prosperity, when the laws of political life were strictly obeyed, when the public peace was preserved, when their Senate was in high estimation among the people, when the Empire flourished and was under a regular administration, and there was no such thing as tyranny and arbitrary power among them.

But to finish the oracular predictions concerning this city, I come now to Zosimus, a very ancient historian, if compared with Tzetzes and Zonaras. This author writes that Constantinople had arrived at such a state of grandeur and magnificence that no city in the world could be compared with it for greatness and prosperity. And he proceeds:

> Yet after a long search I could find no divine oracle or prophecy predicting any increase in happiness to Constantinople. At last accidentally, having read

many historians and other authors for the purpose,
I met an oracular prediction of a sibyl named
Erythraea Phaelles, or Phaenno of Epirus. This
woman, they tell you, was inspired and uttered
oracles. To them Nicomedes, the son of Prussias,
conformed, especially in such predictions that
might be some advantage to him. He therefore
entered into a war with his father.

The oracle runs thus:

Attend, great king of Thrace, and learn thy
    doom;
Thy stately city soon thou must depart,
And thy defenseless sheep shall follow thee;
The savage lion's irresistless power
Shall plunder thee, and ravage all thy stores.
Thou from thy princely grandeur soon shall fall;
The dogs that now in state stand round thy
    throne
Shall rouse the sleepy wolf, bold to assert
His liberty, nor drag thy servile chain.
Bithynia's realm shall then become a prey
To fierce devouring wolves, and Jove's decree
Transfer thy empire hence to fair Byzantium.
Happy, thrice happy monarch would thou be,
Could you repel with force the ravenous wolf,
Thus timely warned by me: For I am forced
To speak and tell the will of heaven to man.
Wide desolation now attends thee, Thrace;
A heavy vengeance waits; long hast thou tried,
And daringly provoked the neighboring states;
And now a cloud of woe hangs over thy head,
Which daily swelling to a larger size,
Shall burst in blood and ruin all about thee.

This oracle, or prophecy, says Zosimus, truly foretells,

though in an enigmatical manner, all the calamities that would befall the Bithynians, because of an excessive tribute that had been demanded of them, and also presages their speedy subjection to the empire of Constantinople. Although this did not happen until a long time after, let no one infer from this that the time for the accomplishment of the prediction was expired before it came to pass. For all time is only a moment with God, who is eternal. The historian says:

> This interpretation of the oracle I observed to be true by comparing the outcome of things with the words of the prophecy. If any other interpretation seems more agreeable, any one is at liberty to follow it.

To confirm this explanation of it even more, he tells us how Constantine the Great and his sons oppressed not only Bithynia but the whole world with severe exactions, so that whole cities, unable to pay the levies, remained desolate.

The learned Tzetzes, mentioned before, explains this oracle in another manner and says that it was delivered by Phaenno:

> This sibyl was famous long ago for her oracles and foretold some things many ages since that were accomplished only a little before the times we live in, such as the conquest of Persia over the empire, the slavery and subjection of the emperor to them, his dethronement by his people and nobles, the wars of the Scythians with the eastern empire, by whom she seems to mean the Turks.

Although it is very ancient, amid the present ruins of Constantinople, this oracle never appeared so manifestly true as now. But to proceed in my narration of other monuments of antiquity.

On the brow of the fourth hill, which lies eastward, you see a church built in honor of almighty God, which has been much celebrated in the writings of modern historians. Its inside walls are encrusted with several kinds of marble. It has two porches or vestibules, many lesser cupolas covered with lead, the largest of which is supported by four pillars of red variegated marble, each of which measures seven feet in circumference. There is another cupola that bears on four arches, which are supported by four pillars of Theban marble.

On the south side of the fourth hill a pillar is erected, which closely resembles that which, as I observed, was lately standing in the Exacionion, but is now removed to the precinct of the Seraglio. Around its base there runs a wreath of laurel work and the standard of the Cross, curiously cut in bas relief.

At the foot of the fifth hill is a double wall that encloses a street now called Phanarium because, as the inhabitants tell you, when the city was formerly besieged it was built in the space of one night by candlelight. I am induced from the authority of Dionysius to believe that Mellacopsas stood near this street. The reason why it was so called I have shown in my *Treatise on the Bosporus*. On top of the fifth hill stands the Palace of Selim the Grand Seignor, with a caravansaray and his tomb. Near it is a very large cistern in a pleasant meadow, which is despoiled if its roof and pillars.

# III

## The Seventh Hill
## and
## The Fourteenth Ward

THE AUTHOR OF THE *DESCRIPTION OF THE WARDS*
relates that the fourteenth ward is looked upon as part of
the city. Yet, because it is divided from the other wards
by an intermediate area of land and enclosed with its own
walls, it resembles a small city by itself. The author adds,
among other particulars, that the entrance is somewhat
level. The right side of it, however, rises to an ascent,
almost to the middle of the main street. It falls to a sharp
incline and contains a church, the palace, and other
buildings.

It is very probable, one would think, or at least it looks
to be so, that anyone who had never seen Constantinople
could learn from this description in what part of the city
the fourteenth ward stood. But since nothing of the
ancient buildings remains there is at present not even so
much as a bridge or the very channel of the river; there is
some room for inquiry as to where its situation was. For
I am entirely ignorant of the gate where its entrance
begins, the one somewhat on a level. It is possible that I
might also discover the location of it if I knew where the
right side of the ward was that rose into an ascent. It is
plain that this ward did not stand on the fifth hill from the
fact that the author tells us that it was divided from the
other wards by some intermediate space. Had this ward
been divided from other wards only by a small tract of
land, it would have been very injudicious in the
inhabitants to have enclosed it with a wall by itself, when
it stood so near the walls of the city. I would observe
farther that it is inconceivable that there could be any

bridge on the fifth, sixth, or seventh hills of the city or outside the walls of the city, nor is there any valley running between the fifth or the third hill where there is any bridge or any water, unless it can be imagined that it had some small creek, which is now filled up, with a bridge over it. If it could be assumed that there formerly stood any bridge beyond the sixth hill, in the street called Avasarius, we could conclude it to be none other than what was built over the Bay of Ceras, near which are still seen the piles of a bridge. In all probability the sixth hill was wholly inhabited because of the proximity and quality of the roads from Thrace. This is more probable if one considers that the suburbs called Hepdomum were seated on the sixth hill, which incited Theodosius II, because of its proximity to Constantinople, to enlarge the walls of the city.

# IV

# The Hepdomum, a Part of the Suburbs; The Triclinium of Magnaura; The Cyclobion; The Statue of Mauritius; His Armory; and The Place Called the Cynegion

THE SUBURBS CALLED THE HEPDOMUM STOOD ON THE third hill, which is now enclosed within the walls of the city. This is plain from the location of the Church of St. John the Baptist, which even at this time the Greeks call the Ππόδρομος or forerunner of our Savior. This church is situated on the eastern side of the city. It is almost entirely demolished by the Mohametans, and nothing of it remains but a few marble pillars, expecting the last effort of their sacrilege.

This was a costly and magnificent building, as appears among other evidence from the Cistern of Bonus, which was built by a nobleman of that name and situated a little above it. It was three hundred paces long; its roof and columns are entirely ruined, and its site at present is turned into a garden. Sozomen says that Theodosius the Great brought over the head of St. John the Baptist from a village called Coslaus, near Pantichium in Chalcedon, and placed it before Constantinople in the Hepdomum and there built a large and handsome church to the honor of God. The same author attests that when Theodosius marched his army against Eugenius, as soon as he came out of the city, he offered his prayers to God in the Church of St. John the Baptist, which he had built in the Hepdomum.

Procopius pays too great a compliment to Justinian when he reports him to have built this church in the forementioned suburbs. Zonaras tells us that in the reign of Constantine Pogonatus the Hagarens besieged the city with a numerous fleet that extended from the promontory situated in the Hepdomum westward as far as Cyclobion. Other historians mention the same thing, namely that they were stationed from the said promontory or the Triclinium of Magnaura, as far east as the palace called Cyclobion.

From this passage I would observe, by the way, that Magnaura was a place on the Hepdomum. Cedrinus asserts that Philip of Macedon built a round solar there and placed in its court his own statue and built an armory there. Others write that Emperor Mauritius built the Triclinium of Magnaura and that he erected his statue and built the armory there. Over the Triclinium are inscribed these verses:

Heraclius and his son Constantine,
With conquest crowned and laden with success,
Under the auspicious influence of the Cross,
Built, with surprising speed, this beauteous
structure.

The Cistern of Magnaura, which stood near the palace,
was demolished by Heraclius and, as Cedrinus related,
was afterwards cleansed and rebuilt by order of Philip,
king of Macedon. Some attest, if not consistently with
truth, yet more appositely, that when Emperor Anastasius
was expiring there during a terrible storm of wind,
lightning and thunder, he cried out with a loud voice:
"*Magna perimus aura.*"

Pulcheria, the sister of Theodosius II, when removed
from the administration of the government, retired into
the Hepdomum and lived privately. Zonaras relates that
as he came near the city Emperor Nicephorus, surnamed
Phocas, was received by the Prasin faction with great
acclamations, and that he was crowned emperor in the
Hepdomum by the patriarch of Constantinople.

The reason why those suburbs are called the
Hepdomum is from the number seven, which was formerly their number. They retained their ancient names
even after they were enclosed within the city. Procopius
related that Justinian built a Church of St. Anne in the
ward that ought to be called the second. An anonymous
writer of the *Empire of Constantinople* gives a reason
why it may be called the second. "In the place," he says,
"called the second there stood the statue of Justinian
Rhinometus. Bardus Caesar Michael, the grandfather of
Theophilus, demolished it and broke it to pieces."

This place is called the second because after Justinian
was banished by Leo the Patrician to Cherso and had
remained there ten years, he applied himself to Terbelus,
king of the Bulgarians, whose daughter, Theodora, he

married. The king gave him an army, which he led against Constantinople to recover his empire. But when the inhabitants denied him entrance, he privately stole into the city through the passage of an aqueduct to a place where there still remained the foundation of a pillar he had set up, and which his adversary had destroyed. After recovering his dominions a second time he erected a second pillar there and built a church in the same place, which was dedicated to St. Anne.

But, as I observed a little before, Procopius relates that Justinian built this church in the second ward. Here, I am of the opinion, before the reign of Theodosius II, who built the walls of the city, there stood the suburbs of the seventh hill, that is — according to Cedrinus and others — in the twelfth ward. There were, say these writers, the most dreadful earthquakes that overturned the wall of the city in the Exacionion and leveled many beautiful houses and magnificent churches in the Porta Aurea of the city. They add that in the second ward the shock was felt as far as St. Anne's Church. I mentioned this observation to many of my acquaintances, lest anyone should imagine that the δεύτερον χώριον was one of the fourteen wards mentioned in the treatise entitled *An Ancient Description of Constantinople.*

I am surprised that Procopius, who was so exact in describing so many buildings of the city, never mentions them, since they are noted by Justinian in his *Constitutions.* There is a church situated on the seventh hill between the Palace of Constantine and the Adrianopolitan Gate. Though for many ages it stood within the walls, on three sides it formerly stood outside the walls of the city, as it was customary to build the Greek churches.

A portico runs around it. Its walls inside are encrusted with square pieces of several kinds of marble, the fissures of which are covered from top to bottom with modules of astragals, some of which are adorned with berries and others are worked around without them. Above these incrustations rise three fasciae and three ornaments resembling an astragal, two of which are round and the uppermost of them is square. Higher yet are three faciae; above these are the dentils and over the dentils a Corinthian foliage.

It will evidently appear from what I shall mention later that the suburbs called the Hepdomum were in the fourteenth ward of the city, where a palace also stood. Out of many ancient palaces there remains at present not so much as the name of one of them, except the one situated on the seventh hill, which is called the Palace of Constantine, besides a few pillars and a cistern in which the Grand Seignor's elephants are stabled.

In the plain on the shore, situated at the foot of the sixth hill eastward, is the Palatine Gate called Cynegion. Outside the gate is a fine growth of plane trees. Near the gate inside the wall were formerly three large arches, now filled up, through which the inhabitants used to sail their three-tiered galleys into a creek built inside the city for the convenience of the neighboring palace. This creek is now entirely ruined and turned into a garden. The Cynegion, according to modern writers, is a place of some note, so that even Suidas himself thought it not impertinent to insert in his *Lexicon* the following story:

> Criminals condemned to die were thrown into the Cynegion, which was adorned with some statues. Theodorus, the town clerk, going there with Imerius, Keeper of the Records, saw a short but very thick statue. "Look upon the man who built the Cynegion," says Imerius, meaning himself. I returned in answer that Maximinus built it and that Aristides measured out the ground. Whereupon one of its pillars immediately fell and crushed Imerius to pieces so that he died on the spot. Terrified at the sight, I hastened to the church

where I told what had happened. I attested to the fact with an oath to those who questioned the story. Some of the emperor's domestics and servants, when their attendance duty was over, walked me to the place. Surprised at the death of Imerius and the fall of the pillar, a certain philosopher named Johannes told them that he had discovered from a small animal that a man of some note should die. Believing him, Philip of Macedon ordered the little creature buried in the place where the accident happened.

Justinus III commanded Tiberius and Leontinus, after they had reigned for three years, to have their chains taken off, tied body to body, dragged through the forum and the theater by horses. After he had trampled on their necks, he ordered them to be slain in the Cynegion in sight of the people. I look upon this theater to be the one called *Theatrum Venatorium*. For since there was such a theater in Rome, so was there one at Constantinople. For Procopius reports that the theaters, hippodromes and the Cynegia were greatly neglected and fell into ruin through the avarice of Justinian.

# V

# The Blachernae,
# The Triclinium of the Blachernae,
# The Palace, the Aqueduct and
# Many Other Places of Antiquity

THE AUTHOR OF THE BOOK ENTITLED *THE ANCIENT Description of the Wards* attests that a church stood in the fourteenth ward but does not name it. Nor does he take notice of the Blachernae, although it was so called before the taking of Constantinople by Severus, as I shall immediately make clear. The Blachernae stood outside the walls, not only in the time when that book was written, but even in the reign of Justinian, who, as Procopius writes, built a church that he dedicated to the Virgin Mary in front of the walls of the city in a place called the Blachernae:

> When he enters this church the spectator will admire its large and bulky building, still secure from the danger of falling by the strength of its foundation. You may behold in it a stately magnificence, without any mixture of gaiety or too much embellishment.

It is my opinion that Justinian only repaired this church. Zonaras reports the Pulcheria, the wife of Marcian, built a church in the Blachernae and dedicated it to the Virgin Mary. Pomponius Laetus tells us that this church was built by Theodosius. Cedrinus writes that Justin, the nephew of Justinian, added two arches to the church in the Blachernae. It is therefore plain from what Procopius has written on this occasion that the Blachernae stood outside the walls of the city, as it is no less evident from the testimony of Agathius. "When the barbarous nations," he says, "approached Constantinople by the permission of Justinian, all the churches situated outside the walls from the Blachernae to the Black Sea were stripped of their armaments, which were kept inside the city."

There is visible at present near the gate called Xylon and the western angle of the city, between the foot of the sixth hill and the turning of a mosque situated outside the city — which the people say was dedicated to the Virgin Mary — a running spring that the Greeks tell us was consecrated to her. The place where the spring is is called the Blachernae. On my first coming to Constantinople some remains of it were to be seen, but now nothing appears visible even in ruins.

From the bottom of the sixth hill, which rises above the Church in the Blachernae, there shoots an aqueduct with two pipes; one of which is stopped with a cock and the other flows in a constant stream. I noted before that Emperor Andronicus brought this aqueduct from the River Hydrales into the ward of Blachernae, where there was no river water until his time. Emperor Anastasius built the great Triclinium in the Blachernae that went under his name even in the time of Suidas. Zonaras and others assure us that Emperor Tiberius built the public bath in the Blachernae.

It is certain from some modern histories that there was an imperial palace in that place in the time of Zonaras even down to the reign of Emperor Manuel. The reason why it is called the Blachernae is mentioned by Dionysius of Byzantium in his *Navigation of the Bosporus*, from whom I shall just touch on some places described by him that reach from the foot of the fifth hill to the furthermost angle of the city and the sixth hill:

Beyond Mellacopsas — which, I noted before, was at the foot of the fifth hill — there are two places that afford good sport in fishing all year. One on the shallows under the promontories, the other under the deep hollow shores that are never ruffled by the wind. The first of these is called Indigenas, from some great man who was a native there; the other Pyracius, from Pyraeus, a port of Athens; or as some believe, from some ancient inhabitant. There is a place between them called Cittos, from the great plenty of ivy it produces.

There is also a steep place called Camara, which adjoins that of Pyracius. It is much exposed to the wind and therefore often feels the roughness of the sea. From there, up higher, stands Thalassa, which is the boundary of the Ceratine Bay, where the rivers begin to flow into it. It is so called either because of their nearness to the sea, whose salt waters they mingle with their freshness, or because it stands calm and more out of the wind; or rather, because the constant influx of the rivers into it brings down daily a muddy substance into the sea that very much thickens it, even though it serves for nourishment to the multitudes of fish with which it abounds. The first place that stands on this calm sea is called Polyrrhetius, from a man named Polyrrhetus. The next is Vateiascopia, so called from the deep sea that is around it; a third is the Blachernae, which is a barbarous word; and the last place is the marshes.

# VI

# The Bridge Near the Church of St. Mamas
# Its Hippodrome
# The Brazen Lion and
# The Sepulcher of Emperor Mauritius

CERTAIN HISTORIANS AND SUIDAS THE GRAMMARIAN have handed it down to us that near the Church of St. Mamas there stood a bridge that had twelve arches, for there was a great flood of waters at that place. In the same place a bronze dragon was also set up because it was reported that a serpent had lived there sometimes that had deflowered many virgins. This story was occasioned by the name of a man who was called Basiliscus, one of Numerianus Caesar's lifeguard, who lived there and built a church that Zeno afterwards pulled down.

Constantine, called Iconomachus because he was a professed enemy of images, ordered a certain Andreas, a sculptor and man of some note in the Blachernae, to be whipped to death in the Hippodrome of St. Mamas. Zonaras tells us that Emperor Mauritius was buried in the Church of St. Mamas that was built by Pharasmenes, a eunuch and gentleman of the bedchamber to Justinian. Cedrinus writes that the Church of St. Mamas stood near the gate called Xylocercon.

Others report that Crunna, king of the Bulgarians, surrounded Constantinople with an army from the Blachernae to the Porta Aurea. Distrusting the strength of his forces to take the town, he hastened to this church, set fire to a palace that was near it, and on his retreat carried off a bronze lion placed in the Hippodrome, a bear, a dragon, and some curious pieces of marble. Speaking of the persons who were banished on St. Chrysostom's account, Sozomen says that when they were gotten outside the walls, they met in a place situated in front of the city, which Constantine ordered to be cleansed and fenced around and made into a hippodrome. This, I take it, was the place that was afterwards called the Hippodrome of St. Mamas. Zonaras adds on this occasion that Emperor Leo, frightened by a fire that then raged in the city, flew to the Church of St. Mamas and remained there for some time. Cedrinus mentions that the emperor diverted himself with horse racing near the Church of St. Mamas the Martyr, situated in the Stenon.

It is plain from the above-mentioned authorities that this church was situated in the Blachernae and that there was a bridge there. This is further confirmed by Johannes Tzetzes in his *Varia Historia,* where he says that the sea that extends from the Straits of Abydus to the Bridge of the Blachernae is called the Hellespont. It is also evident that this bridge stood where the stone piles of the old bridge are now seen when the water is low, as it is in summer, and where they stand between the suburbs called the Blachernae and the suburbs that the Turks call the Aibasarium. This, I am confident, is the same bridge that the *Ancient Treatise on the Wards of the City* calls the Wooden Bridge and places in the fourteenth ward, in which, as I observed, were the suburbs called the Hepdomum. I desire the reader to note one thing from Suidas: that St. Mamas Bridge had either twelve stone arches, or else that he was writing about another Church of St. Mamas situated in another place.

# VII

# The Seventh Hill,
# The Twelfth Ward,
# The Pillar of Arcadius

I TAKE IT FOR GRANTED FROM THE LOCATION OF THE Pillar of Arcadius now standing on the seventh hill and called the Xerolophon — which is divided from the other six hills by a broad valley — that that is the twelfth ward, which lies level a great way from the entrance of the city at the Porta Aurea and is lengthened on the left by a gentle descent and bounded by the sea. It contained the Porta Aurea, the Trojan Porticos, the Forum and Haven of Theodosius, and a pillar with winding steps inside built in the Xerolophon by Arcadius. The hill still preserves the same name. On this pillar the emperor placed his statue, which was thrown down in the reign of Leo Conon by an earthquake that shook the whole city, overturned many churches and houses, and buried multitudes of people under it.

Cedrinus assures us that this pillar was in all respects like that of Theodosius erected in the Taurus. It has a base, a pedestal, and a capital. The shaft of the pillar, with its pedestal and capital, consists of twenty-one stones. Above the capital are two stones. The pedestal alone is built with five stones so closely cemented together that, if the pillar had never felt the shocks of an earthquake or the decays of time, it would have appeared to have been one entire stone. These stones are placed one above another and are hollow inside. Each of them is the whole circumference of the pillar, out of which are cut the steps and windows that beautify and lighten it.

I took it upon myself to measure the compass of the shaft from the stone that covers it at top down to the lowest step of the pedestal. This stone, therefore, through which there is cut a door, by which you ascend above the abacus of the capital, is about thirteen feet, nine inches high and is itself the roof and arch of the whole pillar. The door is six feet, two digits high and three feet, nine inches broad. The second stone is six feet high. In it is cut the uppermost step above the abacus of the capital. The third is five feet and four digits high and contains the abacus and the whole capital. The fifth is five feet, less two digits, high. The sixth is four feet, nine inches high; the seventh five feet and two digits; the eight four feet and four digits. The ninth is six feet high; the tenth five feet; the eleventh four feet and fourteen digits; the twelfth four feet, nine inches; the thirteenth five feet; the fourteenth five feet, two digits; the fifteenth five and a half feet; the sixteenth the same; the seventeenth five feet and ten digits; the eighteenth six and a half feet; the nineteenth five feet and four digits; the twentieth six and a half feet; the twenty-first, where the shaft of the pillar begins, six feet and four digits high.

The pedestal consist of six stones. The uppermost of these is four feet, nine inches high. The second is the same height; the third four feet; the fourth four feet, six inches; the fifth the same. The sixth and last is four feet high. In all it has fifty-six windows and two hundred thirty-three steps of two kinds. Some rise up square, others in circular windings in the manner of some shell fish.

You ascend the pedestal by five square winding steps. Every winding has a small floor at the top that leads you from one winding to another. The first and second windings have six steps each; the third eight; the fourth and fifth nine each; the lowest of them all, which lies level with the threshold of the door, is ten digits high, twelve inches wide, and two feet, nine inches long. The other square windings are like this; and the floor at the top of each of them is two feet, nine inches square. On the fifth winding stands the shaft of the pillar, the first steps of which are ten digits high; near the wall they are a foot wide, in the middle a foot and nine inches; they are two feet, nine inches long. The steps above them are all nine digits high. The inside of the shaft of the pillar measures twenty-eight feet in circumference. The wall that encloses the steps is two feet and three digits in its lowest part; in its highest it is one feet, nine inches thick.

If I am considered too curious for taking the dimensions of every stone, this trait more justly belongs to the man — Thucydides commends him highly for it — who took the height of the enemies' walls by counting the rows of bricks of which they were built. I was a bit apprehensive about the savagery of the inhabitants should they catch me dropping my line, had I measured it on the outside. I therefore had to take the inside dimensions; and by joining the height of one stone to the height of another, I discovered its altitude.

There are two steps consisting of many stones, which first appear on the ground level. Above them is the third step, which is cut out of a stone three feet and four digits high and thirty-three and a half feet in circumference. On the stone that makes the third step stands the pedestal. The first of the five stones that make it up is five and a half feet high from the threshold of the door. Its ornaments are a plain plinth three feet, five digits high; a small tore five digits high; an apophyge with a reglet of nine inches; another reglet above it of two digits; and an engraved cornice, which is nine inches high. On three sides the frieze is curiously engraved with trophies; the northern side, where the door is, is not engraved at all. The cornice of the pedestal bends downward. At the bottom is a reglet, above that an astragal adorned with berries; then an ovolo, and above that an astragal wreathed like a rope. Higher yet is a folial band. A kind of abacus projects beyond the pedestal; on each side of this there are two faces of laurel work, the largest of which curved down right to the bottom of the abacus. On the sides of this abacus there is a sculpture of seven naked boys, each holding a laurel fascis in his hand. At every angle of this abacus there stands an eagle, and above it is the plinth of the pillar adorned with foliage that projects very little. Above the plinth is a tore adorned with laurel work, which is filleted with a spiral band. Above the tore there rises an apophyge, upon which stands the shaft of the pillar, which is carved with scenes of war and of battles.

The sculpture is much like that that adorns the Pillar of Trajan in Old Rome. The trachelium, or top of the shaft, is fluted perpendicularly. The lower part of its capital is adorned with apophyges, an ovolo, and an abacus, which projects two feet and fourteen digits beyond the shaft. The abacus is seventeen feet on all sides and nine inches round. Above the abacus is a door, above which the pillar rises in the form of a cone, where there is another door over ten feet high. We may consider this pillar to be of the Tuscan order, because both the base and the capital are finished in the Tuscan style.

# VIII

# The Statues and the Ancient Tripod
# Of Apollo
# Standing in the Xerolophon

SUIDAS WRITES THAT THE XEROLOPHON WAS FORMERLY called Thema because it was a kind of repository and contained fifteen winding apartments, the statue of Diana and Severus, who built it, in addition to a thermation and a tripod from which many oracles were delivered. In this place its founder used to offer sacrifices. Among others he sacrificed a virgin.

Priscian, whom I find mentioned by Benedictus Aegius, indefatigably curious in his search for antiquity, observes that the Azoles sometimes inserted the letter "F" in a word, as I have noted in some inscriptions on a very ancient Tripod of Apollo still remaining in the Xerolophon, the words of which are written like this: Δημοφάϝων, ΛαϝονάϝωΝ. He tells us that it is customary in another place, among the Aeolians, to place an "F" between two vowels of the same word, as in ὄϝις, ovis, ΔάϝΟς, Davus, ϖϝον, ovum. "I have seen," he says, "the same in some old inscriptions, in very ancient characters, on some tripods, especially on the Tripod of Apollo, which is in Constantinople, as Δημοφόϝων for Δημοφόων, Λαϝοκόϝων for Λαοκόων."

Others add that there were similar insertions in the Xerolophon a little above the base of the pillars of Marcian, Valentinian, and Theodosius II. Zonaras tells us that Simeon, a prince of the Bulgarians, a man of cruel and turbulent spirit, marched an army against the Crobatians. When he was conquered and had lost his army, in part because of the poor condition of the roads, somebody informed the emperor that the statue looking westward placed above the arch in the Xerolophon was carved for the statue of Simeon the Bulgarian and that if anyone cut off the head of the statue, Simeon would immediately die. The emperor commanded the head of the statue to be chopped off and soon received the news that Simeon was dead from a violent pain in the stomach; and he noted to the minute the time of his death.

The Port of Theodosius was in the same place where the gardens that are now called the Blancha stand at present. These gardens are enclosed by a wall and are situated on a plain adjoining the shore of the Propontis at the foot of the sixth hill. The mouth of the port stood eastward, from which the pier extended westward in a direct line where the walls of the city stand at present. The pier was twelve feet thick; and — as I found by walking it — it was six hundred of my paces long. It is now entirely ruined.

The gardens, which are very spacious, abound with salads and pot herbs but have very few fruit trees. These gardens are watered with pools that they have in them and that are the remains of the old port. I discovered from the pier and the location of the place that it was over a mile in extent.

Outside the city wall at the mouth of the port, not altogether unfit for ships at present, you still see a fortress in ruins, surrounded by the sea. The anonymous writer of the *Empire of Constantinople* asserts that it was first called Thema, afterwards the Forum of Theodosius; though it seems to me instead to be the Forum of Arcadius, because the Pillar of Arcadius adjoins it. For the Forum of Theodosius in all probability stood near the Port of Theodosius. This is no more than what conforms to the rules of architecture, which prescribe that a market should be built near a port.

I am of the opinion that it was formerly called the Port of Eleutherius if we may credit those writers who affirm that Constantine the Great built a wall from the ridge of the first hill to the Port of Sophia and the Port of Eleutherius, built by Constantine the Great to prevent the inundations of the sea. It is called the Port of Eleutherius because he was surveyor of the works when it was built. It was for this reason that there was a marble statue erected to him in that port, bearing on its shoulders a basket made of marble and holding in its hand a marble spade. They add that Irena and her son Constantine built him a noble seat, and that the Hippodrome that was built by Theodosius the Great and demolished by Irena stretched from that seat as far as the Amastrianum. Zonaras writes that after she was removed from the government by her son Constantine, Irena lived in a house that she built in the Port of Eleutherius.

The porticos to which the *Ancient Description of the Wards of the City* gives the epithet *Troadeae,* others mention as *Troadesiae* and tell us that Constantine the Great built the walls of the city as far as the porticos called *Porticus Troadesiae* — that is, the Trojan Porticos — and the Porta Aurea, which stood in the twelfth ward. I am of the opinion that they were called the Trojan Porticos because they contained some things of a type similar to the one called the Porticus Varia. "It is reported," he says, "that in the portico formerly called Plesiactia and now Paecilla, or the Porticus Varia, a celebrated painter drew the face of Laodice on the picture of Elpinica."

I would not have known it by the name it goes by at present had it not been for a spring near it that they call Χρυσοπηγη, deriving its name from the Porta Aurea. This spring flows constantly to this day and is drunk from with great relish by the Greeks, who hold all springs near their churches to be sacred. Nothing of the church remains at present, although Procopius does take notice of it:

Justinian built two churches to the Virgin Mary in front of the walls of the city, one in the Blachernae, the other in a place called Πηγη, where there is a large wood of cypresses, a verdant meadow, and a delightful garden, which produces a great store of fine fruit, and where there is also a gentle spring, which affords very good drinking water. One of the churches stood near the sea shore, the other near the Porta Aurea. Both of them were near the end of the city walls and were impregnable fortresses for it upon occasion.

From this I would remark that in the time of Justinian the angle of the city that they call the Angle of the Seven Towers was not within the city; but that the land wall from the Porta Aurea straightened the angle of the city to a more narrow compass, as appears from the location of the Monastery of Studius, which stood on a piece of ground that was formerly considered to be in the suburbs but now stands further within the walls than the Angle of the Seven Towers. He proceeds to tell us that Justinian rebuilt the Temple of Ja — which time had wholly defaced — at a vast expense at the entrance of the Porta Aurea on the right hand for the service of the true god.

The observation I would make from this is that the Porta Aurea stood near the seventh hill, called the Xerolophon. This is also confirmed by Zonaras, who writes that in the time of Leo many churches and houses, the statue of Arcadius placed on a pillar in the Xerolophon, and the statue of Theodosius the Great placed on the Porta Aurea, as well as the city walls reaching to the Continent on the plain side, were overthrown by an earthquake. Cedrinus asserts that the statue of Victory near the Porta Aurea was overturned by the same earthquake. Other historians mention that by the same earthquake that happened on the Fifth of the Calends of November, many scared buildings and many others of common use, with multitudes of people, were destroyed; and that the statue of Constantine the Great that stood on the Gate of Attalus, with the gate itself, was demolished.

It is therefore a great mistake among those who take the Porta Aurea to be the same gate that is now called Oria and is situated in the northern part of the city. This, as I observed before, was called the Port of Neorius, since it is plain from what I have mentioned that the Porta Aurea was in the western part of the city. This is also evident from the *Ancient Description of the Wards of Constantinople,* which tells us that the length of the city from the Porta Aurea to the sea shore, in a direct line, is fourteen thousand and seventy-five feet. Cedrinus notes that the elephants stabled in the Porta Aurea were much the same kind as those with which Theodosius made his public entry into the city.

It is said that Theodosius II, who built the walls of the city as far as the Blachernae, brought the statues of those elephants that are placed on the Porta Aurea from the Temple of Mars in Athens. Cedrinus asserts that King Philip of Macedon built the great Church of Mocius the Martyr and a Church to St. Anne in a place called Secundus. Procopius says that both these churches were built by Justinian.

I have seen some remains of the Church of Mocius near a large cistern built by Justinian on the top of the seventh hill. All its pillars are standing, and it still goes under the name of Mocius. Some historians and Suidas the Grammarian say that this cistern was built by Anastasius Dicorus. It may be worth the inquiry as to whether the Moneta, which the *Ancient Description of the Wards* places in this ward, was the Temple of Juno Moneta or the Treasury. For the Grand Seignor to this day uses the castle with seven towers as a treasury. Suidas writes that the statue of Juno was supported by a bronze arch made somewhat in the form of a pair of barber's scissors but makes no note of where it stood. I therefore desire that the reader lay no great stress on what I have said about the Moneta.

# IX

# The Columns Now Remaining On the Seventh Hill

THE CHURCH STANDING HERE IS CALLED STUDIOS because it was built by a certain Studius, an eminent citizen of Constantinople. It was he, Suidas says, who built this church with a handsome monastery. In his *Constitutions* Justinian notes him when he says that there were two biers placed in the sacred treasury, one to the memory of the famous Studius, and the other to the memory of the magnificent Stephanus. The monastery built by Studius was called Studium, which is now entirely demolished.

The church remains, although converted into a mosque. In its porch are four pillars with a curiously finished trabeation. On the inside of the mosque there are seven green pillars on each side streaked with black veins that look as if they were inlaid with pieces of stone of another kind. Each of them measures six feet and six digits in circumference. Their capitals and architraves are finished in the Corinthian style, as are those that stand in the vestibule. In the upper part stands another order of six pillars. In the courts of the mosque is a cistern. Its roof, which is brick-work, is supported by twenty-three lofty Corinthian pillars.

The monastery of Studius is now within the walls of the city, though it formerly stood outside them, near the way you go from the Pillar of Arcadius to the Gate of the Seven Towers. The passage of this gate is at present filled up; its jambs are two Corinthian pillars of spotted marble, streaked with green veins, which sustain eight smaller pillars, which support three arches above.

On the left side of the gate are six marble tables, all of which are enclosed, some with round, some with square, pilasters, upon which are carved many fine statues. All of them are naked, of exquisite workmanship, in a fighting posture, with clubs in their hands; the tallest of which have winged cupids engraved over them. On the right side of the gate are six more tables, enclosed like the former. On the lowest of these there lies a young man with his face turned upwards and his legs folded, holding a musical instrument in his hand. Over him there hangs a little figure in the likeness of a cupid, and above the cupid there rises a woman. On the highest table there is carved a naked statue with a club in his hand; his right arm is covered with a lion's skin; and with his left hand he is leading dogs. Above him is the statue of a lioness with full dugs. On another table are carved two farmers carrying baskets full of grapes; and on another is the statue of a flying horse. The bridle is held by a woman, behind whom stand two more women. At the top of the table there is another woman in a recumbent posture, and opposite her a young man lying on the ground. I took particular note of these figures because of their antiquity and their admirable sculpture.

On the seventh hill I also saw, among others, four mosques of curious workmanship. Their vestibules and pillars were all of marble. Three of them stood on the eastern side of the hill, two of whose vestibules were adorned with six lofty and large pillars; two of which were of Theban marble, and the other four of different kinds of marble veined with a dark green. The other stands near the Pillar of Arcadius, recently built by the consort of Süleiyman, the Grand Seignor. It has a handsome caravansaray and a college, where Turkish and

Arabian learning is professed. In it I counted more than sixty pillars of different kinds. On the top of the hill there are two other mosques, one of which has baths and colleges joined to it. Its vestibule is beautified with six pillars of Theban marble that each measure six feet in circumference. Their bases and capitals are finished in the Turkish style. The shafts of the pillars are very ancient, especially of those two that face the door of the mosque, whose hypotrachelions at top are more slender than the shafts, though in their lower parts they are equal to them, just as a person's neck is smaller in circumference near the head than the shoulders. It is adorned with one annulet that rises like a ring. Above it there is another annulet, which is broad and flat. I saw no hypotrachelion the whole time I was in Constantinople that came so near the model of Vitruvius as this. He offers his judgement that the hypotrachelion ought to be contracted in its upper part, as you may see in his third book, *De Ionicis*. There is another mosque on the same hill, the vestibule of which is beautified with six very lofty pillars; in the college court there are fourteen, and as many in a portico adjoining it.

# X

## The Thirteenth Ward of the City Called the Sycaene Ward The Town of Galata Sometimes Called Pera

THE *ANCIENT DESCRIPTION OF THE WARDS* NOTES that Galata was formerly a part of the city. The thirteenth ward of New Rome, the author says, is the Sycaene Ward, which is divided from it by a narrow bay and preserves intercourse with it by boats and shipping. It is situated on the side of a hill, except for a broad tract of land at its foot, which lies level. Stephanus says that the town of Sycae was situated opposite New Rome and that in his time it was called Sycae Justinianae; but he does not give the reason why it was so called. Probably it was because Justinian either repaired or rebuilt it; for which reasons cities most frequently change their names.

I wonder why Procopius never took notice of this place, since he has given us an exact description of all the edifices of the bay called the Chrysoceras that were either built or repaired by Justinian; unless, perhaps, a mistake was made in Procopius by inserting the word *Jucundianae,* instead of *Justinianae,* when he tells us that Justinian rebuilt the palaces of the suburbs in the Chalcopratia, as also in the place called Sycae Jucundianae. If the fault is not in Procopius, it is an error in Stephanus, who writes *Justinianae* for *Jucundianae.* But it is clear that Stephanus wrote long before the time of Justinian; so that if there is any blunder, it is not one of Stephanus' but of Hermolaus, a grammarian of Constantinople, who abridged the *Commentaries* of Stephanus and dedicated them to Justinian.

If I might give my opinion, I would call it Sycae Justinianae rather than Jucundianae, because it appears to me that it should be so not only from comparing some books of Procopius and Justinian that have been published but also from the authority of several manuscripts. In his *Constitutions* Justinian asserts that "it is agreeable to equity that if a corpse is carried to the grave a great distance, the deacons attending it should have some acknowledgement." He adds a little later that he is of the same opinion "if the corpse is buried within the new walls of the city or this side of the Sycae Justinianae." This is only a small procession and it does not require much time or pains to walk there; "but," he says, "if the body is carried beyond the walls of this flourishing city, or beyond any other stairs than those that lead to Sycae...." There is no need to add what follows. I would only think it reasonable to add that the word πέρασμα, which the Latins interpret *terminus*, or a boundary, properly signifies *trajectus*, a ferry, or the "stairs" from which you sail from one place to another.

It is evident from what I have quoted that the town called Sycae is on the other side of the bay facing Constantinople, although Stephanus has not declared what part of the city it lies opposite. Notwithstanding, I observe from the above-mentioned *Treatise* that the sixth ward reached from the Forum of Constantine to the ferry opposite Sycae, which is now called the Pera, or Galata, Ferry.

Since I want to pay proper attention to the authority of some more modern historians, I shall produce some testimony from them. They assert that Absimarus, the commander-in-chief of the forces that besieged Constantinople, harbored in the port of Sycae opposite the city. Evagrius writes that the heads of Longinus and Theodorus, stuck upon poles, were sent to Constantinople by Johannes, a Scythian, and by the emperor's command were fixed on the shore of Sycae opposite Constantinople, a pleasant spectacle for the inhabitants of the city! He adds further that Vitalianus made an incursion as far as Sycae, and that when he came to anchor there, Emperor Anastasius sent Marinus, an Assyrian admiral, to fight him. Both fleets prepared for the engagement; one facing Constantinople, the other Sycae. For some time they kept their positions; after some small skirmishes and attacks on both sides, the fight began near the places called the . Vitharia. Having lost most of his men, Vitalianus was forced to bear off, so that there was not the least appearance of an enemy in all the Bosporus.

Nor am I induced to change my opinion on the authority of Strabo, who seems to place Sycae at some distance from the bay:

The Bosporus, straightening from the Promontory for five stadia or furlongs, widens at the harbor placed below Sycae to thirty furlongs; and from Sycae to the Chrysoceras it contracts again to five furlongs.

Nor would this opinion contradict what I have said before in any way if my author had meant by the Ceras of the Byzantines what, it is plain, Pliny did, namely, the Bosporian Promontory where Byzantium stood. But Strabo immediately adds that the Ceras was a bay that was sixty furlongs long; and therefore it appears to me that the mistake lies either in the *Codex Strabon.* or in the historian himself, as is fully evident from the authority of Dionysius, a very ancient writer of the *History of Constantinople,* which was his native place. This author has recorded that Sycodes, or Sycae, is the same place near the bay called Ceras where Galata stands at present, as I have clearly shown in my *Treatise on the Bosporus.*

The people of Pera, therefore, are grossly in the wrong when they tell us that Pera was first built by the Genoese; when it is plain that Pera was built long before they were supposed either to have purchased the town or to have received it as a reward for their sea services from some emperor of Constantinople. Justinian places Sycae within the walls of the city, and Agathius assures us that it was enclosed with walls when he writes that the people of Constantinople were in such consternation upon the approach of the enemy that the forces of Justinian were obliged to climb the walls of Sycae to make a more vigorous defense.

Sycae is called a city by Stephanus, as it also is by some modern historians; but more ancient authors who lived before Galata was taken by the Genoese call it the citadel of Galata. They tell us further that a fleet of the Saracens was stationed from the Magnaura to the Cyclobion, and that after it had remained two days in that position, part of it was driven to the citadel of Galata by a storm as far as the Clydion, where the emperor of Constantinople destroyed it from the Acropolis with liquid fire. Zonaras writes that when Emperor Michael was besieged by both sea and land, he was so terribly distressed that he was forced to lay a boom across the sea from the Acropolis to a small town on the opposite shore. There is to this day a gate at Galata that is called the Boom Gate.

It is, however, beyond dispute that Galata was more than once enlarged by the Genoese. This appears from the walls that they have built around it several times. It is fortified on the east by double, and on the west by triple, walls, denoting the gradual growth of the town. At present you may see ancient Sycae enclosed in the middle of Galata, situated opposite the sixth ward and the Sycaene Ferry, all built on the side of a hill, just as it is represented in the *Ancient Description of the Wards,* except for one broad piece of ground that lies level on the shore at the foot of the hill. This tract of land was at least a hundred Roman paces wide. At present, between the hill and the bay, there is visible a plain of equal, if not of greater, width; because over such a length of time it has been widened — as may be observed daily — by the abundance of filth and nastiness that is cast around it. To make it sink to the bottom the inhabitants have fixed wooden troughs on piles that they drive into the earth with an engine, much like a ram. By this means the plain on the shore is enlarged and made more commodious for havens. But so that the reader may understand more perfectly where the Sycaene Ward formerly stood, I will describe the layout of Galata as it stands at present.

## XI

## A Description of Galata
## The Temples of Amphiaraus,
## Diana, and Venus,
## The Theater of Sycae,
## The Forum of Honorius

THE SYCAENE WARD, WHICH IS COMMONLY CALLED
Galata, or Pera, should more properly be called the
Peraean Ward. So it is that Josephus called Judaea,
because it lay on the other side of the River Jordan. So it
is that Strabo calls that part of the country that lies on the
other side of the Euphrates. The reason alleged by the
inhabitants as to why it is called Galata is, as they tell you
— impressed by the allusion of the name — that *milk* was
formerly sold there. I have no doubt about it: if they only
knew that Galata was formerly called Sycae they would
derive its name from the word "fig" and pretend to justify
their mistake on the authority of Dionysius, their
countryman, who says that it was originally called Sycae
from the fairness and abundance of that fruit, which grew
there.

Their conjectures would have been better founded,
however, if they had derived the name of Galata from the
Galatae, backed by the authority of Johannes Tzetzes, a
citizen of Constantinople and a very industrious grammarian, in his *Various History,* written over four
hundred years ago. This author tells us that Brenus, a
Gaul and commander-in-chief of the Gauls, whom the
Greeks call Γαλάται, "passed over the sea" from there to a
possession of Byzantium and that this place was called
Pera for that reason and was called Galata after their
arrival.

This place is situated partly on a hill and partly on a plain at its foot. This hill is enclosed on the east and west by two valleys, each of which is about a mile in length. The ridge of the hill shoots from north to south, and no part of it is less than two hundred paces wide and of equal length with the valleys that enclose it; and it joins the plain on the Continent. The south side of this hill and the plain below it are bounded by the Bay of Ceras, which makes it almost a peninsula of a semicircular shape in the form of a drawn bow with only this difference: its western point is larger by half and not quite as long as the eastern.

As it is enclosed by its walls, Galata is four thousand, four hundred paces around. Its width varies in many places. In the middle of the town it is six hundred paces wide. The bay and the walls stand twenty paces apart. The plain that runs between the bay and the hill is one hundred and eighty, and the hill itself four hundred paces broad. The eastern side of Galata, at its first entrance, is four hundred paces wide; after which it contracts to a width of only two hundred and sixty paces. Its western side, which stands outside Old Galata, rises on a moderate ascent that winds southward and joins a small descent that terminates westward near the walls of Old Galata.

The town of Galata therefore stands on a triple descent, one of which winds from north to south, another falls easterly, and another west. The slope that crosses its width stretches from north to south and is so steep that in many places you are forced to climb it by steps so that you ascend the first floor of the houses, which stand on one level, by ladders. The eastern and western sides of Galata have a double slope; one from north to south, the other east and west, so that not only the parts of it that lie in a straight line, but also those streets that are winding or lie crossways have their descents. The eastern side of the town is more on a slope than the western side. To be brief: Galata is of such steepness that if all the houses were of equal height, the upper rooms would have a full view of the sea and of all the ships sailing up and down in it.

Not only Galata but almost the whole city of Constantinople would have the same privilege if the law that was first made by Zeno and afterwards ratified by Justinian were in full force. This law expressly forbids anyone to hinder or obstruct an open and entire view of the sea, or indeed a side view of it, and enjoins the inhabitants to build at least a hundred paces distance from it.

The level part of the town, which runs between the bottom of the hill and bay is nowhere less than two hundred paces broad. Towards its ends it is much broader; and in some places it widens to a length of five hundred paces. The town is three times as long as it is wide. It extends in breadth from north to south, in length from east to west. Its western side is wider than the eastern and almost of an equal width with the middle of the city. In a length of five hundred paces it is no less than five hundred paces wide. The eastern side of Galata is more narrow; there it is no more than two hundred and sixty paces wide.

The shore around the town is full of havens. Between the walls and the bay there is a stretch of shore where there is an abundance of taverns, shops, victual houses, besides several wharfs where they unload their shipping. It has six gates, at three of which there are stairs from which you sail over to Constantinople. Galata is so situated to the north of Constantinople that it faces the first, second, and third hills and the first and second valley of the city. In front it has the Bay of Ceras and Constantinople and behind it some buildings of the suburbs. Many of these buildings stand partly on top of the hill and partly on its sides. The town itself does not rise to the ridge of the hill.

Where Galata rises highest there still stands a very lofty tower. Here there is an ascent of about three hundred paces, full of buildings, and beyond that is the ridge of the hill, which is level, about two hundred paces broad and two thousand paces long. Through its middle runs a broad way full of houses, gardens and vineyards. This is the most pleasant part of the town. From here and from the sides of the hill you have a full view of the Bay of Ceras, the Bosporus, the Propontis, the seven hills of Constantinople, the country of Bithynia, and Mount Olympus, always covered with snow.

Besides these there are many other additional buildings that adorn the hills and vales adjoining this town. It has the same number of hills and valleys as Constantinople itself so that the inhabitants, whenever they please, can make the town one third larger than it is at present. If the grandeur of the Byzantine Empire continues a hundred years longer, it is not improbable that Galata may seem to rival Constantinople itself.

They who write that Byzas, the founder of Byzantium, built the Temple of Amphiaraus in Sycae are somewhat in the wrong, although not grossly mistaken. Dionysius of Byzantium tells us that behind Sycae stood the Temple of Amphiaraus, which was built by those who transplanted a colony to Constantinople under the command of Byzas. Both the Greeks and the Megarians honored Amphiaraus as a god. But although the Temple of Amphiaraus did not stand in the place that Dionysius calls Sycae, the word *sycae* meant a large tract of land after it was made a city, so that the temples of Amphiaraus, Diana Lucifera, and Venus Placida all stood within its limits, as I have fully made clear in my *Treatise on the Bosporus*. But there are no remains of these buildings at present, nor of those edifices that the *Ancient Description of the City* tells you were in the Sycaene Ward. The oldest man now living cannot so much as tell where those temples stood in ancient times; nor has he ever read or heard whether there was such a place as the Sycaene Ward.

We can guess only so far from the rules of usage of architecture that the Theater and Forum of Honorius stood at the bottom of the hill on a plain, where theaters are generally built, as I observed in my travels through Greece. When I first came to Constantinople there was standing a forum on level ground near the haven where a caravansaray is now built in the ruins of a church dedicated to St. Michael. This forum was well supplied with water by an ancient subterranean aqueduct. In short, there is nothing to be seen of old Sycae at present. Those ancient pillars we see in some mosques in Galata are said to have been imported by the Genoese. Some of them are of very ancient workmanship and well finished. The Cistern of St. Benedict, now despoiled of its roof, and three hundred pillars that supported it — now turned into a cistern for watering the priest's gardens — shows it to be a very ancient and expensive work.

*

FROM WHAT HAS BEEN WRITTEN ON THIS SUBJECT THE reader may learn how renowned Constantinople has been for its monuments of antiquity. It would take up another volume to enlarge upon the public buildings of the Mohametans at present and to explain for what uses they were intended. I shall just touch upon a few things that are the most remarkable.

As it now stands the city contains more than three hundred mosques, the most magnificent of which were built by their emperors and pashas and are all covered on top with lead and marble, adorned with marble columns, the plunder and sacrilege of Christian churches, as these were previously beautified with the spoils of the heathen temples. It has over a hundred public and private baths, fifty of which are very spacious and of two lengths, much like those I have described, built by their Emperor Mohamet. Their caravansarays and public inns are more

than a hundred in number. In the middle of their courtyards the most famous of these are furnished with
fountains of water brought from the fields adjoining the
city. The emperors have particularly distinguished
themselves in this respect. In this way Eusebius expounds
in praise of Constantine:

> In the middle of their fora you may see their
> fountains adorned with the emblems of a good
> shepherd, well known to those who understand the
> sacred scriptures, namely the history of Daniel and
> the lions carved in brass and shining with plates of
> gold.

Valens and Andronicus, at a vast expense, made rivers
at a remote distance tributary to the town, partly by
directing their courses under arches at this time appearing
above ground, and partly by channels dug under it.
Several other emperors, with no less cost, made themselves fish ponds and subterranean lakes, called cisterns
by later ages, in every ward of the city principally to
supply them with water in case of a siege. But the enemies
of Constantinople presently lie at such a distance from
them that they have either entirely ruined their cisterns or
converted them to another use.

I shall take no notice of the stately houses of their
noblemen and pashas, nor of the Grand Seignor's palace,
which spreads all over Old Byzantium and is constantly
supplied with rivers that flow in on it from distant parts
of the neighboring country. I pass over their lakes and
conduits, placed in every part of the city, that serve them
not only with water to drink but also carry off its filth to
the sea and wash away those impurities of the town that
clog and encumber the air, and for which great cities are
generally looked on as unwholesome.

I shall not mention now that almost all the buildings of
Constantinople are low and made out of the ruins that the
fire and earthquake had spared; that many of them are not

two stories high, rebuilt with rough stones or with burnt, and sometimes unburnt, bricks. I also omit the houses of Galata built by the Genoese.

The Greeks who profess Christianity have lost their six hundred churches and do not have one left of any note except the church belonging to the monastery where their patriarch dwells. The rest are either entirely ruined or prostituted to Mohametan worship. The Franks have about ten, the Armenians only seven. The Jews have upwards of thirty synagogues, which are hardly sufficient to hold the numerous congregations of that populous nation.

The reader will view the ancient monuments of Constantinople in a better light when he peruses the *Ancient Description of the Wards of the City,* finished before the time of Justinian. When this treatise was first written Constantinople was so fully populated that those who inhabited the fora and the main avenues were very tightly packed. In fact, their buildings were so closely joined to one another that the sky was scarcely discernible at their tops.

The buildings in the suburbs were very thickly crowded together as far as Selymbria and the Black Sea. Indeed, even some part of the neighboring sea was covered with houses supported by props underneath. Constantinople was renowned for these and many other monuments in antiquity. None of them remain at present except the Porphyry Pillar of Constantine, the Pillar of Arcadius, the Church of St. Sophia, the Hippodrome, now in ruins, and a few cisterns.

No historian recorded the antiquities of Old Byzantium before it was destroyed by Severus; although it is reasonable to believe that there were very many of them, especially if one considered that it long flourished in those times of heroism, when art and ingenuity were in high esteem and when Rhodes — in no way preferable to Byzantium — was beautified with no less than three thousand monuments. It is easy to form a judgment of what beautiful scenes of cost and workmanship were contained within it from the strength and proportion of its outside walls. We know for a certainty, however, that Darius, Philip of Macedon, and Severus demolished many of their antiquities, and that when they had ravaged the whole city, the Byzantines made a noble stand against the forces of Severus with statues and other materials that were part of the ruins of the city.

I have already partly accounted for the ruins of these curiosities; I shall now briefly mention some other causes that contributed to it. The principal one of these was the division of their emperors among themselves; frequent fires, sometimes accidentally, sometimes set by design not only by their enemies from abroad but by their own factions and civil dissensions among themselves. Some of these fires burned with a constant flame for three or four days straight. These fires raged so terribly that they not only consumed what was purely combustible; but they also wasted the marble statues and images and buildings made of the toughest and most solid materials whatever. In fact, so fierce were they that they devoured their own ruins and laid the most mountainous heaps of rubbish level with the ground.

Nor were the ancient monuments of Old Byzantium demolished only by their emperors but even by those emperors who had the greatest regard and affection for the city. The chief of these was Constantine the Great, who, as Eusebius reports, spoiled the temples of the heathen gods, laid waste their fine porches, entirely unroofed them, and took away their statues of brass, gold, and silver, in which they took glory for many ages. To add to the infamy, he exposed them to mockery and ridicule in all the most public places of the city. To disgrace them even more, he tells us that he filled the city with his own statues of brass, exquisitely finished. Eusebius concludes that Constantine was so incensed against the heathen monuments that he made a law for their utter abolition and the utter destruction of their temples.

How far Eusebius himself and other Christian authors were provoked against them is plainly discernable in their writings. They inveighed against the images of their gods with the same severity that they do against our statues at present. Emperors Basilius and Gregorius were bitterly enraged not only against the images themselves but against those who wrote too freely in their justification.

I shall not mention many other emperors, successors of Constantine, who were so exasperated, even with the images of the Christians, that they not only destroyed them but proceeded with such rigor against those who devised or painted or engraved them that they were entitled the *Iconomachi,* or champions that fought against images. I shall say nothing of the earthquakes mentioned in history that happened in the reigns of Zeno, Justinian, Leo Conon, Alexius Comnenus, which demolished not only the most considerable buildings of Constantinople but almost the whole city with its walls so that they could scarcely discover its ancient foundation had it not been for the Bosporus and Propontis, the eternal boundaries of Constantinople that enclose it.

I pass over the large wards of the city that lay a long time in ruins through the poverty of the inhabitants, after frequent fires and the ravages of war. They were later rebuilt, although the streets are promiscuously huddled up without regularity or order. These were the causes, as Livy related about Old Rome after it was burnt down, that not only the ancient common shores but the aqueducts and cisterns formerly running in the open streets now have their courses under private houses, and the city looks rather like one solid lump of building than divided into streets and lanes.

I shall not mention how the large palaces of their emperors, located in the middle of the city, nor the seats of the nobility enclosing great tracts of land, nor how the old foundations still appearing above ground, nor the remains of buildings discovered by the closest investigation under it, are almost entirely defaced. During the time I lived in Constantinople, had I not seen so many ruined churches and places and their foundations, since filled with Mohametan buildings, so that I could hardly discover their former layout, I would not so easily have guessed what destruction the Turks had accomplished since they took the city.

Although they are always attempting to beautify it with public buildings, at present it looks more dingy in the day than it did formerly at night, when, as Marcellinus tells us, the brightness of their lights, like southern sunshine, reflected the luster from their houses. The clarity of the day now only serves to show the meanness and poverty of their buildings, so that were Constantine himself alive, who rebuilt and beautified it, or others who enlarged it, they could not discover the location of their ancient structures.

The difficulties I labored under here in the search for antiquity were very great. I was a stranger in the country, had very little assistance from any inscriptions, none from coins, none from the people of the place. Having a natural aversion for anything that is valuable in antiquity, they rather prevented me in my inquiries so that I scarcely dared tackle the dimensions of anything; and I was menaced and cursed by the Greeks themselves if I did. A foreigner has no way to allay the heat and fury of these people, except by a large dose of wine. If you don't invite them and tell them "you'll be as drunk as a Greek," they'll treat you in a vary coarse manner. Their whole conversation is frothy and insipid, retaining none of the customs of the old Byzantines except a habit for fuddling.

It is not the least among these inconveniences that I could not have recourse to so many authors in describing Constantinople as a writer may have in describing Old

Rome. They are so fond of change and novelty that anything may be called "antique" among them that is beyond their memory or was transacted in the first stages of human life. Not only have the magnificent structures of ancient times been demolished by them, but their very names are quite lost. A more than Scythian barbarity prevails among them. The Turks are so tenacious of their own language that they gave a new name to all places that are forced to submit to their power, even though it is ever so impertinent and improper. They have such an abhorrence of Greek and Latin that they look on these tongues as sorcery and witchcraft.

All the assistance I had was my own observation, the memory and recollection of others, and some insight into ancient history. Principally with these helps I discovered the layout of the fourteen wards of the city. The inhabitants are daily demolishing, effacing, and utterly destroying the small remains of antiquity, so that whoever wants to engage in the same inquiries after me, even though they may far exceed me in industry and application, they will still not be able to make any further discoveries of the monuments of the fourteen wards.

But it is not my intention to prefer myself over other writers; if I can be of assistance to future times in any way, my end is answered. I hope I need make no apology for recording in history such monuments as are falling into ruins; and if my stay in Constantinople was somewhat longer than I intended, I hope it will not impute on me, since it was occasioned by the death of my Royal Master. It was by his command that I traveled to Greece, not with any design of staying long in Constantinople but to make a collection of ancient Greek manuscripts. Not with any intention of describing only that city, but as a further improvement of human knowledge that I might delineate the layout of several other places and cities.

Upon the death of my king, not having sufficient reimbursements, I was forced to travel through Asia and

Greece for this purpose with a small allowance. I can assure the reader that I did not undertake this voyage with any prospect of sensual pleasure, any view of worldly interest, or any pretense of popular applause. No, I could have lived in ease, more to my own advantage and in a much better state of health, as to all appearance, in my own country.

Not all the dangers and inconveniences of a long and laborious voyage could ever move me to a speedy return. How I came to engage myself in such unfortunate travels, I know not. I was very apprehensive about the troubles and dangers that I must necessarily undergo and that, indeed, have befallen me before I ventured on such an undertaking. Yet I would willingly persuade myself that my resolutions here were good and my design honorable, confirmed in the opinion of the Platonists that "we ought to be indefatigable in the search for truth," and that "it is beneath a man to give up when his inquiries are useful and becoming."

\* \*
\*

CONSTANTINOPLE FROM THE SEA OF MARMARA

# GLOSSARY

ABACUS: a square platter; the square, flat slab above the *capital* on the top of a *column*.

ANNULETS: little rings turned around Corinthian *capitals,* also known as shaft-rings.

APOPHYGE: from the Greek word ἀποφυγή, signifies that part of a *column* where it seems to fly out of its base; a curve at the top and bottom of a column where the shaft meets the *capital* and *base.*

ARCHITRAVE: the first or lowest member of the *entablature.*

ASTRAGAL: derived from the Greek word αστραγαλος and signifies the little joints in the neck. It is an architectural member joined to *bases, cornices* and *architraves;* a small molding with a circular section, often decorated with a bead and reel motif.

BASE: the foot of a *column* that supports it; the part on which the shaft of the column bears.

CAPITAL: the "head" or crowning part of a *column* or *pillar.*

CARAVANSARAY: an inn for the reception of strangers and travellers.

COLUMN: an upright, circular member, usually tapered; the classical column consists of the *base, shaft* and *capital.*

CORNICE: the third, highest and projecting part of the *entablature.*

DENTIL: a member of the Ionic, Corinthian, Composite and rarely Doric, *cornice,* small square blocks cut at regular intervals, which give the appearance of a set of teeth, hence the name.

DIGIT: a unit of measurement slightly less than an three-quarters of an inch.

ENTABLATURE: the upper part of the classical order, consisting of the *architrave, frieze* and *cornice.*

FASCIAE: the horizontal bands that make up the *architrave,* which usually consists of two or three fasciae projecting out over one another and often separated by narrow moldings.

FURLONG: a unit of distance equal to 220 yards.

FRIEZE: the round part of the *entablature* between the *architrave* and *cornice*; it is usually decorated, but may also be plain.

HYPOTRACHELION: the most slender part, or neck, of the *column,* which touches the *capital;* the groove around a Doric column between the *shaft* and the neck.

INTERCOLUMNIATION: the distance between one *column* and another measured in diameters.

LABARUM: a long piece of wood crossed near the top by a shorter piece, on which hangs a military flag; an imperial standard of the Late Empire.

MODIUS: a bushel in English measure; 32 quarts; the Greek modius is a half-pint less than a peck.

OVOLO: or "egg," the egg-shaped architectural member placed first on the top of Ionic *capitals;* a rounded, convex molding, also called quarter-round.

PACE: the ordinary steps taken by a person walking; not exactly the Roman pace, since the measurement used here varies according to the grade of the ground discussed.

PEDESTAL: the lowest member of the classical order that supports the *column* or colonnade.

PILLAR: a free standing, upright member, that need not be circular or conform with any of the classical orders; used interchangeably here with *column.*

PLINTH: the square or rectangular, projecting base of a wall or column *pedestal.*

SCOTIA: a concave, sometimes fluted, molding, often used on the base, where it is placed between two *torus* moldings or between a torus and an *astragal.*

SHAFT: the body of a *column* or *pillar,* between the *base* and the *capital.*

TORE, or TORUS: the third architectural member in the *base* of a *column,* which turns around it like a ring; a large, semicircular, convex molding.

TRABEATION: construction method using the post and lintel system, common to all classical architecture.

VOLUTAE: spiral scrolls, usually on an Ionic *capital*. The word means "wreathed" and is that part of the capitals of the Ionic, Corinthian and Composite orders that is supposed to represent the twisted bark of trees.

* *
*

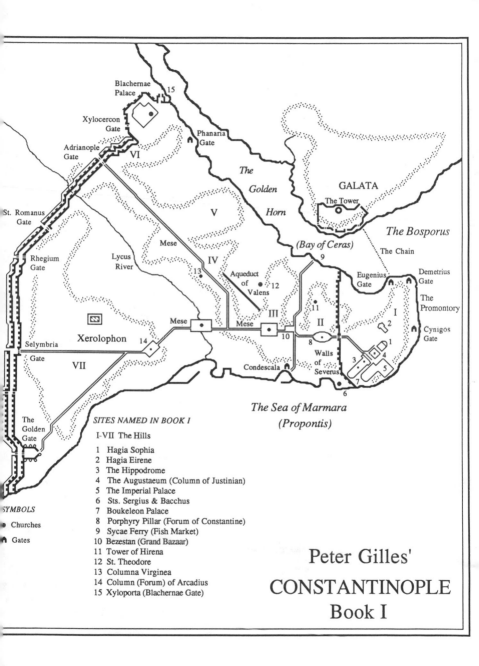

Blachernae Palace

15

Xylocercon Gate

Phanaria Gate

Adrianople Gate

VI

The

Golden

GALATA

The Tower

St. Romanus Gate

V

Horn

The Bosporus

Rhegium Gate

Lycus River

Mese

IV

(Bay of Ceras)

The Chain

9

13

Aqueduct of Valens

12

Eugenius Gate

Demetrius Gate

The Promontory

III

11

I

Mese

Mese

II

2

Cynigos Gate

Xerolophon

14

10

8

1

Selymbria Gate

VII

Walls of Severus

3

4

5

Condescala

7

The Golden Gate

The Sea of Marmara

6

(Propontis)

*SITES NAMED IN BOOK I*

I-VII  The Hills

1   Hagia Sophia
2   Hagia Eirene
3   The Hippodrome
4   The Augustaeum (Column of Justinian)
5   The Imperial Palace
6   Sts. Sergius & Bacchus
7   Boukeleon Palace
8   Porphyry Pillar (Forum of Constantine)
9   Sycae Ferry (Fish Market)
10  Bezestan (Grand Bazaar)
11  Tower of Hirena
12  St. Theodore
13  Columna Virginea
14  Column (Forum) of Arcadius
15  Xyloporta (Blachernae Gate)

SYMBOLS

● Churches
⌂ Gates

Peter Gilles'

CONSTANTINOPLE

Book I

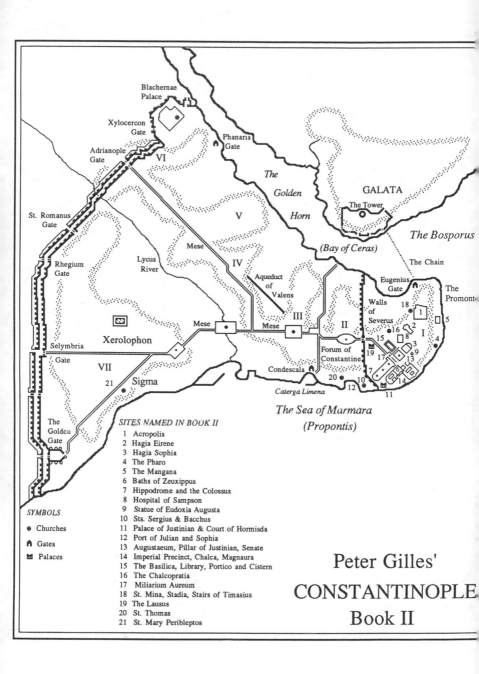

Blachernae
Palace

Xylocercon
Gate

Phanaria
Gate

Adrianople
Gate

VI

*The*

Golden

GALATA

The Tower

St. Romanus
Gate

V

Horn

*The Bosporus*

Mese

*(Bay of Ceras)*

Rhegium
Gate

Lycus
River

IV

The Chain

Aqueduct
of
Valens

Eugenius
Gate

*The Promont*

Walls
of
Severus

18

1

5

Selymbria
Gate

Mese

Xerolophon

Mese

III

II

16

2

15

19

17

I

4

Forum of
Constantine

3

9

13

VII

21

Sigma

Condescala

20

7

10

14

11

*Caterga Limena*

12

*The Sea of Marmara*
*(Propontis)*

The
Golden
Gate

SITES NAMED IN BOOK II
1   Acropolis
2   Hagia Eirene
3   Hagia Sophia
4   The Pharo
5   The Mangana
6   Baths of Zeuxippus
7   Hippodrome and the Colossus
8   Hospital of Sampson
9   Statue of Eudoxia Augusta
10  Sts. Sergius & Bacchus
11  Palace of Justinian & Court of Hormisda
12  Port of Julian and Sophia
13  Augustaeum, Pillar of Justinian, Senate
14  Imperial Precinct, Chalca, Magnaura
15  The Basilica, Library, Portico and Cistern
16  The Chalcopratia
17  Miliarium Aureum
18  St. Mina, Stadia, Stairs of Timasius
19  The Lausus
20  St. Thomas
21  St. Mary Peribleptos

SYMBOLS

●  Churches

⌂  Gates

⌸  Palaces

Peter Gilles'

CONSTANTINOPLE

Book II

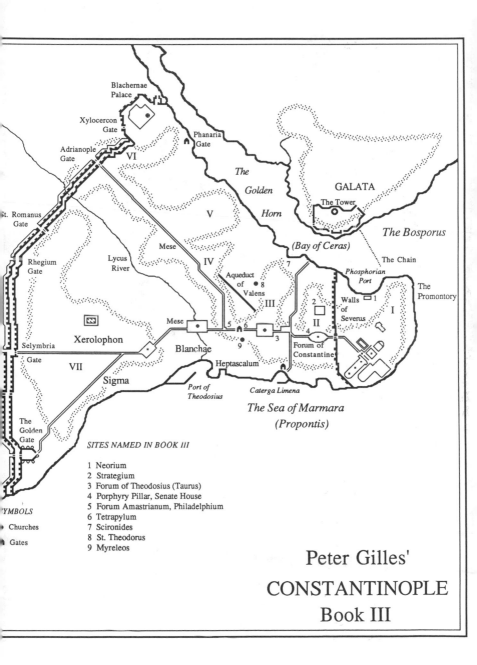

Blachernae
Palace

Xylocercon
Gate

Adrianople
Gate

VI

Phanaria
Gate

*The*

*Golden*

*Horn*

V

GALATA

The Tower

The Bosporus

(Bay of Ceras)

The Chain

St. Romanus
Gate

Rhegium
Gate

Mese

Lycus
River

IV

7

Phosphorian
Port

The
Promontory

Aqueduct
of ● 8
Valens

III

Walls
of
Severus

I

Selymbria
Gate

Xerolophon

Mese

5 6

2

II

4

9 3 Forum of
Constantine

Blanchae

Heptascalum

VII

Sigma

Port of
Theodosius

*Caterga Limena*

*The Sea of Marmara*
*(Propontis)*

The
Golden
Gate

SITES NAMED IN BOOK III

1 Neorium
2 Strategium
3 Forum of Theodosius (Taurus)
4 Porphyry Pillar, Senate House
5 Forum Amastrianum, Philadelphium
6 Tetrapylum
7 Scironides
8 St. Theodorus
9 Myreleos

*YMBOLS*

● Churches

▲ Gates

# Peter Gilles'
# CONSTANTINOPLE
## Book III

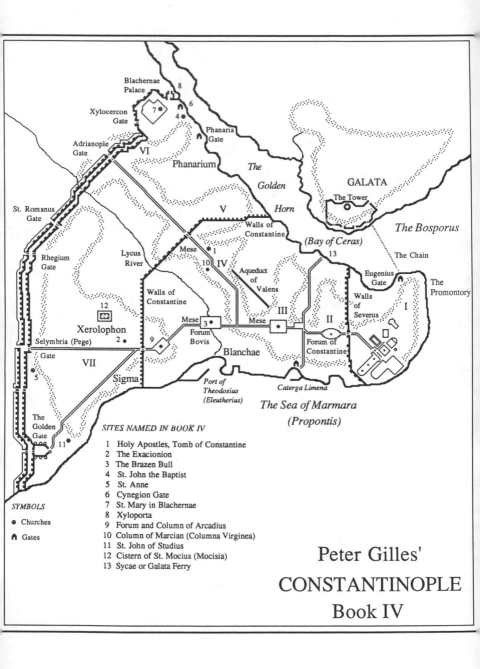

SYMBOLS
- Churches
- Gates

SITES NAMED IN BOOK IV
1 Holy Apostles, Tomb of Constantine
2 The Exacionion
3 The Brazen Bull
4 St. John the Baptist
5 St. Anne
6 Cynegion Gate
7 St. Mary in Blachernae
8 Xyloporta
9 Forum and Column of Arcadius
10 Column of Marcian (Columna Virginea)
11 St. John of Studius
12 Cistern of St. Mocius (Mocisia)
13 Sycae or Galata Ferry

Peter Gilles'
CONSTANTINOPLE
Book IV

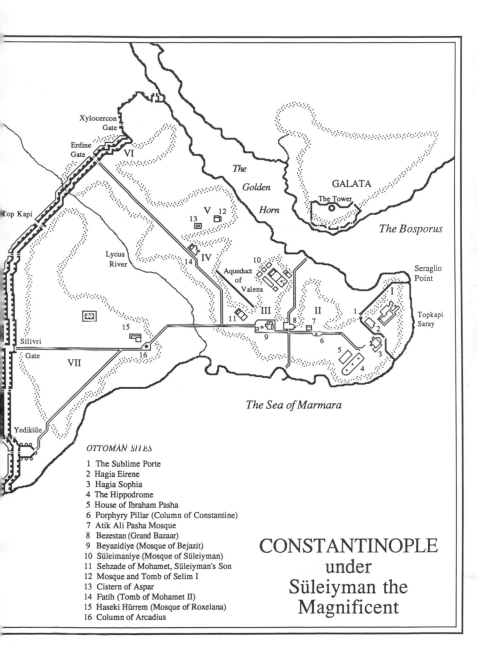

Xylocercon
Gate

Erdine
Gate

VI

Top Kapi

*The*
*Golden*

GALATA

The Tower

*Horn*

V 12

13

*The Bosporus*

Lycus
River

14 IV

10

Aqueduct
of
Valens

Seraglio
Point

I

Topkapi
Saray

11 III

II

1

9

8 7

2

15

Silivri
Gate

16

5

3

VII

6

4

Yediküle

*The Sea of Marmara*

OTTOMAN SITES

1  The Sublime Porte
2  Hagia Eirene
3  Hagia Sophia
4  The Hippodrome
5  House of Ibraham Pasha
6  Porphyry Pillar (Column of Constantine)
7  Atik Ali Pasha Mosque
8  Bezestan (Grand Bazaar)
9  Beyazidiye (Mosque of Bejazit)
10  Süleimaniye (Mosque of Süleiyman)
11  Sehzade of Mohamet, Süleiyman's Son
12  Mosque and Tomb of Selim I
13  Cistern of Aspar
14  Fatih (Tomb of Mohamet II)
15  Haseki Hürrem (Mosque of Roxelana)
16  Column of Arcadius

# CONSTANTINOPLE
## under
## Süleiyman the
## Magnificent

# BIBLIOGRAPHY

## WORKS BY PIERRE GILLES

*De Bosporo Thracio libri tres.* Lyon: Guillaume Rovillium, 1561; Leiden: Elsevier, 1632, 1635.

*De topographia Constantinopoleos et de illius anti-quitatibus libri quatuor.* Lyon: Guillaume Rovillium, 1561; Leiden: Elsevier, 1661.

—.*The Antiquities of Constantinople.* Transl. John Ball. London: Private printing, 1729.

"Elephanti nova descriptio missa ad reverendissimum cardinalem Armaignacum ex urbe Berhoea Syriaca." in *Ex Aeliani de Historia animalium libri xvii,* p. 499.

*Ex Aeliani de Historia animalium libri xvii de vi et natura animalium.* Lyon: Sebastien Gryphius, 1533.

*Lexicon graecolatinum.* Basil: V. Curio, 1532.

*Liber unus de Galicis et Latinis nominibus piscium.* Lyon: Sebastien Gryphius, 1533.

## WORKS ON PIERRE GILLES

Ebersolt, Jean. *Constantinople byzantine et les voyageurs du Levant.* London: Pindar Press, 1986.

Hamy, E.T. "Le père de la zoologie française, Pierre Gilles d'Albi." *Nouvelles Archives du Muséum d'histoire naturelle.* 4th ser., 2 (1900): 1 ff.

Pascal, Louis, "Pierre Gilles." *Nouvelle Biographie Générale.* Paris: Didot Frères, 1857, 20: 542-44.

Reulos, Michel, and Peter G. Bietenholz. "Pierre Gilles." *Contemporaries of Erasmus.* 3 vols. Toronto, Buffalo, London: University of Toronto Press, 1985-87. 2 (F-M): 98.

Van der Vin, J.P.A. *Travellers to Greece and Constantinople. Ancient Monuments and Old Traditions in Medieval Travellers' Tales.* 2 vols. Leiden: Nederlands Historisch-Archaeologisch Institut te Istanbul, 1980.

## WORKS ON CONSTANTINOPLE

### Topography and Architecture

"Byzantium," in *The Princeton Encyclopedia of Classical Sites.* R. Stillwell, William L. Macdonald, Marian Holland McAllister, eds. Princeton, NJ: Princeton University Press, 1976, pp. 177-79.

*Dumbarton Oaks Papers.* Washington, DC: Dumbarton Oaks Center of Byzantine Studies.

Guilland, Rodolphe Joseph. *Etudes de topographie Constantinople Byzantine.* Berlin: Akademie-Verlag, 1969.

Janin, R. *Constantinople byzantine.* 2nd ed. Paris: Institut français d'études byzantines, 1964.

—*La géographie ecclésiastique de l'Empire byzantine: Les églises et les monastères de Constantinople.* 2nd ed. 1,3. Paris: Institut français d'études byzantines, 1969.

Krautheimer, Richard. *Three Christian Capitals.* Berkeley: University of California Press, 1983.

Mathews, Thomas F. *The Byzantine Churches of Istanbul: A Photographic Survey.* University Park, PA: Pennsylvania State University, 1976.

Müller-Wiener, W. *Bildlexikon zur Topographie Istanbuls.* Tübingen: Wasmuth, 1977.

Van Millingen, Alexander. *Byzantine Constantinople.
The Walls of the City and Adjoining Historical Sites*.
London: John Murray, 1899.

History and Culture

Atil, Esin. *The Age of Sultan Süleyman the Magnificent*.
Washington: National Gallery of Art, and New
York: Harry N. Abrams, 1987.
Downey, Glanville. *Constantinople in the Age of
Justinian*. Norman, OK: University of Oklahoma
Press, 1960.
Dragon, G. *Naissance d'une capitale. Constantinople et
ses institutions de 330 à 451*. Paris: Presses
universitaires de France, 1974.
Freely, John. *Blue Guide: Istanbul*. New York: W.W.
Norton, 1983.
—*The Companion Guide to Turkey*. Englewood Cliffs,
NJ: Prentice-Hall, 1984.
—*Stamboul Sketches*. Istanbul: Redhouse Press, 1974.
Hetherington, Paul. *Byzantium, City of Gold, City of
Faith*. London: Orbis, 1983.
Maclagan, Michael, *The City of Constantinople*. New
York: Praeger, 1968.
Mango, Cyril. *Byzantium: The Empire of New Rome*.
New York: Charles Scribner's Sons, 1980.
Miller, Dean. *Imperial Constantinople*. New York: John
Wiley, 1969.
Phillips, James. *Early Christian and Byzantine
Constantinople*. 2 vols. Monticello, IL: Vance
Bibliographies, 1982.
Rice, David Talbot. *Constantinople from Byzantium to
Istanbul*. New York: Stein & Day, 1965.
Runciman, Steven. *The Fall of Constantinople*.
Cambridge: Cambridge University Press, 1965.

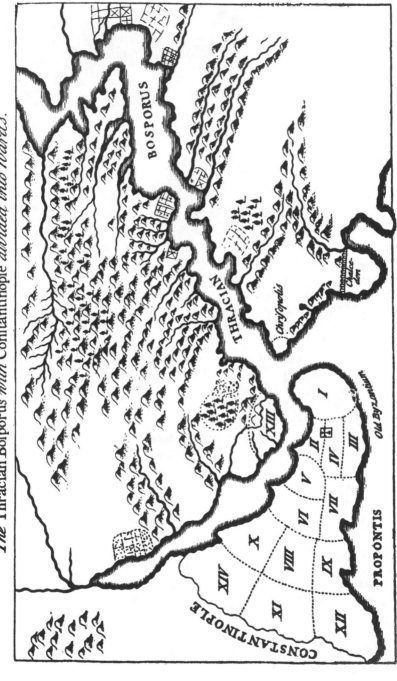

The Thracian Bosporus *with* Constantinople *divided into Wards.*

BOSPORUS

THRACIAN

Chrysopolis

Chalce-don

XIII

Old Byzantium

I

II

III

IV

V

VII

VI

X

VIII

IX

XIV

XI

XII

PROPONTIS

CONSTANTINOPLE

# INDEX

239

Bulgarians 49
Bupalus, sculptor 123
Bushel 160
Byzas 1, 2, 8, 107, 118, 120, 215
Byzes 1
Calliades, general 107
Callimachus 128
Capitol 13, 152, 157-58
Capoochees 22
Caravansaray of Beyazit 32, 155, 156
Caravansaray of Mohamet 38, 173
Caravansaray of Selim 38, 184
Caravansaray of Süleiyman 32-33
Carya 171
Carosia 153, 161
Castle of Galata 54
Catacosmus, emperor 61
Caterga Limena 75, 92
Cedrinus, Georgius on Amastrianum 161; on Basilica 104; on Baths of Constantius 163; on Baths of Zeuxippus 71; on Bay of Ceras 47, 54; on Blachernae 192; on Brazen Bull 178; on building of walls 189; on Chalca 102-3; on Church of Chalcopratia 113; on Church of Mosius 204; on Church of St. Achatius 166; on Church of St. Anne 204; on Church of St. Mamas 195; on Church of Sts. Sergius and Bacchus 89, 90; on Church of St. Sophia 60-61, 67; on Cistern of Theodosius 153; on clocks 108; on earthquake 170; on fires 73-74, 90,

103, 109, 110, 114, 122, 127, 139, 149, 157; on founding of city 8; on Hepdomum 187; on Lausus 122; on Library 110-11; on Miliarium Aureum 117; on Palace of Sophia 91-92; on Port of Sophia 90; on Porphyry Pillar 132; on Pillar of Arcadius 197; on Pillar of Justinian 99; on Pillar of Theodosius 150; on Porta Aurea 203-4; on Pyctacia 92; on Sigma 93; on Strategium 127; on Taurus 153; on Temple of the Sun and Moon 161; on Tetrapylum 151; on Tetrasceles 152; on Triclinium of Justinian 124; on Valens 164
Ceras, Bay of, mentioned in relation to other sites, 7, 15, 18-21, 24, 31, 45, 47, 53-54, 125, 127, 154, 167, 171, 186, 210, 213, 214-15
Chalca 73, 74, 100, 102-4, 106, 110, 114-15
Chalcopratia 6, 111, 113-14, 122, 208
Chariot Racers 85-87
Chrysaphius Zomas 94
Chrysoceras 17, 52, 208, 210
Chrysopolis (Scutari) 4, 7, 93, 127, 128
Chrysostom, St. John 58, 74, 100, 162, 195
Chrysotriclinium 124
Church of Procopius 85
Church of St. Achatius 162, 165-66
Church of St. Agathonicus 57

\* \*
\*

*This Book Was Completed on November 1, 1987*
*at Italica Press, New York, New York and Was*
*Set in Times Roman. It Was Printed on*
*55 lb Glatfelter Natural Paper with*
*a Smyth-Sewn Binding by*
*McNaughton & Gunn,*
*Ann Arbor, MI*
*U. S. A.*
*\* \**
*\**